500 Tips and Techniques for PeopleSoft Development and Troubleshooting

500 Intermediate and Advanced Peo0pleSoft Technical Tips

100+ Common Technical Issues and How to Resolve Them

100+ Commonly Used Code Examples

2025 Edition

By

Shawn Chen

Contents

500 Tips and Techniques for PeopleSoft Development and Troubleshooting

ACKNOWLEDGEMENTS

This book would not have been published without the help of Ali Khan and the editing and publishing team at Amazon Publishing Pros. Ali worked as the project manager for publishing this book on major book platforms and various book chain stores. The Amazon Publishing Pro team assisted in editing, proofreading, designing the book's covers, promotion of this book, etc. My daughter Kerol Chen also helped on the editing and proofreading.

Also, I would like to express my gratitude to the following colleagues who I have closely worked with during my 20 years of PeopleSoft career: Eileen Wang, Lily Wu, Danny Yoo, Eddie Mak, Dustin Kim, Simon Bayhon, Justin Chen, Dejesh Vora, Carlos Jesus, Khurana Ankur, Mehak Soni, Sumant Kshisagar, Ratika Arora, Carmela Roberts, Rob Chan, Kevin De Kock, Dave Hall, Mark Rumbles, Nishaan Parbhoo, Amanda Morgan, Sarah Hill, Derek Konieczny, Ita Mariasin, Paul Smith, Shirley Marshall, Janet Lynch, Madeline Barr, Aashish Dhand, Satabdi Roy, Dominik Rachwal, and Dave Kurysko.

ABOUT THE AUTHOR

Shawn Chen is a PeopleSoft technical expert who began his IT career in 1994 as a software engineer and gained over 20 years of experience working in PeopleSoft. He has worked as a PeopleSoft technical consultant with many different organizations including government entities, banks, universities, and corporations. Shawn has worked on the PeopleSoft Finance and Supply Chain Management (FSCM), Human Capital Management (HCM), Campus Solutions (CS), Customer Relationship Management (CRM)and Enterprise Performance Management (EPM) systems.

During his 20+ year PeopleSoft career, Shawn has worked with various organizations, including University of British Columbia, Accenture, IBM, Deloitte, Attain Solutions, the Provincial Government of Alberta, the Provincial Government of Newfoundland, Export Development Canada, 407 ETR, WorkSafe BC, the Regional Municipality of York, the Regional Municipality of Peel, Canadian Imperial Bank of Commerce, Scotiabank, Canadian Tire, Ryerson University, Tarion Warranty Corporation, and McMaster University.

When Shawn was working with all these diverse businesses, he gathered numerous tips he found useful and published them into this book.

Shawn holds a bachelor's degree in Computer Engineering and a Master's degree in Biomedical Engineering from Zhejiang University in Hangzhou, China, one of the top three universities in China.

Shawn is the founder and CEO of the PeopleSoft Upgrade Technology and Service Ltd, located in Toronto Canada. The company's website is https://psupgradepro.com. He is the creator of the PeopleSoft upgrade code retrofit application PS Retrofit which can be downloaded at https://psretrofit.com. This software application is currently the best PeopleSoft upgrade code retrofit accelerator and automation tool on the market.

Shawn immigrated from China to Canada in 1998, and he has lived in Canada since then. He currently lives in Toronto, Canada. In his spare time, Shawn enjoys playing tennis, golf, biking, hiking, and traveling. As an advanced level long-term tennis player, he once won a men's singles championship at a local tennis club's annual tournament in Toronto.

You can visit Shawn's YouTube PeopleSoft Technical Tips channel located at https://youtube.com/@PeopleSoftTechnicalTips. Shawn has created over 90 videos with the tips provided in this book and shared them through the YouTube channel.

You can visit Shawn's web site at https://shawnchenbook.com, and contact Shawn at shawnchentoronto@gmail.com.

WHAT IS PEOPLESOFT?

PeopleSoft is an e-business software product line owned by Oracle that was initially designed to offer human resources and finance applications. Over the years, it has expanded its offerings to include tools and applications for general business processes, such as customer relationship management (CRM), and applications for specific industries, such as higher education. Today, the PeopleSoft application engine programs enable users to develop, test, and run batch or online projects that perform high-volume background processing against data.

Peoplesoft was founded in 1987 by Ken Morris and David Duffield. Originally located in Walnut Creek, California, it later moved to Pleasanton, California. In 2003, PeopleSoft merged with its rival JD Edwards. In 2004, Oracle acquired PeopleSoft for approximately $10 billion.

PeopleSoft now provides users with an integrated ERP software package that assists in the everyday execution of various business operations. It is used by human resource departments, finance management departments, customer service departments, and performance management departments in large corporations. The suite of applications includes human resource management systems (HRMS), financial and supply chain management systems (FSCM), customer relationship management (CRM), and enterprise performance management systems (EPM). The latest version of PeopleSoft (9.2) introduces the Selective Adoption function, which allows users to customize the software while retaining strategic customizations.

The original architecture for PeopleSoft was a suite of products built on a client-server (two-tier) approach with a dedicated client. However, the entire suite was later rewritten as an n-tier web-centric design called PeopleSoft Internet Architecture (PIA). This new format enables all of a company's business functions to be accessed and run from within a web browser.

PeopleSoft products are now available via the Oracle Cloud. Users can access and deploy PeopleSoft applications using Oracle's Cloud Infrastructure.

PEOPLESOFT DEVELOPMENT GUIDELINES

AND BEST PRACTICES

- A PeopleSoft development team should adhere to Software Development Life Cycle (SDLC) to optimize workflow and ensure quality.

- When coding, it is essential to consider all possible scenarios, write logic code meticulously, and avoid making any assumptions. If any assumptions are made, it is recommended to jot down notes and review them during the testing and code debugging phase.

- For each development task, it is advisable to create a separate file folder and store all related files and documents, including requirement documents, functional and technical specifications, and scripts.

- During development, it is beneficial to create task notes using the Note application. These notes should include important information such as user details, objects being created or modified, project name, test IDs, navigation path, etc. Each task note should be placed within the folder that stores all the related documents for that task.

- Regularly saving changes is crucial. In the event of an unexpected computer breakdown or network disruption, failing to save changes can result in the loss of all modifications made since the last save.

- After creating or modifying new code, it is highly recommended to thoroughly review and check the code or changes. Rushing into testing without careful consideration can lead to careless errors that may take ten times longer to debug and fix.

- Creating a backup of a program before making significant changes is advisable, especially if there is only one copy of the program.

- Whenever copying existing code and pasting it to a new location, it is important to meticulously review each line of code and ensure that necessary changes are made. This is particularly crucial when copying and pasting a large block of code.

- Special attention should be given to the code that processes date values, as it often causes issues due to incorrect syntax.

- Minimizing repeated code reduces the chances of bugs and contributes to quicker development time for future enhancements.

TIP LINKS

Tips

How to enable a field as a page anchor?

How to override the search record of a component?

What are the advantages of using views as search records?

How to create a dynamic drop-down list?

How to create a dynamic prompt?

How to create a dynamic prompt in a grid?

How to create a dynamic view?

How to resolve the issue of the Ok button at the bottom of the Properties dialog box is hidden?

How to use SQL to find the menu group, menu item name, menu label, and item label of a component?

What is the difference between component buffer and data buffer?

How to create Event Mapping?

How to resolve the issue of Unable to click the Ok button in a Properties window to save a change in Application Designer?

How to hide a subpage or multiple page controls together?

How to find out the names of a field and its record on a page without using Application Designer?

How to enable filed level auditing and record level auditing?

What are the different ways to restart an application engine program after it abends?

What is the difference between %Select and %SelectInit in Application Engine?

How to terminate and branch out in Application Engine?

How to exit from an application engine program successfully with a Warning status?

How to perform a dynamic call section in an Application Engine program?

How to perform a dynamic call section to create a single AE program that can function as both a batch process and an online process?

How to use SQL to find which project an Application Engine program is in?

How to call a SQL object in a SQL action in Application Engine?

How to configure and publish a synchronous web service after migrating a PS project containing the web service from one environment to another?

How to set up a JMS node for integrating with a third-party Java-based application?

How to integrate your PeopleSoft system with a third-party system using synchronous service operation and rowset-based messaging?

How to create a REST web service and test it?

How to copy the entire component, a header/line page rowset, or only the changed rows of data from a component into a message object?

What is the difference between PeopleSoft Vanilla and Keep Customizations when selecting a Target Orientation in Compare and Reports and how to use the setting?

How to migrate Approval Workflow Engine (AWE) configurations?

How to migrate Page and Field configurations?

How to migrate navigation collections?

How to migrate event mappings?

How to migrate Fluid objects?

How to enable nVision report drill down in Excel?

How to perform nVision report output formatting with nPlosion?

What is the execution order of PeopleCode events?

How to check if the value of a field on a page has been changed by user?

How to select all fields from a table and ensure only one single row is returned based on the key field values using %SelectByKey and %SelectByKeyEffdt?

How to create a string with a repeated charactor or a substring?

How to perform left padding or right padding on a string?

How to copy field values between different records?

What is the difference between the DoSave() function and the DoSaveNow() function?

What are the differences between the Transfer(), TransferPage() and DoModalComponent() function?

What is the difference between the Transfer() function and the TransferExact() function?

How to call a secondary page from a main page?

What is the difference between SQLEXEC and CREATESQL?

How to control component save processing?

Code Examples

How to call an Application Engine from record PeopleCode?

How to put two or more SQL statements in one SQL action in Application Engine?

How to pull data from a table/view and write it into a BI Publisher XML file using PeopleCode?

How to schedule to run the full data publish process with PeopleCode?

How to publish a message for incremental sync?

How to subscribe a message for full sync?

How to subscribe a message for incremental sync?

How to publish a row-set based message?

How to publish a non-rowset based message?

How to subscribe and consume a rowset based message using PeopleCode?

How to subscribe and consume a non-rowset based message using PeopleCode?

How to use SQL to update the status of an IB message from DONE to NEW so that the message can be reprocessed?

How to create an Application Engine program that can log and auto re-submit the error and timeout IB messages?

How to pass a variable to a new window opened by the TransferExact() function and the DoModalComponent() function?

How to retrieve the data in an unknown table using the CreateArrayAny() function?

How to save the results from a SQL query to a file using the CreateArrayAny() function?

How to set an edit table for a record field at run-time?

How to perform quick and dirty bulk delete of records with the same key value?

How to keep a small set of data in working memory without having to set up a temporary table in the database?

How to check if there are any rows returned from SQLExec("Select")?

How to select all fields from a table and ensure only distinct rows are returned ?

How to obtain the value of a field in a grid?

How to obtain the value of a field of the current row in a grid?

How to loop through all rows in a grid or a scroll and do data validation?

How to reference a rowset on a scroll on the level 2 of a page?

How to access/traverse component buffer data from level 0 to level 1, level 2 and level 3?

How to populate a grid with selected rows from a table or view?

How to sort a grid on specific columns?

How to execute a Unix command from PeopleCode?

How to get the value of a component record field from the component buffer?

How to cause a time delay (sleep) from PeopleCode?

How to check whether a file exists in the file system?

How to delete a file from the file system?

How to check the PeopleTools Release version in PeopleCode?

How to build nested logic in PeopleCode?

How to insert a new row into a table using PeopleCode?

How to pass a URL to a PeopleCode built-in function?

How to set a dynamic prompt table in PeopleCode?

How to call a java class in PeopleCode?

How to debug code by writing variable values to a file?

How to set trace in PeopleCode?

How to find records and fields used in a PeopleSoft Page using a SQL query?

How to use the %EffdtCheck meta-sql element to select the effective date rows?

How to increment the number automatically with strings?

How to clear the default values of a drop-down list and create a new drop-down list?

How to create a drop-down list of the months in the order from January to December?

How to load a flat file with a control file using file layout, save the data into a table with edit, save any errors into a log file, and send out a notification email if the file cannot be found in a folder?

How to export data from a table to a flat file using a file layout?

How to export data from a table or a view to a flat file and save the data into a history table with the same table structure?

How to delete data from another table when deleting a row from a grid on a page?

How to perform record field edit from PeopleCode?

How to get the web site name from a sign out URL?

How to build a file validation routine?

11

Errors

Table does not exist when using the select or describe a statement in the SQL client after building a record in Application Designer

Could not read shared cache RDM

User receives "password has expired" error when trying to login to Application Designer

Page data is inconsistent with database

Data being inserted doesn't exist

You are not allowed to update your own data

No matching values were found

Data being added conflicts with existing data

"Invalid Value" error in a drop-down list

Class Row method GetRowset scroll {Record} is invalid

SQL Access Manager SQL error: the account is locked

Invalid Drop-Down List in page definition

A page URL with parameters does not go to the page as supposed to

Invalid identifier

PeopleTools has stopped working

Open file operation failed. <FilePath>\PSBUILD.LOG

No matching buffer found for level

A SQL error occurred. Please consult your system log for details

Application Engine Request is not active -- processing suspended

A Process Request shows the status of 'INITIATED' or 'PROCESSING' but is no longer running

Unique constraint violated

Error generating report output in BI Publisher report

Bursting is disabled in BI Publisher report

Can't find project or library in Excel to CI

Property or collection {Record} was not found in the component interface at the given level in Excel to CI

Wrong grid layout on a Fluid page

Pagelet is missing from the EMPLOYEE portal for homepage tab name on a Fluid homepage

Java Exception: java.lang.OutOfMemoryError: Java heap space

Invalid row number for class Rowset method GetRow

You are not authorized to access this component

QDM could not load query definitiom

You do not have permission to edit or view <OBJECT NAME>

Unable to extend tablespace

Looping chain of synonyms

Cannot resolve the collation conflict between 'Latin1_General_BIN' and

'SQL_Latin1_General_CP1_CI_AS' in the equal to operation

Program stopped by user request in SQR

APPLICATION DESIGNER

1. Translate tables are effectively dated.

2. A change to the name of a field will affect all the records, views, and pages that field is being used; therefore, you should only do it after you have done the impact analysis.

3. All date fields allow null value by default; all character fields do not allow null value by default.

4. When working with effective dated records, always ensure that the effective dated logic is in place and the correct date value is used.

5. Pressing the Tab key does not trigger any field change event, whereas pressing the Enter key does.

6. To create a separate tab in a grid, insert a grid tab separator from the Insert menu.

7. The primary index of a table is generated from the primary key fields of a record definition.

8. You can check the indexes of a record/table by going to Tools -> Data Administration -> Indexes.

9. You can add secondary indexes via Application Designer. Go to Tools -> Data Administration -> Indexes, choose Add Index, specify whether it is a unique or non-unique index, and select the fields of the new index from the list of all the fields of the record.

10. Set a field as a Duplicate Order Key field instead of a key field if there can be duplicated values in the field.

    The purpose of a Duplicate Order Key is to allow you to store records with the same key structure. An example would be a record with one key emplid, set as a duplicate order key. You would be able to insert duplicate emplids into the table without issue.

11. A field can be a Related field (of a Display Control field) and a Display Control field (of other Related fields) at the same time.

   The Display Control and Related fields must be in the correct order on the order page. The Display Control field must be positioned before the associated Related field; otherwise, a warning dialog box appears when you save the page.

12. To make a field as the field of a drop-down list, the field needs to be set as a List Box Item in the prompt table of the field.

13. You can specify different prompt tables in PeopleCode so that you can have dynamic values for a prompt field.

14. What is the difference between signed and unsigned numbers?
   A signed number can be negative (have a sign), whereas an unsigned number will only be positive.

15. All the work/derived record fields that are being used by a page must be placed on the page in order for the page to work effectively; otherwise, a Field Does Not Exist error message may be encountered. Note that the work/derived record fields can be set to invisible.

16. How to create a table in which one of the fields is unlimited in length?
   Setup the field in Application Designer, make it a field type of Long Character, and set the maximum length to 0. When you use it on a page, make it a Long Edit Box.

17. During development and testing, you can press Ctrl-Shift-N to open an Incognito tab in Chrome without having to clear browser cache.

18. The default display order of the rows of a grid is determined by the key structure of the record definition or the view that the grid is mainly based on. If the record definition or the view is

effectively dated, the display order of the rows will be the key field ahead of the EFFDT field first and then the EFFDT field. Date fields are sorted in descending order by default.

19. When making a change to an existing object, perfom a reference check on the object being changed and ensure all possible implications are identified. Carefully look at the reference check results and specifically pay attention to the component interfaces that may be affected.

20. How to enable a field as a page anchor?

A field that has the "Enable as Page Anchor" checkbox turned on works in conjunction with another push button with the destination set to Page Anchor. Clicking on this type of push-button will reposition the page to the location where the target page anchor is.

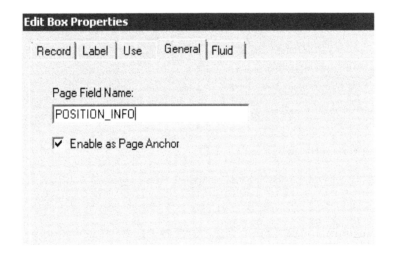

21. How to override the search record of a component?

Overriding the search record allows us to use the same component in different situations without modifying that component. You can override a component's search record with a different record in the configuration of the menu item for the component.

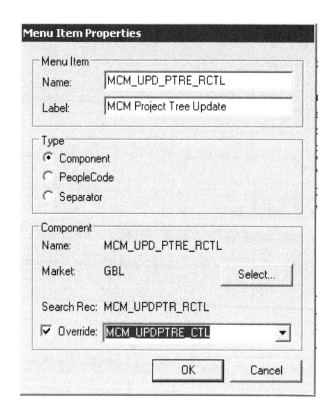

22. What are the advantages of using views as search records?

There are advantages of using search views instead of search table. As the search view is created with selected fields there will not be much stress on app server and there by improves the performance. Search view also gives additional search criteria. Thus, it can be used to provide row level security.

23. How to create a dynamic drop-down list?

If the value selected from the first drop-down list is part of a compound key of the second drop-down list, PeopleTools will automatically filter the results of the second drop-down list based on the value selected from the first.

To create dynamic drop-drown lists, you should build a view for the second drop-down list with the first drop-down field as a key field. When you select a value in the first drop-

19

down list, a second drop-down list will be automatically updated to show only values respective to the value selected on the first prompt.

The key structure on the view for the second drop-down is very important. In which you should have something like this,

Field A - has values of the first drop-down list – make it a key field

Field B - has values required for the second drop-down list – make it a key field and a list box item field.

24. How to create a dynamic prompt?

Prompts allow users to choose a value from a predefined list of control values for a field on a page while performing transactions.

Below are the record field properties of the COMPANY field in the record DEPT_TBL,

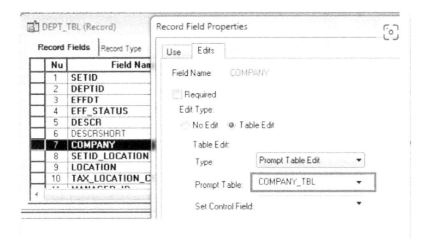

In this case, the user has no control over the values that will be prompted. The system will list all available values from the COMPANY_TBL record. Dynamic prompts provide users with control over the prompt values and how they are generated. For example, you can build a prompt dynamically at runtime based on a specific field value.

Let's explore this further with two scenarios:

Scenario 1: Dynamic Prompt using Dynamic View

In the delivered PeopleSoft functionality, Compensation Rate Codes are created to be used by all companies. However, this results in a large number of Compensation Rate Codes being generated for users when they define a person's compensation on their Job data.

However, the business may need to customize delivered PeopleSoft pages that enable HR Users to access and view only Compensation Rate Codes, which are applicable to a person's company.

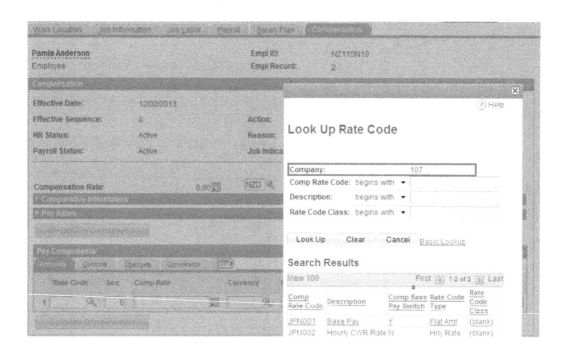

The selection options should be limited to compensation rate codes that are relevant to each individual company. One approach to achieve this is by utilizing the Dynamic View record type, which is an effective method for implementing dynamic prompts.

Step 1: Create a record of type Dynamic View using Application Designer as follows,

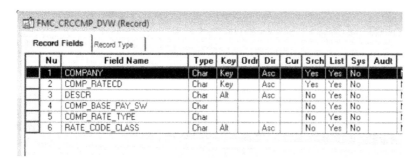

Make the Fields COMPANY & COMP_RATECD as both Search key and List Box item and all other fields as List Box item only.

Step 2: In the COMPENSATION record, open the record field property of COMP_RATECD, go to the Edits tab and assign the newly created dynamic view FMC_CRCCMP_DVW as the prompt table edit.

21

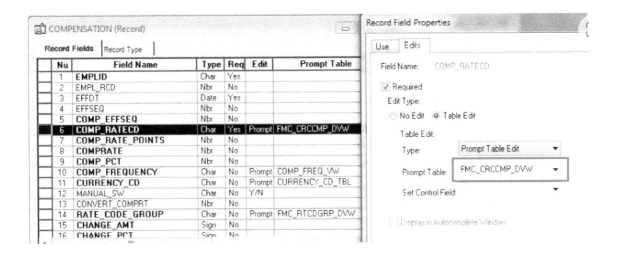

Step 3: Add below PeopleCode in the RowInit record field event of COMP_RATECD field

```
&Company = JOB.COMPANY.Value;

If %Component = "JOB_DATA" Or Then

    &fmccrcdyvwsql = SQL string which fetches the
compensation rate codes WHERE    COMPANY = &Company
(Current person's company)

    COMPENSATION.COMP_RATECD.SqlText = &fmccrcdyvwsql;

End-If;
```

Where &fmccrcdyvwsql is SQL string which will pull the compensation rate codes valid only for the current person's company.

Note, the above SQL is valid only when the below component is customized to define the Compensation rate codes based on the company:

Navigation - SetUP HRMS -> Foundation tables -> Compensation rules -> Comp rate code table

Scenario 2 Dynamic Prompt using Derived Record Field

The prompt table for a field can be different depending on the value that user selects from another field.

This is also called a dynamic prompt, and it can be implemented using a field that is defined in record type Derived/Worked and is another way of implementing dynamic prompts.

Now, let us see how it's been implemented. This example shows how to change the Pay Group drop-down lists based on the value that user has selected for the field of Pay System Flag.

Step 1: Add a field EDITTABLE6 in the derived record named - DERIVED.

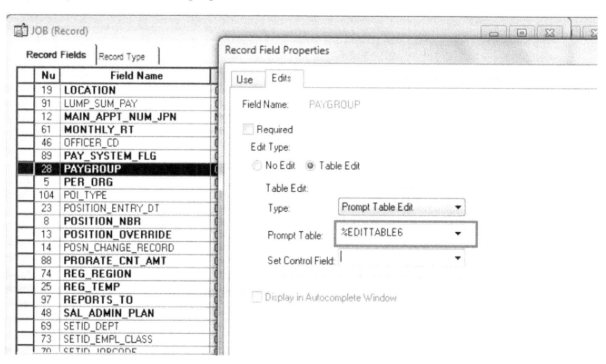

Step 2: Open the record field properties of the field PAYGROUP in JOB table

Step 3: Add below PeopleCode in the FieldChange event of the field PAY_SYSTEM_FLG

23

```
If JOB.PAY_SYSTEM_FLG = "GP" Then

    DERIVED.EDITTABLE6.Value = RECORD.GP_PYGRP;

Else

    If JOB.PAY_SYSTEM_FLG = "PI" Then

    DERIVED.EDITTABLE6.Value = RECORD.PAYGROUP_TBL;

    End-If;

End-If;
```

Below is the difference of the above 2 scenarios.

Scenario 1 - Dynamic prompt is created using the Dynamic View record definition, and the rows selected in the prompt are controlled by SQL query supplied to the SQL TEXT property of the record field based on certain conditions.

Here, rows displayed in the prompt can be controlled, but the structure of the prompt remains the same because the underlying prompt record doesn't change.

Scenario 2 - Dynamic prompt is created using a field added in a record definition of type Derived/Worked the field name is used as the bind variable (%FieldName), which is mentioned in the record field properties. Then in the PeopleCode, record definitions are assigned to this bind variable based on a certain condition which becomes the prompt record.

Here, the structure of the displayed prompt appears different each time because the underlying prompt record is changed.

25. To set or change the title of a column in a grid at run-time, you can use the following PeopleCode,

```
&MyGrid = GetGrid (%Page, "XXX_CUST_VW");

&MyGridColumn = &MyGrid.GetColumn ("PLATE");

&MyGridColumn.Label = "License Plate";
```

26. To display the row sequence numbers on a grid, open the grid properties, go to the Label tab and check the Show row headings (runtime) checkbox in the Body Area.

27. How to create a dynamic prompt in a grid?

Through dynamic prompt we can dynamically change the underlying prompt table for a particular field depending upon previous selection. To create dynamic prompt for a field in a grid, you need to insert the EDITTABLE field of the DERIVED Record into the grid, make it invisible, and put the following code in the RowInit event of the field.

```
If XXX_FIN_PLAN.PLAN_TYPE.Value = "ONC" Then
   GetRow().DERIVED.EDITTABLE.Value = Record.XXX_ONC_ACT;
Else
   If XXX_FIN_PLAN.PLAN_TYPE.Value = "BEN" Then
      GetRow().DERIVED.EDITTABLE.Value =
   Record.XXX_BEN_ACT;
   End-If;
 End-If;
```

28. To get a list of all fields in a record definition in the text format, you can query the database as follows,

```
SELECT * FROM PSRECFIELD
WHERE RECNAME = {RECNAME}
ORDER BY FIELDNUM;
```

29. What are the default settings in Application Designer Options?

The recommended default settings are when an object is modified, saved, or deleted. Do not insert related definitions with the current definition, andreload the last project at start up.

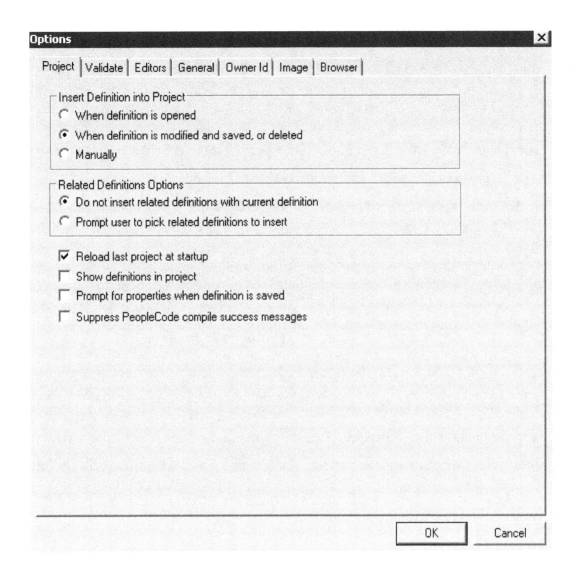

30. Deferred processing mode can be set on the page field level, page level, and component level. If you specified deferred processing mode for a component, you could specify whether a page within a component or a field on a page also performs processing in deferred mode. The default is for all pages and components to allow deferred processing.

If you specify that a field or page allows deferred processing but do not set the component to deferred processing mode, then the deferred processing mode is not initiated. Hence, you must set the component first.

31. To make a FieldChange event PeopleCode working, in cases such as graying out or ungraying radio buttons or drop-down lists, you need to change the page from allowing deferred processing (by default) to not allowing deferred processing.

32. You do not need to alter a record definition when its record field properties are changed; only save the change. The record field property changes include:
- Changing record field edit properties from translate to prompt table.
- Assigning a default value at record field properties level.

You can determine if the change made in-Application Designer will affect the database; these changes are something like changing a field's length or adding a field. Likewise, if you change the key structure - this would change the index. These types of changes would affect the database structure and would therefore merit a rebuild in application designer.

33. How to create a dynamic view?

Dynamic Views can prove to be powerful prompting mechanism when you come across a requirement where the values fetched by the prompt table needs to be changed based on some system variables such as %OperatorId or %EmployeeId. Take a situation where you want to filter the data present in the prompt table based on the logged in user. In this case you need to use dynamic views as a prompt table.

Take a situation where you have an address id as a field on the page. Your requirement will be to bring up the address id's for the particular logged in user alone. But if a system administrator logs in, then you should display address id's corresponding to all the users. In this case you have to use up dynamic views. The step should be followed will be as follows.

1) Create a record (say PROMPT_DVW) and add necessary fields that need to be prompted.
2) Set up the key structure in the way you would like the prompt page to be appeared.
3) Save the record as dynamic view type. No need to build or write sql for these kinds of records.

4) On the record field property of the address id field, set the dynamic view as the prompt table.

5) Now on the appropriate event (RowInit, FieldChange etc) write the below code.

```
/* Note: ADDRESS_ID is the field which requires prompt. We are
not writing anything on the dynamic view people code events.
*/
If %OperatorId = "Admin" Then
RECORD.ADDRESS_ID.SqlText = "select ADDRESS_ID, DESCR from
PS_BASE_TABLE";
Else
RECORD.ADDRESS_ID.SqlText = "select ADDRESS_ID, DESCR from
PS_BASE_TABLE where EMPLOYEE_ID = '"|%EmployeeId|"'";
End-If;
```

The SqlText property will dynamically act as a view sql and bring up the corresponding result in the prompt page.

You can use a dynamic view to create a dynamic drop-down list, which lists the different sets of values depending on the value retrieved for a field such as Emplid. In the dynamic view, you can use %OperatorID to get the value of Emplid from PSOPRDEFN table, and then you can get a list of distinct values by joining tables in a select SQL.

F.I., you can create a dynamic record with the DEPTID field and the DESCR field, and use the following SQL.

```
SELECT DEPTID, DESCR
FROM PS_XXX_DEPT_OPR_VW
WHERE OPRID = %OperatorID;
```

You can then specify the Edit table of the drop-down list field to be this dynamic view.

34. Search keys must be specified in a record definition or a view in order for it to be the Search Record or the Add Search Record of a component.

35. By default, a grid will be automatically populated by the data from its base table or view; but the data auto-population can be disabled by setting the grid as No Auto Select in Use – Data Options in the grid property.

36. How to resolve the issue of the Ok button at the bottom of the Properties dialog box is hidden? As the Properties dialog box is pretty long, the Ok button at the bottom of the Properties dialog box is often hidden by the Windows Taskbar and become invisible and therefore a change cannot be saved.

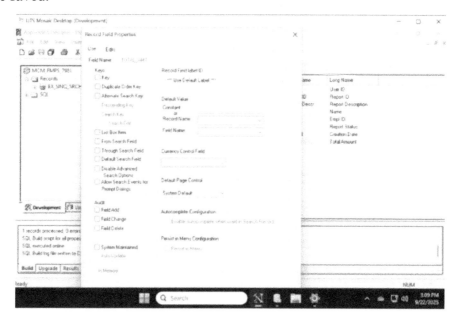

These are the steps to reveal the Ok button in the Properties dialog box if the taskbar overlapped it.

The first step is right-click the taskbar at the bottom of the Windows and select Taskbar settings.

The second step is enabling the option for Automatically hide the taskbar.

If you are using the remote desktop server to access the Application Designer, sometimes you may have to hide the task bar of the Windows on both the remote desktop server and your local computer in order to reveal the Ok button.

If the OK button is still not showing up after hiding the Window taskbar, you can press the Tab key three times to move the cursor to where the Ok button is located, and press Enter, and your change will be saved.

37. How to use SQL to find the menu name, menu item name, menu label, and item label of a component?

You can use the following SQLs to find the menu name, menu item name, menu label, and item label of a component.

```
SELECT * FROM PSMENUITEM WHERE PNLGRPNAME = XXXXXXXXXXXXX;
SELECT B.MENUGROUP, B.MENULABEL, A.BARLABEL, A.ITEMLABEL,
   A.PNLGRPNAME  ,A.BARNAME
 FROM PSMENUITEM A, PSMENUDEFN B, PSPNLGRPDEFN C
 WHERE A.MENUNAME = B.MENUNAME
 AND C.PNLGRPNAME = A.PNLGRPNAME
 AND C.PNLGRPNAME = 'XXXXXXXXXXXXX';
```

38. You can implement row-level security by having a query search for data using a query security record definition defined for the record on which you want to apply row-level security.

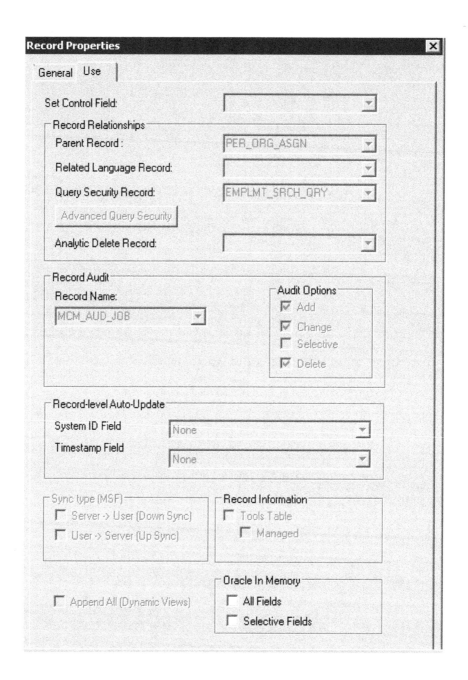

39. To track down the PeopleCode causing a SaveEdit error or a warning message, you may need to check all the record fields behind the page from the Order tab of the page, not just the record fields of the record that appears to have caused the issue. This is because all the records on a page, except those working records, may be affected by a SaveEdit event on saving.

An online trace will be helpful in tracking down the cause of an issue when needed.

40. To qualify as a Search Record or an Add Search Record of a component, a record definition or a view must include specified search keys.

41. What is the difference between component buffer and data buffer?

    Component buffer is an area in memory, which stores data for the currently active component. Whenever you open a component the entire data for that component is retrieved upfront and stored in the application server. Component buffer is a temporary buffer allocation. Component buffer contains active component data i.e. level 0 data.
    Data buffer contains multiple components of data.

42. Use the following statements to show variable values when debugging

```
        WinMessage("EMPLID is " | &Emplid);
```
Or,
```
    MessageBox (0, "", 0, 0, "EMPLID is" |&Emplid);
```

43. If you are making a change to an existing record, such as adding a new field, deleting an existing field, or changing the name of a field, always check whether there are views that are built based on the record definition; if there are any, the view(s) may have to be modified and rebuilt.

    You may need to do a definition reference check on all the views affected, check those pages that utilize the views, and see if the change causes any errors.

44. You must have developer or supervisor access to Change Control to lock and unlock definitions. If you have supervisor access, you can also lock all definitions at once, which can be helpful when performing upgrades to ensure that definitions are not modified in the middle of the process.

    You can also have Application Designer lock unlocked definitions for you each time you open them.

    Tools -> Options -> Change Control -> Lock Definition when it is opened

Now, whenever you open a definition, it is locked automatically unless you have only restricted access to Change Control. In this case, the system will notify you that you have restricted access and will ask whether you want to open the definition in read-only mode.

45. How to create Event Mapping?

Event Mapping is a useful feature that was introduced in PeopleTools 8.55. The basic concept is straightforward: Event Mapping enables you to inject custom code before or after delivered event code. There are some key benefits of Event Mapping:

- Your Custom PeopleCode is kept separate from delivered code

- You have Complete access to component buffer

To create a new Event Mapping in PeopleSoft, you follow a structured process using the Related Content Framework and Application Designer. Here's a step-by-step guide based on PeopleTools 8.55 and later, including enhancements in 8.59.

1. Create an Application Package and insert a new Application Class in it.

2. Write code in the Application Class.

Here is the sample code of an Event Mapping Application Class. It checks the values entered for the project id field on the bill line and the bill distribution line and generates an error message if only one of the two values is entered, or, if the two values entered for the project id field are different.

```
import PT_RCF:ServiceInterface;


class BI_LINE_PROJ implements PT_RCF:ServiceInterface
   method execute();


end-class;


method execute
   /+ Extends/implements PT_RCF:ServiceInterface.execute +/
   Local Rowset &HDR_RS, &LINE_RS;
   Local integer &I;


   &HDR_RS = GetLevel0();
   &LINE_RS = &HDR_RS(1).GetRowset(Scroll.BI_LINE);


   If
GetLevel0()(1).GetRecord(Record.BI_HDR).GetField(Field.BILL_SO
URCE_ID).Value <> "SPRDSHEET" Then


      /* Check values entered for two Project fields */
      /* Value exists in the bill line but not the accounting
distribution line */
      If All(&LINE_RS(1).BI_LINE.PROJECT_ID.Value) And
         None(BI_LINE_DST.PROJECT_ID.Value) Then
         Error MsgGet(22000, 41, "A value for Accounting
Distribution Project ID is required.");
         Exit;
      End-If;
```

```
        /* Value exists on the the accouting distribution line
and also the bill line but they are not the same */

        If All(&LINE_RS(1).BI_LINE.PROJECT_ID.Value) And

            All(BI_LINE_DST.PROJECT_ID.Value) Then

            If &LINE_RS(1).BI_LINE.PROJECT_ID.Value <>
BI_LINE_DST.PROJECT_ID.Value Then

                SetCursorPos(Page.BI_HDR_X,
BI_LINE.BUSINESS_UNIT_PC, CurrentRowNumber());

                Error MsgGet(22000, 31, "Values entered for
Project ID are different.");

                Exit;

            End-If;

        End-If;


    End-If;

end-method;
```

3. Define a Related Content Service

The navigation to define a Related Content Service is typically through PeopleTools > Portal > Related Content Service > Define Related Content Service.

Define Related Content Service

Service Information ⑦

Service ID MCM_BI_LINE_PROJ   Object Owner ID [ ] 🔍
*Service Name BI Line Req Proj

Description Set required project fields in BI Line

☐ Bulk Action   ☐ Template

*URL Type Application Class ⌄   [Write help text]   [Copy Service Definition]

▼ URL Information

Application Class Parameters

Package MCM_COMP_CONFIG 🔍   Path 🔍   Class Name BI_LINE_PROJ 🔍

☐ Post mapping definition data   ☑ Escape URL Parameters

Note: parameter names are case-sensitive.

Service URL Parameters

*Parameter Name	Required Flag	*Description		
1	☐		+	−

1-1 of 1 ⌄

Show Formed URL   Test Related Content Service

Display Options

☐ Refresh   ☐ New Window

Select Security Options

☑ Public Access   ☐ Related Content Provider Security   ☐ Related Content Consumer Security
☐ App Class Required

4. Configure Event Mapping

PeopleTools > Portal > Related Content Service > Manage Related Content Service.

36

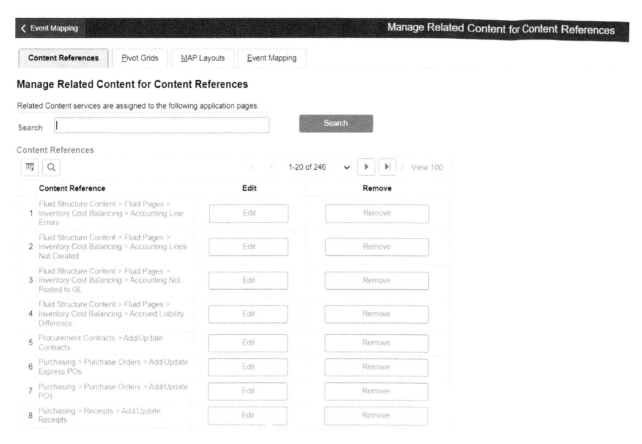

Search by component name

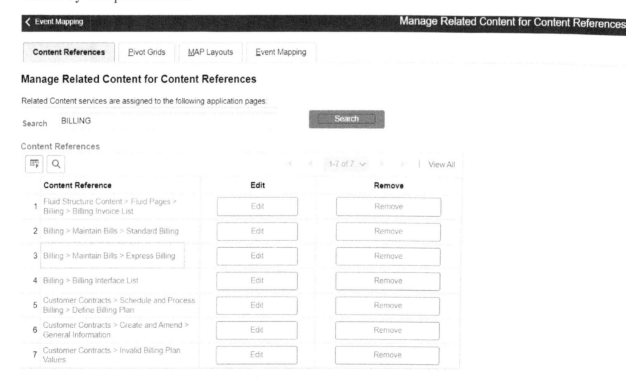

Click the Event Mapping tab

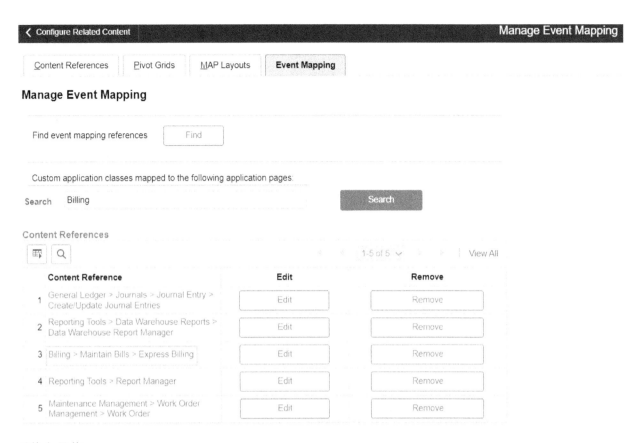

Click Edit

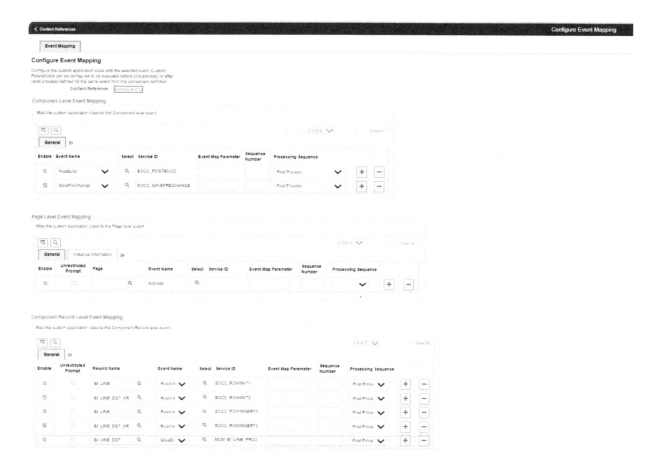

Which Events Support Event Mapping?

The list has been growing ever since Event Mapping was introduced.

Component Level events:

- PostBuild

- PreBuild

- SavePreChange

- SavePostChange

- WorkFlow

Component Record level events:

- RowDelete

- RowInit

- RowInsert

39

- RowSelect

- SaveEdit

- SavePreChange

- SavePostChange

Page level events:

- PageActivate

Field level events:

- FieldChange

Event Mapping Enhancements

Several enhancements have been added in 8.58 to support broader usage of event mapping. Event mapping now supports FieldDefault, FieldEdit, SearchInit, and SearchSave events for component record fields, and SearchInit and SearchSave events for component records.

Event mapping now also supports records and record fields on subpages and secondary pages at any level of nesting, not just for primary pages in the component. This enhancement extends support to the page Activate event for secondary pages and to derived work records.

Time to Use Event Mapping

PeopleSoft users that have heavily customized their PeopleSoft applications should look seriously at Event Mapping to isolate those customizations to provide a better PeopleSoft life cycle. Event Mapping can even be used in concert with other configuration features to dramatically reduce the impact of customizations.

46. How to resolve the issue of Unable to click the Ok button in a Properties window to save a change in Application Designer?

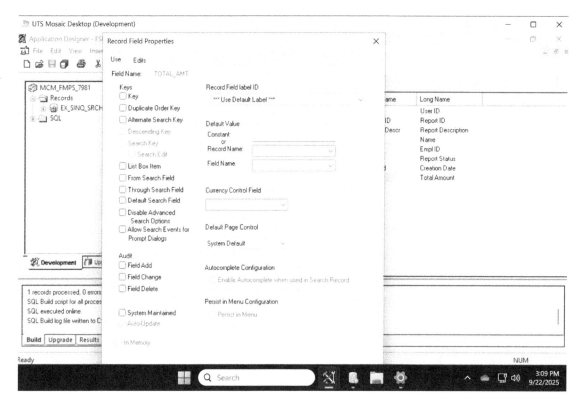

- Right-click the taskbar and select Taskbar settings.

- Enable the option for Automatically hide the taskbar. This can reveal the button if the taskbar was overlapping it.

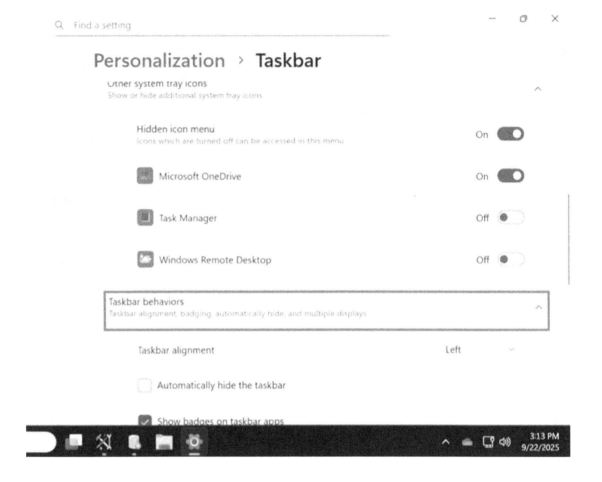

Personalization › Taskbar

Other system tray icons
Show or hide additional system tray icons

Hidden icon menu   On
Icons which are turned off can be accessed in this menu

Microsoft OneDrive   On

Task Manager   Off

Windows Remote Desktop   Off

Taskbar behaviors
Taskbar alignment, badging, automatically hide, and multiple displays

Taskbar alignment   Left

Automatically hide the taskbar

Show badges on taskbar apps

3:13 PM
9/22/2025

Personalization > **Taskbar**

🔲 Task Manager	Off	⬤
☁️ Windows Remote Desktop	Off	⬤

Taskbar behaviors
Taskbar alignment, badging, automatically hide, and multiple displays   ∧

Taskbar alignment	Left ⌄

☑️ Automatically hide the taskbar

☑️ Show badges on taskbar apps

☑️ Show flashing on taskbar apps

Show my taskbar on all displays

When using multiple displays, show my taskbar apps on   All taskbars   ⌄

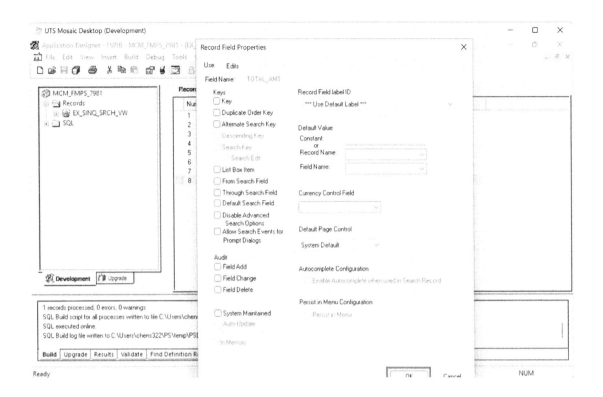

If you are using the remote desktop server to access the Application Designer, you may need to hide the task bar of the Windows of your local computer as well.

Here is an example.

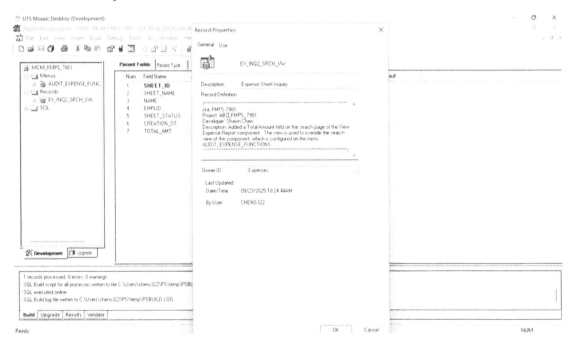

44

47. How to hide a subpage or multiple page controls altogether?

To hide a subpage or multiple page controls altogether, place the subpage or the page controls inside a group box. A group box has a property to hide/unhide all controls inside it when the groupbox is hidden. You must assign the groupbox to a record field (a derived work field would be suitable.) If you do not want the appearance of a group box when controls are visible, you could tweak the appearance of the groupbox such that none of its elements are visible.

48. **Error:** Unable to see the table in the SQL client after building a record in Application Designer

Cause: If it is the first time you try to build a record in a new environment, it can be caused by the fact that your database driver, such as ODBC driver, has not been set up properly on your local machine, if you are using SQL Server on a Windows platform.

Or, you may be missing some roles, f.i., the UPG_ALLPNLS role, which allow you to use Application Designer and build/alter records successfully.

If it is not the first time you try to do this, the reason why you cannot see a created table in the SQL client after you have built a record with Application Designer could be that a public synonym needs to be created for that table.

Solution: Make sure the table name starts with 'PS_'

Typically, when a new record is built, you will have to prefix your select with the schema owner until you have a public synonym created for that table. Therefore, try adding the 'sysadm.' prefix to the table's name in the SQL client.

If it doesn't work, you can try granting all access to the table. In Oracle, you can use the Grant statement. F.i.

```
grant all on PS_XXX_CRACLN_RCTL to public;
```

If you don't have the privilege to do the table grant, you can run it using a DMS script via the Data Mover. F.i.

```
set log H:\Temp\table_grant.log;

grant all on PS_MCM_CRACLN_RCTL to public;
```

You can also contact DBA to see if a public synonym can be created for the table.

Make sure you have all the roles needed for a PeopleSoft developer. Make sure your ODBC driver is set up properly if your Tools is installed locally if you are using Windows and SQL Server

49. **Error:** "Could not read shared cache RDM" error is thrown when logging in

Cause: The space on the network drive where the PS cache directory is located is low.

Solution: Increase the space on the network drive where the PS cache directory is located or change it to a different location.

50. **Error:** User receives "password has expired" error when trying to login to Application Designer

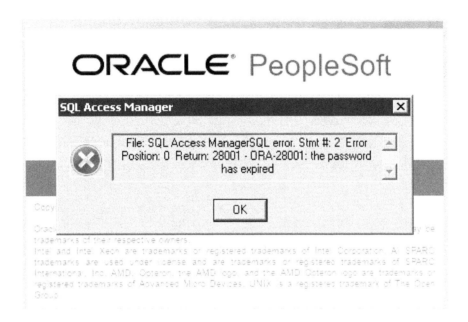

Cause: The SYSADM userid, which is used to access the database behind the scene, has expired.

Solution: Ask DBA to reset the password of the SYSADM userid.

51. **Error**: "Page data is inconsistent with database."

Cause: The record definition does not have any keys; therefore, the database table does not have an index, or the keys in the record definition do not match the keys in the database table.

Another thing to watch out for is any SavePostChange PeopleCode that may be changing the data outside of the buffer and causing it to be out of sync.

Solution: Check your keys and ensure they match the record definition and the database table. If not, update the record definition and/or alter/recreate the database table with the correct keys.

Check if any SavePostChange PeopleCode may change the data outside of the buffer, and fix it if so.

52. **Error:** "Data being inserted doesn't exist" error is thrown when saving a component.

    Cause: The data has been deleted or has been marked as deleted, but the page still references the deleted data

    Solution: Check if the data still exists in the backend.

53. **Error**: When clicking on the lookup of a field on a page, the following error message is shown "No matching values were found"

    Cause: The key structure of the prompt table or view may not be correct

    Solution: Check the key structure of the prompt table/view; the prompt field should be a key field and search key field in the prompt table/view. Some other remaining fields can be set as alternate keys.

54. **Error**: "You are not allowed to update your own data" when saving changes to the employee data.

    Cause: This error typically occurs when you attempt to modify a record that matches your own Employee ID (EmplID). You cannot update your own information inside PeopleSoft, except when doing so through self-service.

    Solution: You can change the EmplID associated with your user ID, or, use the following PeopleCode function to update your own data

    ```
    AllowEmplIdChg(True);
    ```

55. **Error**: "Data being added conflicts with existing data" error is thrown when trying to add new data.

    Cause: Same data has been added to the database before.

    Solution: If it is an effective dated component with both Update/Display and Add mode, and the error happens in the Add mode, check if all the key fields of the level 0 record on the page are Display Only; also check if the search field keys are set correctly for the search record; likewise, check whether the build of the record definition has been properly done, and make sure that some indexes have been created for the table.

56. **Error**: "Class Row method GetRowset scroll {Record} is invalid" when opening or saying a page with a grid or a scroll.

Cause: There can be multiple causes depending on the context of this error

It is usually caused by the level of the rowset is not specified correctly in the PeopleCode.

Solution: Check the page order for the grid main record. You need to have the parent record fields on level 0 or 1 and the child record fields on level 1 or 2. Check your code against the structure of the component.

57. **Error**: "Invalid Value" error in a drop-down list

Cause: An Invalid Value in a drop-down comes when the value retrieved from the database for the field is not a valid value for the field. So if your field is a translated field that has two values X and Y, and if you saved a value Z by some means to that field - the next time you try to view this field system will give you the invalid value error as only X and Y are recognized values for the drop-down. Another common cause is a required field with no default value.

Solution: Check your data integrity first - make sure that no incorrect data exists in the database.

If you want to populate a value other than the translate values to the drop-down, work around the translate value logic by using the AddDropDownItem PeopleCode.

If the error is caused by the fact that there is no default value, and your use case says no value should be defaulted, then consider deferring the field value check. Furthermore, instead of marking it required on the record field properties, you could make it an edit that only fires when an action occurs. For example, when the PO is approved or the project submitted—even deferring it to SaveEdit works.

Alternatively, consider radio buttons.

58. **Error**: Cannot delete the last row in a grid with a required field

Cause: When trying to save a change, required fields are highlighted and prompted for data entry, and the row is not deleted from the database.

Solution: Move the PeopleCode from RowInit and RowInsert event to FieldDefault event.

RowInit PeopleCode causes a new row to generate, which asks for the values for required fields, whereas the FieldDefault PeopleCode does not.

59. **Error**: "Data Exists" error message is thown when a change to a grid with a check box field is being saved

    Cause: Key fields are not set in the record definition behind the grid, hence there is no unique index in the table.

    Solution: Set key fields in the record definition behind the grid in order for the system to identify the unique rows; there is no need to rebuild the record after setting key fields.

60. **Error:** A page URL with parameters does not go to the page as supposed to, and it only stops at the search page of the component the page is within

    Cause: Not all search key values are provided.

    Solution: Provide all search key values.

61. **Error**: "Invalid Drop-Down List in page definition"

    Cause: The issue might be caused by record definitions not being current and missing fields. Or it might be caused by using a dynamic prompt table such as %EDITTABLE.

    Solution: Replace the prompt table with a regular table/view from a dynamic table/view, save the record, and save the page, then go back to the prompt field and change it to the dynamic table/view, and re-save the record. The purpose of doing so is to save the page first so that this error will not be thrown. This should allow you to be able to use the dynamic view/table as the prompt table.

62. **Error**: "SQL Access Manager SQL error. ORA-28000: the account is locked."

    Cause: The database system account used by PeopleSoft (typically SYSADM in Oracle) has been locked.

    Solution: Ask DBA to unlock the database system account.

64. **Error**: "Invalid identifier" error is thrown when trying to build a table from a record

49

Cause: One record field has an Oracle reserved keyword as its name, such as Date, UID, etc.

Solution: Run the record build script in the SQL client, and the error message may suggest which field uses a reserved keyword. Change the field name to something safer.

65. **Error**: "PeopleTools has stopped working" when trying to log in to the Application Designer

    Cause: There can be different reasons, including configuration, network issues, etc.

    Solution: Try to redo a workstation install with a good config file.

66. **Error**: "Open file operation failed. <FilePath>\PSBUILD.LOG" when building a record or a project.

    Solution: Ensure to set a valid path in the Logging tab and Scripts tab in Build Settings.

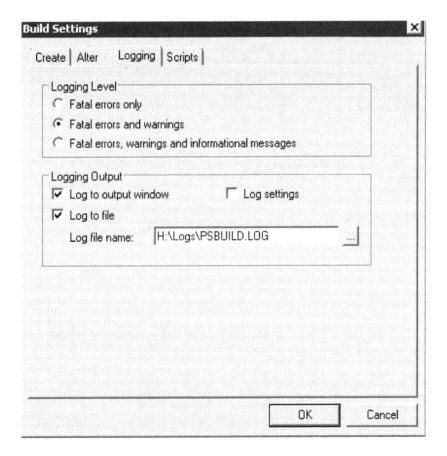

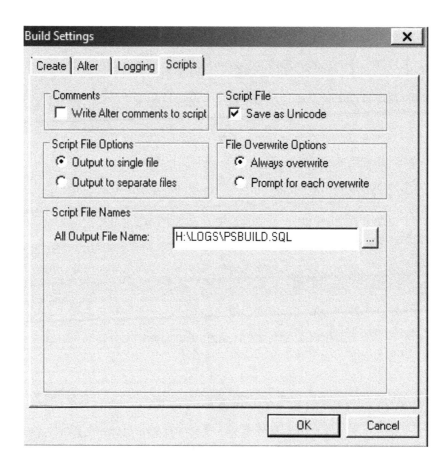

67. **Error**: "No matching buffer found for level."

Cause: There might be a missing row in the level 1 record (parent), but there are rows in its level 2 record (child)

Solution: Check all level 1 records which has a level 2 record under the component interface. You can put on an online SQL trace for a specific user. Get the trace log file from the PS admin.

Search by keyword 'Rollback' and/or 'Error.' Check the select statements and tables right before where the keyword is found. It is likely the table that has the child record data doesn't have a matching row in its parent table.

68. **Error**: "A SQL error occurred. Please consult your system log for details" pops up when opening a page.

Cause: If you get a SQL error when trying to open a page, you should check whether any of the records on the page should have been built or altered, but it hasn't been done yet. The Alter action should be performed on any records that have been modified.

It is often a case where a record or a view was not built, perhaps the search record/view for the component. Or it was caused by a SQL error in the PeopleCode.

Solution: Check the record/view and the SQLs in the PeopleCode behind the page.

Execute the SQLs in the back end and see the results.

Check app server log files, and they may have the details about which specific SQL errored out.

Navigate to the log files, and its path should be like this:

/home/<YourappserverName>/app/psoft/<DBname>/appserv/<DBname>/logs

Search for "Failed SQL stmt," and it will show the SQL statement that is causing the problem.

If it is a delivered page, you may need a PeopleTools patch.

69. How to find out the names of a field and its record on a page without using Application Designer?

Other than using the Application Designer to find out details about a field on a page, you can also use the Inspect Element approach from the browser.

Right-click the field or the page control for which you want to know the names of the field and its record, and then select Inspect.

In the Elements tab of the window that appears, details of the control are shown, including the control's id. The id includes the table and field names.

```
                                    <td height="19"></td>
                                ▶ <td colspan="6" rowspan="2" valign="top" aligr
                                  <td colspan="3" rowspan="2"></td>
                                ▼ <td rowspan="2" valign="top" align="left">
                                  ▼ <div id="win0divVOUCHER_GROSS_AMT">
                                        <span class="PSEDITBOX_DISPONLY" id="VOUCHI
                                        <!-- VOUCHER_GROSS_AMT -->
                                    </div>
                                  </td>
                                ▶ <td colspan="3" rowspan="2" valign="top" aligr
```

div#win0divVOUCHER_GROSS_AMT   span#VOUCHER_GROSS_AMT.PSEDITBOX_DISPONLY

Styles   Computed   Layout   Event Listeners   DOM Breakpoints   Properties

⹀ Filter   :hov .cls + ⛉ ⬅

```
element.style {
}

.pt_classic_plus .PSEDITBOX_DISPONLY, .pt_classic_plus     PSSTYLEDEF_...1.css:10861
.PSDROPDOWNLIST_DISPONLY, .pt_classic_plus
.PSEDITBOX_DISPONLY_NOWRAP {
    position: relative;
    top: 5px;
}

.pt_classic_plus .PSDROPDOWNLIST_DISPONLY,                  PSSTYLEDEF_...1.css:10656
.pt_classic_plus .PSEDITBOX_DISPONLY, .pt_classic_plus
.PSEDITBOX_DISPONLY_NOWRAP, .pt_classic_plus .PSTEXT, .pt_classic_plus
.PSLONGEDITBOX, .pt_classic_plus .PSSRCHINSTRUCTIONS, .pt_classic_plus
.PAPAGEINSTRUCTIONS, .pt_classic_plus .PSXLATTITLE {
    font-family: Arial, Helvetica, sans-serif;
    font-size: 14.6667px;
    color: ■ #000;
```

The free PS Utilities extension for Google Chrome includes a number of features, including a Field Inspector.

Click on the Field Inspector icon in the PS Utilities menu, then select the control for which you require information:

54

70. How to enable field level auditing and record level auditing?

It is recommended to monitor the changes occurring in your key records. PeopleSoft offers two different methods to facilitate record auditing. One approach involves specifying an audit table for a record or table and configuring audit options in the record property, Use tab. By doing so, you can eliminate the need for SQL insert statements in PeopleCode to insert audit data. PeopleSoft provides two levels of auditing: field level auditing and record level auditing. Field level auditing allows you to track every change made to a specific field in a record. You can enable auditing for multiple fields within a record. To enable field level auditing, navigate to the record field properties where you will find three options. Select the desired options from there.

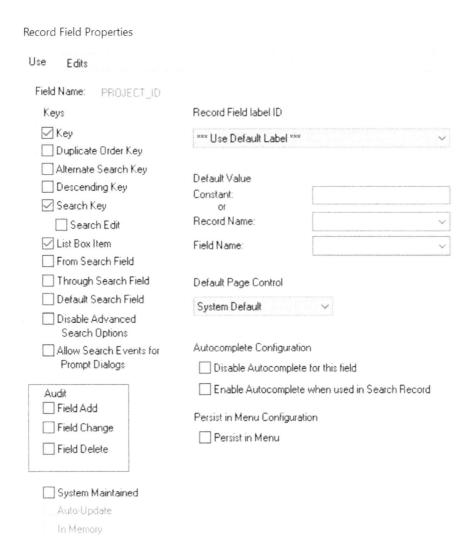

Record Field Properties

Use   Edits

Field Name: PROJECT_ID

Keys
☑ Key
☐ Duplicate Order Key
☐ Alternate Search Key
☐ Descending Key
☑ Search Key
   ☐ Search Edit
☑ List Box Item
☐ From Search Field
☐ Through Search Field
☐ Default Search Field
☐ Disable Advanced
   Search Options
☐ Allow Search Events for
   Prompt Dialogs

Audit
☐ Field Add
☐ Field Change
☐ Field Delete

☐ System Maintained
   Auto-Update
   In Memory

Record Field label ID

*** Use Default Label ***   ⌄

Default Value
Constant:
   or
Record Name: ⌄
Field Name: ⌄

Default Page Control

System Default   ⌄

Autocomplete Configuration
☐ Disable Autocomplete for this field
☐ Enable Autocomplete when used in Search Record

Persist in Menu Configuration
☐ Persist in Menu

Field Add option will track whenever a value is added to that selected field. Checking Field Change option will create an entry whenever you change the value of the field. By checking Field Delete option, a new row is created in the audit record whenever the field value is deleted.

All your audit options are tracked in a PeopleSoft delivered audit record called PSAUDIT. The audit record will capture the details like who changed the field, what time the change was made, what was the change, the field name, old values and new values and the keys for your parent record.

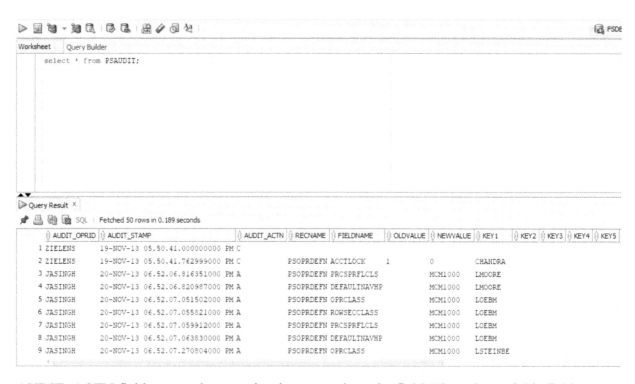

AUDIT_ACTN field stores what was the change made to the field. The values of this field can be interpreted as follows.

A – Added new value or row

C – Changed the existing value or row

D – Deleted the old value or row

K – Row updated, Old Value

N –Row Updated, New Value

O – Original Value

You can check the changes to your base record field by using a query similar to the one below.

```
SELECT * FROM PSAUDIT WHERE RECNAME = '<YOUR RECORD NAME>'
AND FIELDNAME = '<YOUR FIELD NAME>' AND KEY1 = '<FIRST KEY
VALUE FOR YOUR BASE RECORD>' AND KEY2 = '<SECOND KEY VALUE
FOR YOUR BASE RECORD>' <AND SO ON TILL YOU MAP ALL THE
KEYS>
```

Field level auditing is auditing each field on your record and will be creating a new row for change in all the fields. This can grow up your audit record size and end up in performance issue. Also, if you have many fields to audit in a record, then it becomes difficult for you to see through the report to see all the actions done on one particular record as it will result in multiple rows.

To tackle this situation PeopleSoft has provided another level of auditing called Record Level Auditing. With record level auditing, you can enable the audit for entire record and select the fields to be included in the audit. This will be particularly helpful when you have multiple fields in a record to be audited.

Record Properties

General   Use

Set Control Field: BUSINESS_UNIT
  Record Relationships
  Parent Record :
  Related Language Record: CB_HDR_LNG
  Query Security Record:
  Advanced Query Security
Analytic Delete Record:

Record Audit   Audit Options
Record Name: Add
AUDIT_CB_HDR   Change
                                              Selective
                                              Delete

Record-level Auto-Update

System ID Field   None
Timestamp Field   LAST_UPDATE_DTTM

Sync type (MSF)   Record Information
  Server -> User (Down Sync)   Tools Table
  User -> Server (Up Sync)   Managed

                                  Oracle In Memory
  Append All (Dynamic Views)   ☐ All Fields

This is what the AUDIT_CB_HDR record looks like.

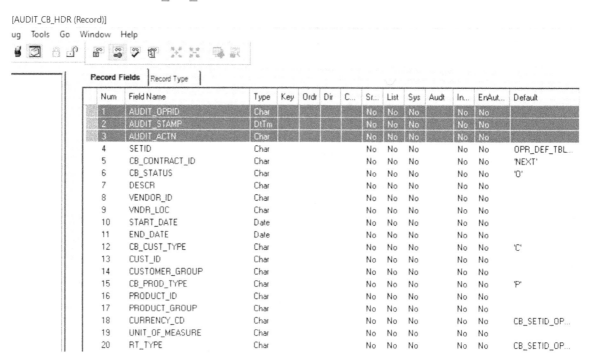

For creating record level audit, you need to create a new audit record for your base record. This record should follow certain standards. The easiest way to create an audit record is to open your record and save it as AUDIT_<Your Name>. Once the audit record is saved you can delete the unwanted fields (fields which need not be audited).

Other important steps you need to make are as follows.

Remove all your keys. Audit records are not supposed to contain keys.

Remove any Query Security record associated with it.

If there are any Parent record associated, then remove it.

Remove any PeopleCode associated with the audit record.

Add the below delivered fields as required

AUDIT_OPRID – This field will capture the operator id of the person who has made the change.

AUDIT_STAMP – This field stores the date time stamp at which the change is made.

AUDIT_ACTN – This field stores what action was taken to the record. The values are as below.

A: Row is inserted

D: Row deleted

C: Row changed (updated), but no key fields changed. The system writes existing values to the audit table.

K: Row changed (updated), and at least one key field changed. The system writes existing values to the audit table.

N: Row changed (updated), and at least one key field changed. The system writes new values to the audit table.

AUDIT_RECNAME – This field stores which record was audited. Include this field only if you are using the same audit record for multiple base records.

Once you are done with it, you are ready with your audit record. Now to enable the auditing for your base table, open the base record properties and go to the use tab. There you should specify the name of the new audit record you have created and check the audit actions that you need to enable for the base record.

As opposed to the field level auditing, you have an additional option called Selective. This will insert a row in an audit table whenever a value of the field included in the audit table is changed in the base table. If you click on change option, then the audit record will capture the row regardless of whether it is included in the audit record or not.

With this, you need to make a special note that the auditing will happen only if the user adds/deletes/changes the data from PeopleSoft application. If the data is changed by SQLs in backend or via any third party, PeopleSoft audit tables will not capture these details. To capture that detail as well, then you need to consider enabling database triggers.

APPLICATION ENGINE

71. Application Engine programs don't have to have a state record; they use a state record only when it is necessary to transfer values. This is because a state record is like a collection of global variables.

72. An Application Engine program can have multiple state records, but only one can be a default state record.

73. An Application Engine temp table (TAO table) needs to be created with its record type selected as a Temporary Table for it to be on the list of temporary tables which can be selected as the temp table for the Application Engine program in the Application Engine properties.

74. When an Application Engine program terminates abnormally, if there is no data in the temporary table, the TAO table, check if TAO1, TAO2, TAO3, etc., tables exist. There might be data in those tables, not the base table.

    You can also check the application engine program to see if there is more than 1 temporary table instance. Open the Application Engine program in Application Designer. Select File, Definition Properties, and then select the Temp Tables tab.

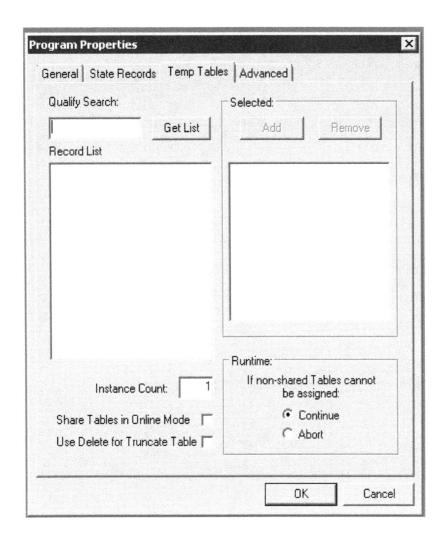

75. When changing the number of instances of the temp table, the table needs to be rebuilt.

76. If data in a table generated by an Application Engine program needs to be deleted for the next run, it is better to delete the data in the table by truncating the table at the beginning of the AE program instead of at the end. This way, the data resides in the table and can be tracked until the next run.

77. PROCESS_INSTANCE should always be the first field of the Application Engine state records. It should also be the only key field. Other commonly used fields are OPRID and RUN_CNTL_ID. This lets you track who is running the application engine program and what run control ID they are using. This is because all the processes need a unique identifier. In PeopleSoft, this unique identifier is called process instance. Since it is a unique identifier, it

must be unique in nature. Therefore, PeopleSoft always generates a new unique number every time for a process instance.

78. What are the different ways to restart an application engine program after it abends?

When an Application Engine program ends abnormally, there are a few ways to start the program over from the beginning after you put in a fix to the program.

- You can select Restart Request from the Process Request Details dialog box;
- You can delete the failed process instance and use a different run control id to run the process successfully, and then change the run control id to the default one

You can use SQL to delete the row that corresponds to the failed program from the Application Engine run control table and your state record.

1) Use the following SQL to manually delete the row in PS_AERUNCONTROL that corresponds to the program you want to start from the beginning.

```
DELETE FROM PS_AERUNCONTROL
WHERE OPRID=OPRID
AND RUN_CNTL_ID=Run_Control_ID;
```

2) If the record type of your state record is a physical table, not a derived record, use the following SQL to delete from your state record the row that corresponds to the failed program run,

```
DELETE FROM PS_MY_AET
WHERE PROCESS_INSTANCE=Process_Instance;
```

Alternatively, you can remove the stuck run controls of a failed Application Engine program by navigating to the following page in the system

PeopleTools -> Application Engine -> Manage Abends

79. What is the difference between %Select and %SelectInit in Application Engine?

The main difference between %Select and %SelectInit is that the former holds the latest value even after the current SQL returns no rows. But, %SelectInit will be assigned with a Null value if the very SQL statement returns no rows. Technically, it reinitializes the buffer.

80. You can use Do Select as the first step and PeopleCode and a SQL as the second and the third step. Both will be controlled by logical loops of the Do Select statement.

81. If you have specified the path and the name of an output file on the run control page of an Application Engine process, but you don't see an output file generated in the process monitor by looking at the View Log/Trace link, check if you have put file extension (e.g., .txt, .csv) after the output file's name on the run control page.

82. How to terminate and branch out in Application Engine?

Terminating or branching out in an AE program can be implemented by using the If/Then logic with the Exit function to go to different steps or sections.

From PeopleCode, you can trigger an error status, or false return, by using the Exit function. Use the On Return value in the PeopleCode action properties to specify how your Application Engine program behaves according to the return of your PeopleCode program. This example shows the On Return property:

Image: Example of On Return action property

This example illustrates the fields and controls on the Example of On Return action property.

By default, the program terminates, similar to what happens when a SQL error occurs. By changing the On Return value to Skip Step, however, you can control the flow of your Application Engine program.

You can use Exit to add an If condition to a step or a section break. For example:

```
If StateRec.Field1 = 'N'
    Exit(1);
Else
    /* Do processing */
End-if;
```

You must specify a non-zero return value to trigger an On Return action. The concepts of "return 1" and "return True" are equivalent; therefore, if the return value is non-zero or True, then Application Engine performs what you specify for On Return, as in Abort or Skip Step. However, if the program returns zero or False, the Application Engine ignores the selected On Return value.

Here are more examples,

```
If XXX_JRNLLAP_AET.PERIOD_ABBRV = "LAP" Then
    Exit (0); /* Continue */
Else
    Exit(1); /* Exit */
End-If;
If XXX_SGS_COM_AET.RERUN_FLAG = "Y" Then
    /* Delete existing data */
    MessageBox(0, "", 0, 0, "Re-run flag is on, deleting
    existing data for RUN_ID = %1",
    XXX_SGS_COM_AET.RUN_ID);
    Exit (0);
```

```
Else

    /* Skip delete and continue processing */

    Exit (1);

End-If;
```

83. How to exit from an Application Engine program successfully with a Warning status?

You can add the AE_APPSTATUS field into the primary state record that your application engine uses.

Based on your condition, update the field value to 1 and then write a warning message into your log. The application engine completes with a warning in the process status and a warning message in the message log.

```
STATE_REC_AET.AE_APPSTATUS = 1;

MessageBox(0, "", 0, 0, "No Message Found.");
```

Here is an example,

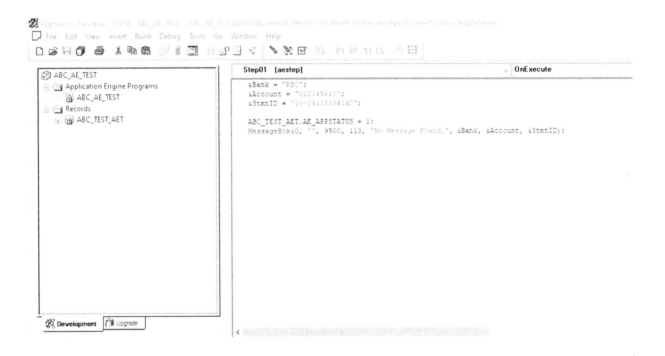

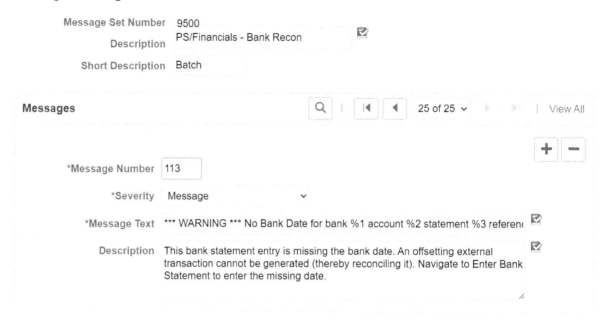

The message catalogue entry for 9500, 113 is as follows,

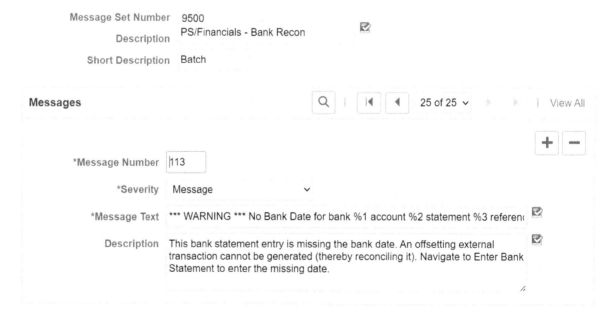

After running the process with the above code in the Application Engine program, the process status of the process instance is shown as Warning.

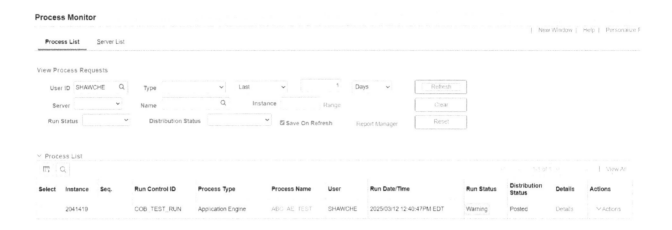

The message log of the process instance is as follows,

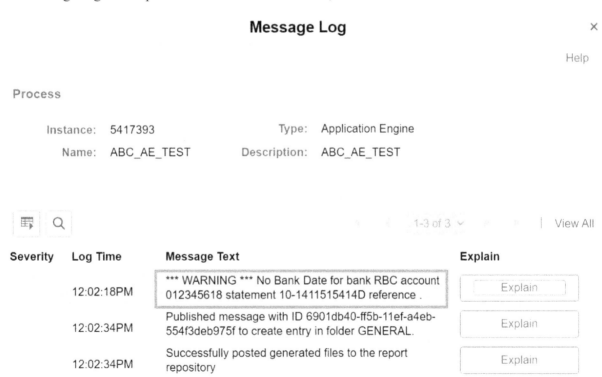

Note, if setting the primary state record's AE_APPSTATUS To 1 using PeopleCode returns Success instead of a Warning status, Oracle issued a fix in PeopleTools 8.61, 8.60.08 and 8.59.20.

84. How to perform a dynamic call section in an Application Engine program?

Firstly, insert the field 'AE_SECTION' into your AE state record. Then prior to the 'Call Section' step, add the following code to a PeopleCode Step, setting the AE_SECTION field to the actual section that needs to be called.

```
If &condition1 Then

      STATE_REC_AET.AE_SECTION.Value = "SECTION1";

Else

      STATE_REC_AET.AE_SECTION.Value = "SECTION2";

End-If;
```

The 'Call Section' command itself should then be defined with no value entered in the section name but with the 'Dynamic' flag ticked. The system will know that dynamic naming is in operation and will check for the AE_SECTION field on the state record. The program will error if the AE_SECTION field does not exist or it points to an invalid section name.

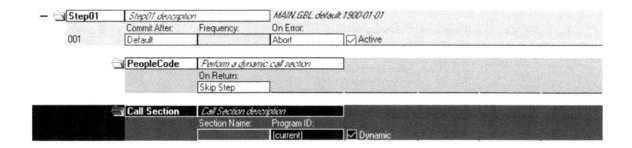

Dynamic sections can be utilized when the App Engine needs to function as both a batch process and an online process. In such scenarios, you might call different sections because the data requirements vary based on whether a run control record has been pre-created, or a different run control has been used.

To call a section in another Application Engine program, insert the field 'AE_APPLID' into your AE state record as well, and add the following PeopleCode to the PeopleCode step.

```
If &condition1 Then

        STATE_REC_AET.AE_APPLID.Value = "PROGRAM1"

        STATE_REC_AET.AE_SECTION.Value = "SECTION1";

Else

        STATE_REC_AET.AE_APPLID.Value = "PROGRAM2"

        STATE_REC_AET.AE_SECTION.Value = "SECTION2";

End-If;
```

85. How to perform a dynamic call section to create a single AE program that can function as both a batch process and an online process?

Using Dynamic Sections in PeopleSoft Application Engine (AE) allows you to create a single AE program that can function as both a batch process and an online process, depending on how it is executed. Below are the steps and best practices to implement this approach:

1) Understanding Dynamic Sections in Application Engine

- A Dynamic Section in AE is determined at runtime based on a parameter.

- You can conditionally execute different logic within the same AE program without hardcoding separate sections.

- This is useful when the AE needs to support both batch and online modes.

2) Key Steps to Implement Dynamic Section for Batch & Online Mode

Step 1: Define Two Sections (One for Batch, One for Online)

- Create two sections in the same AE program:

- Batch Section: Handles bulk data processing.

- Online Section: Handles a single transaction or real-time processing.

Step 2: Use a Parameter to Determine the Execution Mode

- Add a state record field, e.g., AET.PROCESS_MODE:

- 'BATCH' → Calls the batch processing section.

- 'ONLINE' → Calls the online processing section.

Step 3: Create a Dynamic Call Section

- Use the Call Section action with the %Select construct to dynamically call the correct section.

```
%Select(AE_SECTION)

FROM PS_AET_CONFIG

WHERE PROCESS_MODE = %Bind(AET.PROCESS_MODE)
```

- PS_AET_CONFIG is a configuration table that maps PROCESS_MODE values to the appropriate section names.

Step 4: Populate the Configuration Table

Insert records into PS_AET_CONFIG:

PROCESS_MODE	AE_SECTION
BATCH	BATCH_PROCESS
ONLINE	ONLINE_PROCESS

Step 5: Implement Run Control for Batch Mode

- In batch mode, AE is typically triggered using Process Scheduler.
- Use a Run Control Page to allow users to specify batch-specific parameters.

Step 6: Implement PeopleCode for Online Execution

- Call the AE program from a component (PeopleCode):

```
&request = CreateProcessRequest("YOUR_AE_NAME");
&request.RunControlID = "ONLINE";
&request.SetParameter("PROCESS_MODE", "ONLINE");
&request.Schedule();
```

3) Best Practices

- Performance Consideration: Online processes should execute quickly, so avoid processing large volumes of data in the online mode.
- Error Handling: Implement robust error logging using the Message Log and ensure proper rollback handling.
- Testing: Test both batch and online execution paths thoroughly to verify the dynamic behavior.

Example Use Case

Scenario: A payroll calculation process needs to run in batch mode for multiple employees and online mode for a single employee.

- Batch Mode: Processes payroll for all employees using scheduled AE.
- Online Mode: Processes payroll for a single employee from a component.

By following the above steps, the same AE program can be used flexibly for both execution modes.

86. For the application engine programs that you invoke outside of PeopleSoft Process Scheduler, use the Manage Abends page to free or unlock temporary tables used by the program if the program terminates abnormally. Programs running outside of Process Scheduler include those invoked from CallAppEngine PeopleCode and the command line.

Manage abends will clear up the data in all temp tables. Therefore you should rerun an application engine program from the beginning after managing abend, and do not Restart the program.

87. If you want to write an error log to the Process Scheduler Log, your best choice is to use the Application Engine Log Message or MessageBox() within a PeopleCode action.

```
LogMessage("MESSAGE: Consolidating Secondary Customer:" |
&SecondaryCustomer);
or
MessageBox(0, "", 0, 0, "@@@@@ Running in DEBUG mode @@@@@");
or
MessageBox(0, "", 0, 0, &numSent | " of " | (&numSent +
&numFailed) | " Type-1 email(s) sent to SUPERVISORS
successfully.");
MessageBox(0, "", 0, 0, "BusinessUnit=" | &strBU | "; WO_ID="
| &strWO_ID | "; TASK_ID=" | &strTASK_ID);
```

88. How to use SQL to find which project an Application Engine program is in?

Find Definition References doesn't work for an Application Engine program.

You can use the following SQL to find all the projects that contain a specific Application Engine program.

```
SELECT * FROM PSPROJECTITEM
```

```
WHERE OBJECTVALUE1 = '{AE_NAME}' AND OBJECTTYPE = 33;
```

Likewise, you can use the following SQL to find all the projects that contain an Application Engine program section.

```
SELECT * FROM PSPROJECTITEM
WHERE OBJECTVALUE1 = '{AE_NAME}' AND OBJECTTYPE = 34;
```

You can also use the following SQL to find all the projects that contain an Application Engine program step.

```
SELECT * FROM PSPROJECTITEM
WHERE OBJECTVALUE1 = '{AE_NAME}' AND OBJECTTYPE = 35;
```

89. How to call a SQL object in a SQL action in Application Engine?

You can use a SQL object in a SQL action. Here is an example.

```
SELECT A.ITEM
FROM %Sql(XXX_SOURCE)%Table(ITEM_ACTIVITY) A
```

The SQL object can be defined as the database prefix for a cross-database join, such as PSARSRC.PSPROD07.

90. How to use the %EffdtCheck and the %Join meta SQL to build a Where clause dynamically?

You can use the %EffdtCheck and the %Join meta SQL to build a Where clause dynamically. At runtime, these two entire meta SQLs will be replaced with a character string.

You can use the %EffdtCheck meta SQL to dynamically build a Where clause joining one table to its effect date table.

```
%EffDtCheck(DEPT_TBL B, A, %CurrentDateIn)
```

74

Note %EffdtdtCheck doesn't include effective sequence or effective status logic so you'll still have to write that the old fashioned way.

```
%EffDtCheck(DEPT_TBL B, A, %CurrentDateIn)
AND A.EFFSEQ = 1 AND A.EFF_STATUS = 'A'
```

You can use the %Join meta SQL to dynamically build a Where clause joining one table to another with common keys.

```
%Join(COMMON_KEYS, PSAESECTDEFN ABC, PSAESTEPDEFN XYZ)
```

You can also specify a value for a joined key field, Suppose you want to join two tables, but not on the field C3. In addition, you would like to specify a value for C3. Your code could look like the following

```
%Join(COMMON_FIELDS, MY_TABLE1 A, MY_TABLE2 B, C3)
AND C3 = 'XX'
```

Here is an example which uses both meta SQLs,

```
SELECT S.SQLID
  , S.SQLTYPE
  , S.VERSION
  , S.LASTUPDOPRID
  , S.LASTUPDDTTM
  , S.ENABLEEFFDT
  , S.OBJECTOWNERID
  , ST.MARKET
  , ST.DBTYPE
  , ST.EFFDT
  , ST.SEQNUM
  , ST.SQLTEXT
   FROM %Table(PSSQLDEFN) S
   , %Table(PSSQLTEXTDEFN) ST
  WHERE %Join(COMMON_KEYS, PSSQLDEFN S, PSSQLTEXTDEFN ST)
```

```
        AND %EffdtCheck(PSSQLTEXTDEFN ST_ED, ST,
    %CurrentDateIn);
```

When resolved, the above SQL is as follows

```
SELECT S.SQLID
  , S.SQLTYPE
  , S.VERSION
  , S.LASTUPDOPRID
  , S.LASTUPDDTTM
  , S.ENABLEEFFDT
  , S.OBJECTOWNERID
  , ST.MARKET
  , ST.DBTYPE
  , ST.EFFDT
  , ST.SEQNUM
  , ST.SQLTEXT
   FROM PSSQLDEFN S
   , PSSQLTEXTDEFN ST
 WHERE S.SQLID = ST.SQLID
   AND S.SQLTYPE = ST.SQLTYPE
   AND ST.EFFDT=(
 SELECT MAX(EFFDT)
  FROM PSSQLTEXTDEFN ST_ED
 WHERE ST_ED.SQLID=ST.SQLID
   AND ST_ED.SQLTYPE=ST.SQLTYPE
   AND ST_ED.MARKET=ST.MARKET
   AND ST_ED.DBTYPE=ST.DBTYPE
   AND ST_ED.SEQNUM=ST.SEQNUM
```

```
      AND ST_ED.EFFDT<=TO_DATE(TO_CHAR(SYSDATE,'YYYY-MM-DD'),'YYYY-MM-
DD'));
```

These are two very handy meta SQLs.

Please note %EffdtCheck and %Join use all keys when they are expanded, which may not be what you want in all cases. If not all of the key fields are required, you need to join the tables in the old fashion way.

91. How to call an Application Engine from Record PeopleCode?

You can refer to the following code example.

```
If RecordNew(SCH_ASSIGN.EMPLID) Or
   RecordDeleted(SCH_ASSIGN.EMPLID) Or
   SCH_ASSIGN.SCHEDULE_ID.IsChanged Or
   SCH_ASSIGN.EFFDT.IsChanged Then
   &AE_StateRec = CreateRecord(Record.RP_DUR_UPD_AET);
   &nProcessInstance = GetNextProcessInstance();
   &AE_StateRec.PROCESS_INSTANCE.Value = &nProcessInstance;
   &AE_StateRec.EMPLID_PAYEE.Value = SCH_ASSIGN.EMPLID;
   &AE_StateRec.EFFDT.Value = SCH_ASSIGN.EFFDT;
   CallAppEngine("RP_DUR_UPD",                    &AE_StateRec,
&nProcessInstance);
   End-If;
```

92. How to enhance the performance of an Application Engine program using %UpdateStats()?

To optimize the performance of data retrieval from an intermediate table that stores a large volume of data for further processing, you can utilize the `%UpdateStats` command. It is essential to issue a commit just before executing `%UpdateStats`.

77

In scenarios where a table has multiple indexes with overlapping fields, the system determines the appropriate index to fetch results faster. To achieve this, the database maintains meta information known as statistics for the tables. These statistics can be updated manually by the database administrator or scheduled to run at fixed intervals.

The `%UpdateStats` metasql is primarily used for temporary or intermediate tables. These tables hold data only during the Application Engine time frame. Consequently, when the scheduled database update occurs, these tables do not contain any data, leading to improper statistics updates. If you have an intermediate table that stores a substantial volume of data for further processing, it is recommended to call this metasql in the subsequent step. The condition to use `%UpdateStats` is that the step immediately preceding it should issue a commit. Failure to do so will result in incorrect statistics updates. It is advisable to use `%UpdateStats` solely for temporary tables that store a large volume of data. If your tables contain only a few rows of data, index selection and statistics updates are unnecessary. In such cases, invoking `%UpdateStats` may negatively impact performance due to additional commits and database actions.

93. How to run an Application Engine program which doesn't have its own run control page and process definition?

You can run any Application Engine program which doesn't have its own run control page and process definition by going to PeopleTools -> Application Engine -> Request AE. In order to run your application engine program there, you need to go to Process Scheduler -> Processes and add your application engine to the component AE_REQUEST in the Process Definition Options with ALLPNLS as Process Group.

This is especially useful when you need to create custom process requests that require multiple programs to perform parallel processing, or you need to set specific, initial values in a state record. The initial state record value setting is useful in testing when a run control page is not available.

You can also run an Application Engine program through Process Scheduler -> System Process Requests. In order to do that, you need to go to Process Scheduler > Processes and add your application engine to the component PRCSMULTI in the Process Definition Options with ALLPNLS as Process Group.

This is useful when a run control page is not needed for running an Application Engine program.

94. How to put two or more SQL statements in one SQL action using %Execute()?

You can put two or more SQL statements in one SQL action using the metaSQL function %Execute. f.i.

```
%EXECUTE()
TRUNCATE TABLE1;
TRUNCATE TABLE2 ;
TRUNCATE TABLE3;
TRUNCATE TABLE4;
COMMIT;
```

By default, the Application Engine expects a semicolon to be used to delimit multiple commands within an %Execute function statement. You can instruct the Application Engine to use a forward slash (/) delimiter instead by placing a forward slash inside the function parentheses.

```
%EXECUTE(/)
SQLSTATMENTONE
/
SQLSTATEMENTTWO
/
SQLSTATEMENT3
/
```

```
F.I.

%EXECUTE(/)

%TRUNCATETABLE(PS_DEP_BEN_EFF)/

%TRUNCATETABLE(PS_DEP_BEN_ADDR)/

%TRUNCATETABLE(PS_DEP_BEN_NAME)/

%TRUNCATETABLE(PS_DEP_BEN)/
```

Note: When you use the %Execute function, it must be located at the beginning of the statement and must be the only function or command contained in the statement.

95. How to implement parallel processing in Application Engine?

Parallel processing is a technique used to process large amounts of data without compromising performance. This is particularly useful when non-parallel processing would significantly impact performance. To illustrate this concept, consider an application engine program that reads data from tables such as PS_JOB, PS_PERSONAL_DATA, and PS_EMAIL_ADDRESSES via a single SQL object in a peoplecode step. The program performs the necessary data manipulations and writes the results to an extract file. However, the program processes employees sequentially, which can be time-consuming when processing a large number of employees.

To implement parallel processing in this case, follow the below steps,

1) Create a TAO or temporary table. The fields in this table are essentially the unique list of fields or values that the single SQL object is returning.

2) The TAO table should have two key fields, PROCESS_INSTANCE and EMPLID.

3) Before the PeopleCode step is called add a new step to select from the various HR tables and write to this newly created TAO table.

4) SQL step looks something like this.

```
INSERT INTO %Table(XXX_EE_TAO)

SELECT %Bind(PROCESS_INSTANCE), B.EMPLID, C.EMAIL_ADDRESS

FROM PS_JOB A, PS_PERSONAL_DATA B, PS_EMAIL_ADDRESSES C

WHERE ....
```

5) After this add a new step to update statistics on the newly populated TAO table for the indexes to improve the performance when the rows are selected from the instances of this table in further steps.

```
%UpdateStats(XXX_EE_TAO)
```

6) In the PeopleCode step replace the SQL fetch as follows.

```
&EESQL = CreateSQL(FetchSQL(SQL.XXX_EE_SQL),
XXX_EE_AET.PROCESS_INSTANCE);
```

7) In the XXX_EE_SQL SQL object select all fields.

```
SELECT FROM %Table(XXX_EE_TAO)

WHERE PROCESS_INSTANCE = :1

ORDER BY EMPLID
```

8) Add the TAO table under temp tables program properties and provide an instance count of 2 or any other desired instance count. Instance count has to be 1 or more.

9) Under PeopleTools > Utilities > Administration > PeopleTools Options, set the Temp Table Instances to the desired number of instances. The number of temporary tables is determined by the value for the Temp Table Instances setting there plus the number of PeopleSoft Application Engine temporary tables.

10) You can add a step at the beginning or end to purge the TAO table like %TruncateTable (%Table(XXX_EE_TAO)), or use the check-box under program properties "Use Delete for Truncate Table". With this option the TAO table is purged at the beginning of each run.

96. **Warning**: "Application Engine Request is not active -- processing suspended."

Cause: A row exists in the PS_AEREQUESTTBL table for the current process request. The Process Frequency on this row either is set to Don't, or it is set to Once, and the request has already been processed.

Solution: Change the Process Frequency to Always, or use a different Run Control ID.

97. **Error**: Process Request shows the status of 'INITIATED' or 'PROCESSING' but is no longer running

   Cause: The reason for this issue could be a SQL in the App Engine is not running properly, f.i. a SQL to perform some sort of database table operations is not working; it could also be caused the fact that some tables or views may have been changed and need to be rebuilt.

   Solution: Check if there is any SQL used in the App Engine which could potentially cause the issue, run it through the SQL client, fix the SQL, rebuild all the tables and views used by the App Engine. You may need to delete existing data in some tables in order to rebuild them. Rerun the App Engine afterwards. Make certain the App Engine is NOT restartable by checking its properties.

98. **Error**: "Error retrieving Application Engine step"

   Cause: It is likely to be caused by the step being lost when saving the AE program, usually associated with adding a new step and renaming old steps.

   Solution: Remove the step and recreate it again.

99. **Error:** "ORA-00001: unique constraint violated"

   Cause: There're only two types of DML statements, INSERT and UPDATE, which may throw the error. It means that there's a constraint preventing you from having the duplicate value combination. Most likely, it's a unique constraint. That's why your INSERT or UPDATE statement failed to work.

   Solution: Use a different value to perform an INSERT or UPDATE statement.

   Check Constraint Columns. To comply with the unique constraint, you can almost do nothing except for checking the existing data.

   An alternative solution is to drop the unique index if it's not necessary anymore.

   The Unique Contraint Violated error is a common issue which often happens in the batch jobs or scheduled processes. It is a common cause of job/process abends.

   Here are 10 steps you can follow to resolve the problem.

1) Review the error message from the message log of the failed process in the process monitor. It typically looks like this

```
PeopleTools 8.58.04 - Application Engine Server
Copyright (c) 1988-2025 Oracle and/or its affiliates.
All Rights Reserved

PSAESRV started service request at 21.10.11 2025-02-11

File: /vob/peopletools/src/psappeng/psaercur.cppSQL error. Stmt #: 800  Error Position: 0  Return: 805 - ORA-00001: unique constraint (SYSADM.PS_GM_PRJ_RES2_TAO) violated
Failed SQL stmt: INSERT INTO PS_GM_PRJ_RES2_TAO(PROCESS_INSTANCE, BUSINESS_UNIT, PROJECT_ID, ACTIVITY_ID, RESOURCE_ID, BUSINESS_UNIT_GL, CURRENCY_CD, FOREIGN_CURRENCY, TRANS_DT, ACCOUNTING_DT,
DST_ID, TREE_SETID, TREE_NAME, FA_CALC_WAIVED, WAIVED_FA_CLC_MTHD, LEDGER_GROUP, EXIST_BASENODE_FLG, ANALYSIS_TYPE, FOREIGN_AMOUNT, RESOURCE_AMOUNT, TRANSACTION_AMT, RESOURCE_AMT_TMP,
FA_FUNDED_AMOUNT, FA_RESOURCE_AMOUNT, FA_RATE_PCT, ACCOUNT,ALTACCT,DEPTID,STATISTICS_CODE, OPERATING_UNIT, PRODUCT, FUND_CODE, CLASS_FLD, PROGRAM_CODE, BUDGET_REF, AFFILIATE, AFFILIATE_INTRA1,
AFFILIATE_INTRA2, CHARTFIELD1, CHARTFIELD2, CHARTFIELD3, FA_RATE_TYPE) SELECT T.PROCESS_INSTANCE, T.BUSINESS_UNIT, T.PROJECT_ID, T.ACTIVITY_ID, T.RESOURCE_ID, T.BUSINESS_UNIT_GL, T.CURRENCY_CD
T.FOREIGN_CURRENCY, T.TRANS_DT, T.ACCOUNTING_DT, T.DST_ID, T.TREE_SETID, T.TREE_NAME, T.FA_CALC_WAIVED, T.WAIVED_FA_CLC_MTHD, T.LEDGER_GROUP , T.EXIST_BASENODE_FLG , 'SFA' , (
ROUND((((T.FOREIGN_AMOUNT) * ( A.FA_FUNDED_RATE_PCT))) / ( 100)), :1) ) , ( ROUND(((((T.RESOURCE_AMOUNT) * ( A.FA_FUNDED_RATE_PCT))) / ( 100)), :2) ) , T.TRANSACTION_AMT , T.RESOURCE_AMT_TMP
, 0 , A.FA_FUNDED_RATE_PCT , T.ACCOUNT,T.ALTACCT,T.DEPTID,T.STATISTICS_CODE, T.OPERATING_UNIT, T.PRODUCT, T.FUND_CODE, T.CLASS_FLD, T.PROGRAM_CODE, T.BUDGET_REF, T.AFFILIATE, T.AFFILIATE_INTRA
T.AFFILIATE_INTRA2, T.CHARTFIELD1, T.CHARTFIELD2, T.CHARTFIELD3 ,T.FA_RATE_TYPE FROM PS_GM_PRJ_RES1_TAO T , PS_GM_PRJ_ACT_FA3 A WHERE (T.PROCESS_INSTANCE = 5496820 AND T.ANALYSIS_TYPE = 'SFA'
AND A.BUSINESS_UNIT = T.BUSINESS_UNIT AND A.PROJECT_ID = T.PROJECT_ID AND A.ACTIVITY_ID = T.ACTIVITY_ID AND A.FA_RATE_TYPE = T.FA_RATE_TYPE AND A.RATE_EFFDT = ( SELECT MAX (A1.RATE_EFFDT) FROM
PS_GM_PRJ_ACT_FA3 A1 WHERE A1.BUSINESS_UNIT = A.BUSINESS_UNIT AND A1.PROJECT_ID = A.PROJECT_ID AND A1.ACTIVITY_ID = A.ACTIVITY_ID AND A1.FA_RATE_TYPE = A.FA_RATE_TYPE AND A1.RATE_EFFDT <=
T.ACCOUNTING_DT)) AND T.FOREIGN_CURRENCY = :3 AND T.CURRENCY_CD = :4
2025-02-11-21.10.29.548397  AeRcurExecute [676] Exception logged: RC=8.

Process 5496820 ABENDED at Step GM_GMFACS.GMF2220.GMF2222 (SQL) -- RC = 805 (108,524)

Process %s ABENDED at Step %s.%s.%s (Action %s) -- RC = %s

PSAESRV completed service request at 21.10.29 2025-02-11
```

2) Open the Application Engine program for the abended process in the Application Designer, and find the data insert or update SQL step where it abended

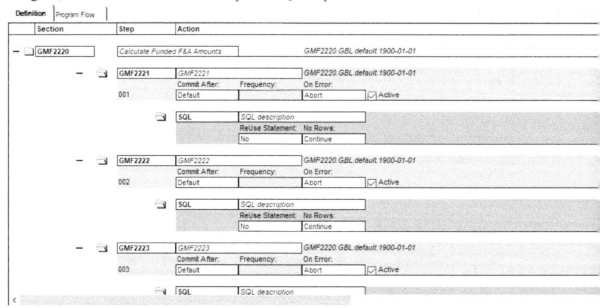

3) Open the data insert or update SQL, resolve its meta SQL, and review it in the Output Window

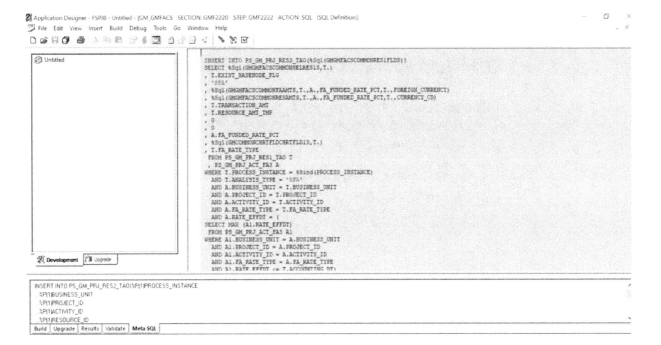

4) Copy the SQL, identify the insert or update source temp tables and insert or update target table, and paste it into a text Editor, such as Notepad;

 *Untitled - Notepad

File   Edit   Format   View   Help

```
INSERT INTO PS_GM_PRJ_RES2_TAO(%Sql(GMGMFACSCOMMONRES1FLDS))
SELECT %Sql(GMGMFACSCOMMONSELRES1S,T.)
, T.EXIST_BASENODE_FLG
, 'SFA'
, %Sql(GMGMFACSCOMMONFAAMTS,T.,A.,FA_FUNDED_RATE_PCT,T.,FOREIGN_CURRENCY)
, %Sql(GMGMFACSCOMMONRESAMTS,T.,A.,FA_FUNDED_RATE_PCT,T.,CURRENCY_CD)
, T.TRANSACTION_AMT
, T.RESOURCE_AMT_TMP
, 0
, 0
, A.FA_FUNDED_RATE_PCT    |
, %Sql(GMCOMMONCHRTFLDCHRTFLD1S,T.)
, T.FA_RATE_TYPE
 FROM PS_GM_PRJ_RES1_TAO T
 , PS_GM_PRJ_ACT_FA3 A
WHERE T.PROCESS_INSTANCE = %Bind(PROCESS_INSTANCE)
  AND T.ANALYSIS_TYPE = 'SFA'
  AND A.BUSINESS_UNIT = T.BUSINESS_UNIT
  AND A.PROJECT_ID = T.PROJECT_ID
  AND A.ACTIVITY_ID = T.ACTIVITY_ID
  AND A.FA_RATE_TYPE = T.FA_RATE_TYPE
  AND A.RATE_EFFDT = (
SELECT MAX (A1.RATE_EFFDT)
 FROM PS_GM_PRJ_ACT_FA3 A1
WHERE A1.BUSINESS_UNIT = A.BUSINESS_UNIT
  AND A1.PROJECT_ID = A.PROJECT_ID
  AND A1.ACTIVITY_ID = A.ACTIVITY_ID
  AND A1.FA_RATE_TYPE = A.FA_RATE_TYPE
  AND A1.RATE_EFFDT <= T.ACCOUNTING_DT)
```

5) Open the record definition of the insert or update target table in the Application Designer and identify all key fields in the table

Record Fields | Record Type

Num	Field Name	Type	Key	Ordr	Dir	C...	Sr...	List	Sys	Audt	In...	EnAut...	Default
1	PROCESS_INSTANCE	Nbr	Key	1	A...		No	No	No		No	No	
2	BUSINESS_UNIT	Char	Key	2	A...		No	No	No		No	No	
3	PROJECT_ID	Char	Key	3	A...		No	No	No		No	No	
4	ACTIVITY_ID	Char	Key	4	A...		No	No	No		No	No	
5	RESOURCE_ID	Char	Key	5	A...		No	No	No		No	No	
6	ANALYSIS_TYPE	Char	Key	6	A...		No	No	No		No	No	
7	FA_RATE_TYPE	Char	Key	7	A...		No	No	No		No	No	
8	BUSINESS_UNIT_GL	Char					No	No	No		No	No	
9	ACCOUNT	Char					No	No	No		No	No	
10	ALTACCT	Char	N...				No	No	No		No	No	
11	DEPTID	Char					No	No	No		No	No	
12	CF12_AN_SBR	SRec					No	No	No		No	No	
13	CURRENCY_CD	Char					No	No	No		No	No	
14	STATISTICS_CODE	Char					No	No	No		No	No	
15	TRANS_DT	Date					No	No	No		No	No	
16	ACCOUNTING_DT	Date					No	No	No		No	No	
17	FOREIGN_CURRENCY	Char					No	No	No		No	No	
18	FOREIGN_AMOUNT	Sign				Yes	No	No	No		No	No	
19	RESOURCE_AMOUNT	Sign				Yes	No	No	No		No	No	
20	LEDGER_GROUP	Char					No	No	No		No	No	
21	DST_ID	Char					No	No	No		No	No	
22	TREE_SETID	Char					No	No	No		No	No	
23	TREE_NAME	Char					No	No	No		No	No	

6) Modify the SELECT part of the SQL to only include the key fields, paste the
   modified SQL into the SQL Developer and try to run it

7) Change the bind variable of the Process Instance field to the process instance number of the abended process instance and re-run the SQL

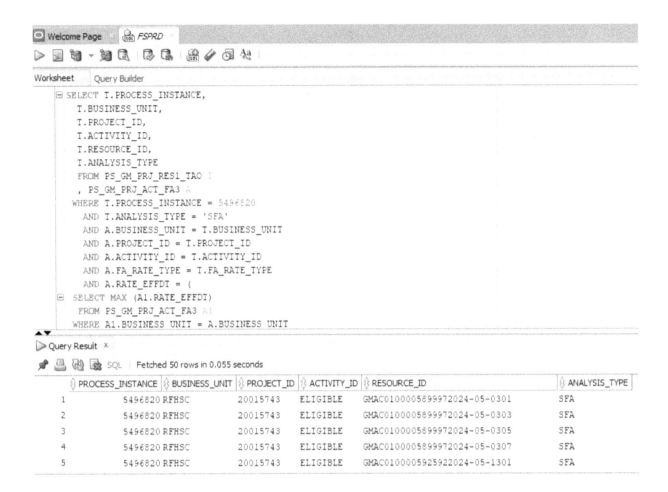

8) If there is no data in the result, check the insert or update source temp table in the production database whether the data still remains in it

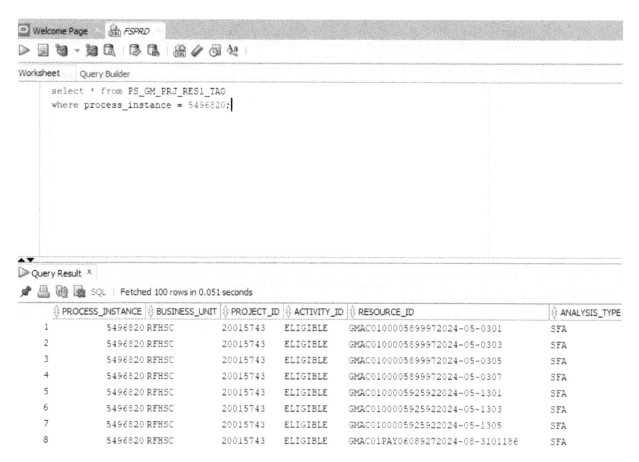

9) If there is no data in the insert or update source temp table, the failed process instance may have been deleted from the process monitor. Let the scheduled job run again as scheduled, or, re-run the process ad-hoc. It would fail again with the All Processing Suspended error. Check the insert or update source temp table again. The data may be in the insert or update source temp table now.

If the data is still not in the source temp table, you may have to replicate the issue in a non-production environment. You may have to refresh the non-production environment with the data from the production environment to have the data for replicating the issue.

After the issue has been replicated in the non-production environment, delete the failed instance in the environment, and then add some error-introducing code in the step which is prior to the step that caused the abend in the Application Engine program to force an abend at that step. With that you should have the data in all the insert or update source temp tables. Rerun the SQL in the SQL developer, and you should see the data now

10) Add a Group By clause with all the key fields and a Having clause with Counts greater than 2 to the SQL, and run it again, and you should find out the culprit which caused the abend of the process in the production environment

100. What are the Application Engine meta variables and how to use them in Application Engine programs?

The main meta-variables are as follows:

%AsOfDate – display the current date and time

%SQLRows – display the number of rows affected by the most recent SQL insert or update, update or delete statement

%AEProgram – display the name of the current App Engine program

%AESection – display the name of the current App Engine Section

%AEStep – display the name of the current App Engine Step

%JobInstance – the process ID of the current Job instance

%ProcessInstance – the process ID of the current Process instance

The easiest way to see the valus of these meta-variables is to insert or update an SQL step into your App Engine, one that performs an insert, delete or update operation. Then immediately after the SQL step, insert a Log Message step. You can refer to message 18030 / 3, as this is a generic message that allows four parameters to be passed into the message. Then, in the parameters section you can list the parameters one after the other, separated by a comma:

```
%AESECTION,%AESTEP,%SQLROWS, %ASOFDATE
```

The App Engine Step should end appearing as follows,

On running the App Engine, you should see a line produced in the log file:

```
'100EMPL' 'Step01' 23 rows updated on '2023-08-04' (18030,3)
```

BI PUBLISHER

101. What are the steps to create/modify a BI Publisher report?

The steps to create/modify a BI Publisher report are as follows,

• Create/update data source in Reporting Tools -> BI Publisher, create or update sample data XML file, and then upload the file;

• Create/update report definition in Reporting Tools -> Report Definitions, create or update template file, and then upload the file;

• Create/update template file in MS Word with BI Publisher Add-In

• You need to install Java Runtime Environment in order to install BIP Desktop Utility, which includes Designer Helper.

• After installation of the Designer Helper, BI Publisher Add-In is available on the menu; you need to import the XML file, and then you can click the fields button to see a list of fields in the XML file, and you can insert the fields to where it should be in the template; you can insert tables and other objects using wizard.

Note the Designer Helper is not a must-have for creating a BI Publisher report; you can manually add fields by copying from existing templates and pasting them into a new template.

102.   You can schedule to run BIP reports in the BI Publisher report scheduler, but if you need to pass parameter values to a BIP report, you need to create a run control page, process definition, Application Engine program, etc.

103. Any special character such as '&' should be changed to the Ascii code in the XML file; otherwise, an error will occur when generating the file.

Also, you should include encoding='ISO-8859-1' in the XML file definition at the beginning of an XML report so that international characters of the Latin language family, such as French, can be displayed.

```
<?xml version="1.0" encoding="ISO-8859-1"?>
```

104. How to tune the performance of an Application Engine that generates a query-based BI Publisher report?

If the performance of an Application Engine that calls a query-based BI Publisher report is slow, you can run the SQL behind that query in the SQL client tool and tune the SQL, or, run the query in the BI Publisher Viewer to check its performance.

105. How to pull data from a table/view and write it into a BI Publisher XML file using PeopleCode?

Running a BI Publisher report in batch doesn't mean it has to use PS Query as a data source. An XML file is the most efficient way to feed the report data.

Here is an example of retrieving data from a table or a view and writing the output into a BI Publisher XML file.

```
&xml = "<?xml version='1.0'?>";

&xml = &xml | "<XXX_TRAN_DETAIL><REPORT_HEADER>";

&xml = &xml | "</REPORT_HEADER>";

&TranDetailSQL = CreateSQL("%SelectAll(:1)" |
&where, Record.XXX_VCHR_ERR_VW);

While &TranDetailSQL.Fetch(&cycle, &section, &bu);

    &xml = &xml | "<CTAP06661>"; /*Start of Report Section*/

    &xml = &xml | "<XXX_VCHR_BLD_CYCLE>" | &cycle
"</XXX_VCHR_BLD_CYCLE>");

    &xml = &xml | "<XXX_VCHR_BLD_SECT>" | &section
"</XXX_VCHR_BLD_SECT>");

    &xml = &xml | "<BUSINESS_UNIT>" | &bu |
"</BUSINESS_UNIT");

    ......

End-While;
```

The &where string variable is used as the where clause to filter out data in the SQL select.

106. Usually, when you create the report definition and templates for the first time, while including template definitions, file definitions get inserted into the PS project automatically. However, if you make any change to the template and upload a new template file, the new file definition does not get inserted into the PS project automatically, and you may miss this object.

So, you need to insert these file definitions manually. However, the file definitions are hard to search since they usually have an awkward naming convention, f.i. "0EEVMWUE4HG5M0C1SDSFG".

Below is the SQL query which will fetch the file definitions associated with your template.

```
SELECT A.TEMPLATE_FILEID

FROM PSXPTMPLFILEDEF A

WHERE A.TMPLDEFN_ID like 'your template id';
```

107. To print .XLS/.XLSX format output reports in process monitor logs/report repository in BI Publisher reports, you need to add the below piece of code in your Application Engine,

```
SELECT PRCSOUTPUTDIR

FROM PSPRCSPARMS

WHERE PRCSINSTANCE = AETRecord.ProcessInstance
```

Next, Assign the value of PRCSOUTPUTDIR to the Report definition object.

```
&oRptDefn = create

PSXP_RPTDEFNMANAGER:ReportDefn("Report_ID");

&oRptDefn.Get();
```

94

```
&oRptDefn.OutDestination = "Value from PRCSOUTPUTDIR";
```

108. **Error:** "Error generating report output" in BI Publisher report

     Cause: XML data file has a formatting error, such as there is extra space between some lines of XML code

     Solution: Check the XML data file generated to see if there is any formatting error or any special character

109. **Error:** "Bursting is disabled" error message pops up when opening a new BI report definition

     Cause: This Burst by field tag must be from the highest-level repeating group (node) in the XML data. For bursting to work, only one high-level repeating group should be in the XML source.

     The structure of the XML file should contain a root node followed by one repeating group node.

     The structure in the case of sample XML is not the structure that has been outlined as a requirement for PeopleSoft BIP Report template consumption.

     The bursting process recreates the XML file (for each burst instance) and, in the process, ignore those nodes that are outside the required structure.

     Solution: You can try to add one other XML tag to the highest-level group of the XML file.

     Or, you can try to move the nodes that are outside the required structure to be under the repeating group node.

COMPONENT INTERFACE

110. When should I be using a component interface?

If you need to insert/update/delete data through PeopleCode, and your PeopleCode will require replicating a lot of existing business logic that already exists in a component, then a component interface is the best approach. Once you learn how to use them, they will be the fastest and most robust solution for such cases.

If you are making simple changes, using a CI becomes overkill as there is an overhead to using a CI on both the system and development time. Similarly, large amounts of batch processing may be too much for a CI to handle or may be considerably slower using a CI.

Also, use CI if there are only 1 or 2 scroll levels in the component. You may want to avoid using a CI to add/update data if there are three or more scroll levels in the CI and use SQL inserts/update statements instead if the required changes are not complicated.

111. For many Delivered components in their Component Interfaces, many collection fields are "Read only", whereas those fields are editable and can be updated online.

The Read Only Access property can be changed in the CIs. You need to make sure that the field properties are not set to Read Only Access if your PeopleCode does not update the value of a field as it is supposed to.

112. When you create a new component interface by selecting a component, fields in GETKEYS, FINDKEYS, CREATKEYS, PROPERTIES are sorted in alphabetical order; after you save the CI, close it and reopen it, those fields are then sorted in the order of the field sequence number.

113. PageActivate event doesn't get trigged when a CI is called. Therefore, put your custom PeopleCode in the PostBuild event instead.

114. How to build a component interface API file using Application Designer?

Go to the Build menu item and click PeopleSoft API, copy the path of a Java class file or a C header file, paste it into Target Directory or browser to the file, and then select the required CIs to build API.

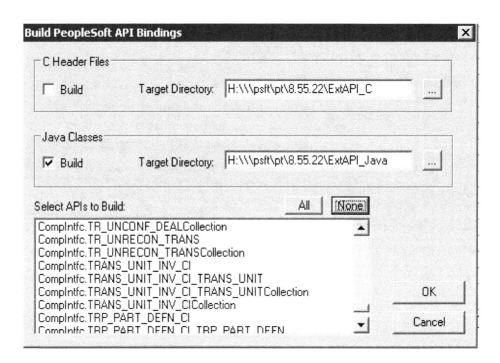

CONFIGURATION MANAGER

115. You need to have local admin privilege to be able to run the configuration manager. Check if you have the local admin privilege by running the command REDGEDIT and see if it opens the Registry Editor window, or by going to Control Panel - > System -> Advanced System Setting -> Advanced and see if you have privilege to create new system environment variables there.

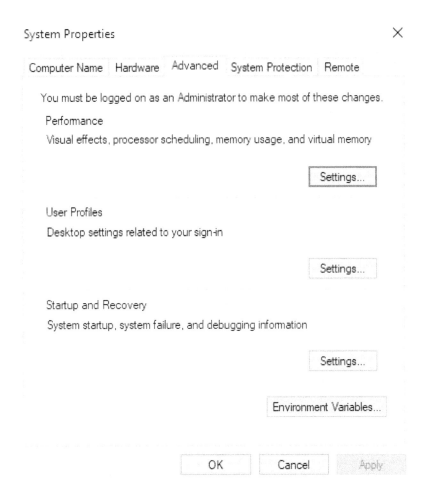

116. How to add a program group for the PeopleTools programs to the Windows Start menu? To add a program group for the PeopleTools programs to the Windows Start menu, go to the folder where PeopleTools are installed, run Configuration Manager pscfg.exe, and go to Client Setup tab, select the programs that you would like to be in the program

group, normally Application Designer, Data Mover, Configuration Manager, and Uninstall Workstation, and then select Install Workstation, and click Apply.

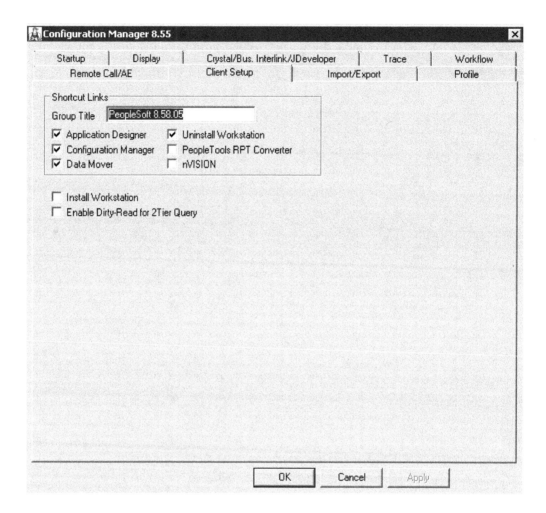

117. Changes made within Configuration Manager do not take effect until you sign on to the system. If you're logged in when you are making changes to Configuration Manager, you'll have to log off and log back in to see the effect of the changes.

118. What are the default Connect ID and the Connect Password that are used in the Configuration Manager?

 Configuration Manager 8.58   ✕

| | Client Setup | | Import/Export | | | Profile |
| Startup | Display | Bus. Interlink/JDeveloper | | Trace | Workflow | Remote Call/AE |

Signon Defaults

☐ Numeric keypad -
Enter Key tabs to
next field

Database Type: Oracle   ⌄

Application Server Name: ⌄

Server Name:

Database Name: FSDEV

User ID: SCHEN

Connect ID: people

Connect Password: ●●●●●●●●●●●●●●●●|

Connect Password (confirm):   ●●●●●●●●●●●●●●●●

User Can Override   Cache Files
☐ Database Type   Directory:
☑ Database Name   C:\Users\chens322\PS\CACHE   …
☑ User ID
                                     Purge Cache Directories…

[OK]   Cancel   Apply

The default Connect ID is *people*.

The default Connect Password is *peop1e*.

DATA MOVER SCRIPT

119. To improve the performance of the data mover scripts, use a local folder instead of a network folder to save output data files and logs.

120. What are the differences between IMPORT, REPLACE_DATA and REPLACE_ALL?
    - The IMPORT command will just import, but not replace any data.
    - The REPLACE_DATA will purge the target table by truncating the data in the table first and then fill it with what you are importing.
    - The REPLACE_ALL command will drop the target table, recreate it, and then import it.

121. There are three different ways to run Data Mover
    - Run from the Application Designer
    - Use the Data Mover shortcut from the PeopleTools Program Group in the Start Menu
    - At a command prompt, enter PS_HOME\bin\client\winx86\psdmt.exe

122. What are the delivered DMS scripts to import and export user profiles, user security, and PeopleTools tables?

    The PeopleSoft delivered Import and Export DMS scripts exist in the $PS_HOME/scripts folder.

    DMS scripts to import & export all user profiles
    - userimport.dms
    - userexport.dms

    DMS scripts to import & export PeopleTools security tables
    - securityimport.dms
    - securityexport.dms

    DMS scripts to import & export only PeopleTools tables without application data
    - mvprdimp.dms

- mvprdexp.dms

EXCEL TO CI

123. How to unhide a hidden worksheet in an Excel to CI spreadsheet?

Open Excel Visual Basic Editor in one of the following two ways

   (i) Click the Visual Basic button on the Developer tab. If the Developer tab is not present, go to File -> Options -> Customize Ribbon, and check the Developer check box under the Main Tabs.

   (ii) Use the Alt + F11 keyboard shortcut.

   Use Ctrl + G to open the Immediate Window.

   Enter:Worksheets("Template").Visible=True.

   Press Enter.

124. **Error:** "Excel To CI: Can't find project or library"

   Cause: The RelLangMicro.xla file is missing

   Solution: Check if the RelLangMicro.xla file has been copied to the same folder where the Excel to CI spreadsheet is copied to. You can copy the RelLangMicro.xla file from the Excel directory in your PeopleSoft home, i.e., <PS_HOME>\Excel.

125. **Error:** "Property or collection {Record} was not found in the component interface at the given level"

   Cause: One or more parent collections are either not mapped, or any of those collection rows' keys were not provided when trying to insert a row.

   Solution: Make sure each of the lower-level row's keys are provided

FLUID

126. Components must be defined as Fluid Mode and should have Display on Small Form Factor Homepage checked if you intend to provide access to the application from a small device.

127. Most main Fluid pages are based on the PSL_APPS_CONTENT layout, which will put a layout-only group box with a Fluid style of ps_apps_content;

128. How to display two fields on the same line on a Fluid page?

   Here is an example. There are three fields on a Fluid page which are shown as below,

If you want to put the above the second field and the third field on the same line, add the style class psc_display-inline to the properties of those two fields.

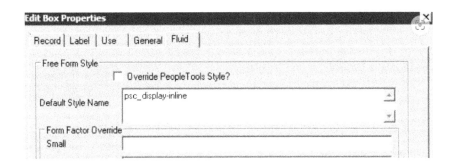

And then add the psc_label-none style class and the psc_padding-left20px style to the properties of the third field.

   Field 1: (none required)

Field 2: psc_display-inline

Field 3: psc_display-inlinepsc_label-nonepsc_padding-left20px

With the change, the three fields will be displayed as follows,

Field 1

Field 2

129. How to add a tile to a Fluid homepage manually without using the tile wizard?

To add a tile for a new custom component on a Fluid Homepage, such as the Employee Self Service homepage, you need first go to Structure and Content, go to Fluid Structure Content -> Fluid Pages, select an existing folder for the new tile or create a new folder,

Go inside the folder, add a new content reference for the new tile (Usage Type -> Target, Storage Type -> Remote by URL), enter the menu name and the component name, specify the value of Market as GBL, and then go to Fluid Homepages, and select a Fluid Homepage, f.i., Employee Self Service, and click Edit, and then click on the Tile Content tab, and check the checkbox of the new tile in its group/folder.

130. How to use a custom image on a Fluid tile?

Follow the below steps:

1) Navigate to PeopleTools -> Portal -> Branding -> Branding Objects
2) Click on the "Image" tab
3) Attach an image here
4) Navigate to PeopleTools -> Portal Structure and Content -> Fluid Pages -><open the Tile to add the custom image> -> Fluid Attributes tab
5) Change the image to the custom image uploaded on the Branding Objects page

131. How to convert an existing PeopleSoft classic component to a Fluid component?

There are 8 steps to convert an existing classic component to a new Fluid UI Component.

1) Create the Fluid Component

2) Create the Fluid Page

3) Add Fluid Pages to the Fluid Component

4) Update PeopleCode References

5) Update, Remove, or Redesign Unsupported Control

6) Enable Search Pages

7) Adjust and Finalize Layout

8) Implement Responsive and Adaptive Behaviors

Check out details in the Oracle Red Paper "Converting Classic PIA Components to PeopleSoft Fluid User Interface" at the following URL: https://peoplesofttechnical.files.wordpress.com/2017/02/converting_classic_pia_components_to_peoplesoft_fluid_user_interface.pdf

The paper provides information and guidance on the above steps. In addition,

1) It gives great instruction with an example of how to convert a Component to Fluid UI.

2) There is a very important section on classic controls that are not supported in Fluid UI, or require some type of conversion.

3) There is an appendix that identifies the delivered PeopleSoft style classes. You will find that appendix extremely valuable when you're looking for the right style to get the UI you want.

132. How to restrict users from adding Tiles on Fluid Homepages, Favorites and Navigation Bar?

The Add To functionality are determined by 3 things:

1) Does the component itself have the Add To functionality enabled in Component Properties (default is enabled): - Open component definition in Application Designer - Access the component's Component Properties. - Click the "Fluid" tab - Check "Add To" option box to see if it is checked

2) Does the user have permission to access the iScript which performs the Add To functionality? You should check: - PeopleTools -> Security -> Permissions &

Roles -> Permission Lists - Open the user's individual permission lists - Go to the Web Libraries tab, and see if there is permission given to: Web Library: WEBLIB_PTNUI Function: PT_BUTTON_PIN.FieldFormula.IScript_SavePin

3) The form factor of the device being used to access the application. The Add To functionality is disabled on the small form factor. So users accessing the application from a small form factor device (such as smart phones) will not see the Add To feature.

The above will determine access to all 3 of "Add To Homepage", "Add To Favorites" and "Add To Navbar". There are no options at a more granular level to control each individual "Add To" item.

133. How to set width and height of an Edit Box field on a Fluid page?

You can use the following Style Class,

psc_control-width50em

You can also use the following Style Class to change the height of a Long Edit Box,

psc_control-height25em

You can change the numbers in the Style Classes to adjust the width and the height.

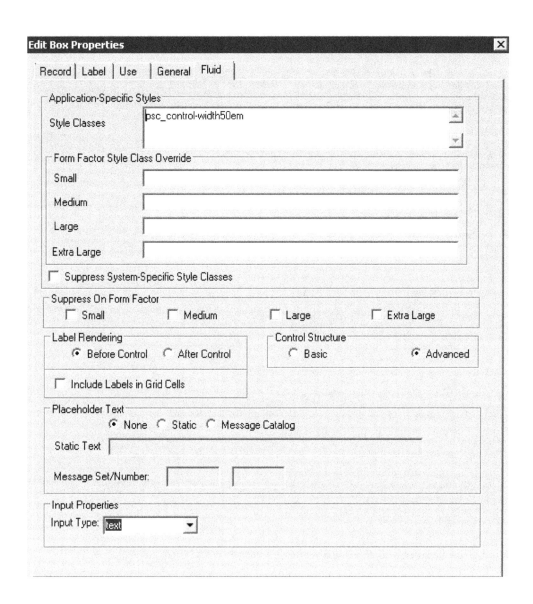

134. How to apply a style to the page controls on a Fluid page?

PeopleSoft Fluid pages are not WYSIWYG like classic pages. Because Fluid pages render differently according to the device form-factor on which they are displayed. This fact, coupled with the integration of standard web-development technologies like CSS and HTML, makes Fluid a much more powerful technology than PeopleSoft classic.

Method 1 - Adding delivered style classes to Fluid page controls

1)Open the page field properties -> Fluid tab

2)Add the class name to Default Style Name box and/or Form Factor Override boxes

Long Edit Box Properties

Record   Label   Use   General   Fluid   Options

Application-Specific Styles

Style Classes | psc_nolabel psc_wrap

Form Factor Style Class Override

Small

Medium

Large

Extra Large

☐ Suppress System-Specific Style Classes

Suppress On Form Factor

☐ Small   ☐ Medium   ☐ Large   ☐ Extra Large

Label Rendering   Control Structure

◉ Before Control   After Control   Basic   ◉ Advanced

☐ Include Labels in Grid Cells

Placeholder Text

◉ None   Static   Message Catalog

Static Text

Message Set/Number:

Method 2 - Creating custom CSS classes using a free-form stylesheet

1)Create a new free-form stylesheet

A custom style sheet can be built as follows,

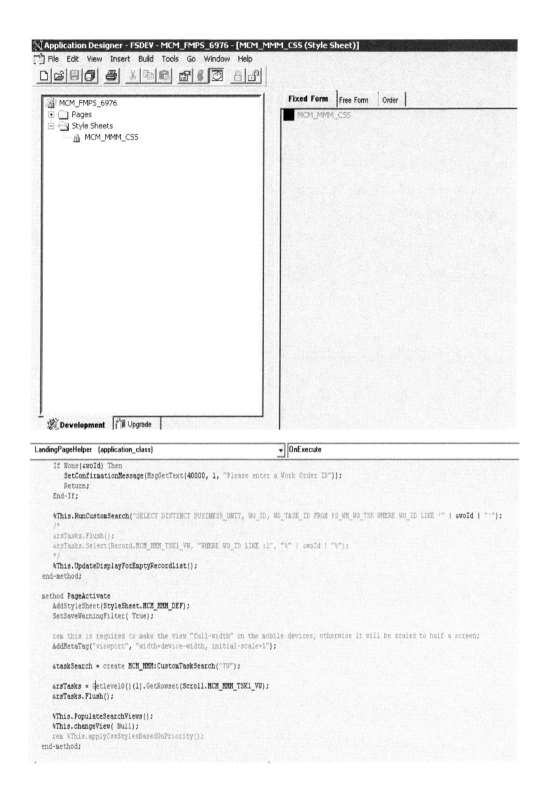

2) Add PeopleCode to an event, such as component prebuild event or page activate event

```
AddStyleSheet(StyleSheet.YOUR_STYLE_SHEET_NAME);
```

135. How to create a PeopleSoft Fluid tile with its data source as PeopleSoft Pagelet?

Step 1: Create PeopleSoft Pagelets:

Navigation to create the PeopleSoft Pagelets:

PeopleTools -> Portal -> Pagelet Wizard -> Pagelet Wizard

Now, in this Example, Embedding the PeopleSoft classic plus YouTube video into PeopleSoft Pagelet.

Specify the title and the description of the pagelet.

Select HTML as the type of data, copy and paste the URL to the Data Source HTML box field.

Specify the visual options related to the display format for your pagelet.

Specify the manner in which your pagelet is published.

Specify the security of your pagelet.

After it, PeopleSoft Pagelet development has been completed.

Step 2: Create content reference with Fluid parameters:

Now, create the content reference in a specific folder with parameters as shown below.

Specify the security of the fluid tile

Specify the attributes of the fluid tile, including the image to be used for the tile.

Step 3: Publish the content reference as Fluid tile:

Next, Publish the Pagelet embedded Content reference in Fluid landing page.

Click on "Add Tile" button.

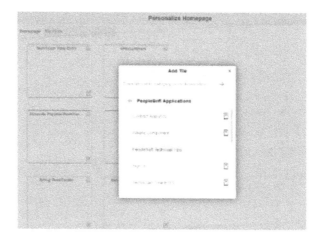

Added Fluid tile in landing page as shown below.

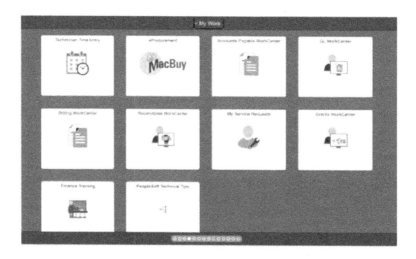

When clicking the tile, the YouTube PeopleSoft Technical Tips channel homepage shows up.

136. How to implement the Attachment Framework on a Fluid Page?

The PeopleSoft Attachment Framework is a feature within PeopleSoft applications that allows users to attach files, notes, and URLs to various transactions and applications. It supports different file types and devices, and can be used across a range of applications.

The key features and benefits of the Attachment Framework include:

- Document Attachment: Enables users to upload and attach files, notes, and URLs to transactions and other data within PeopleSoft.

- Diverse File Types: Supports various file types such as PDFs, spreadsheets, documents, and more.

- Cross-Device Support: Works on desktops, smartphones, and other devices, providing flexibility for users.

- Security and Authorization: Allows for defining security levels for attachments, controlling which users can access specific documents

- Integration with Fluid Framework: The Attachment Framework is integrated with the Fluid Framework

- Configuration: Provides options for configuring the framework, including defining attachment types, authorization IDs, and storage locations.

To implement the PeopleSoft Attachment Framework, you'll need to define your attachment configuration, configure the user interface, and implement PeopleCode logic to handle attachment processing. This involves creating a custom record for attachments, including a subrecord for line or header-level details, inserting a subpage for the user interface, and adding PeopleCode for processing.

The following example shows how to use the attachment framework to enable employees to add attachments on the HCM Employee Self Service > Payroll > Direct Deposit > Edit Account page.

It also allows an HCM Administrator to view the attachments loaded by each employee to their bank accounts on the Payroll for North America > Employee Pay Data > Request Direct Deposit page.

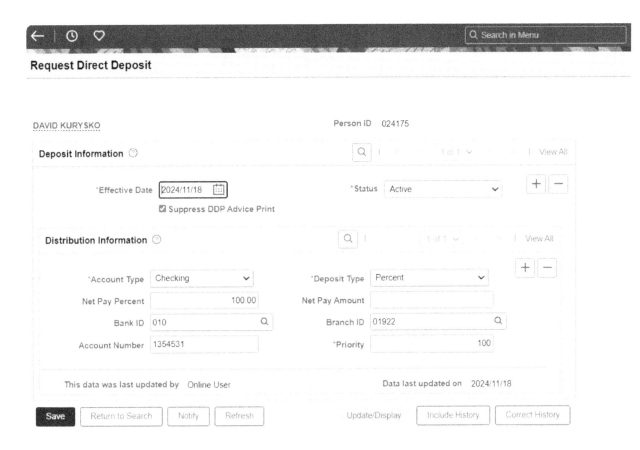

Step 1. Create a custom record for attachment and specify the key Fields based on the required logic. In this example, the EMPLID field has been set as a key field and a search key field, and a Sub Record (HR_ATT_DD_SBR) has been added to the record.

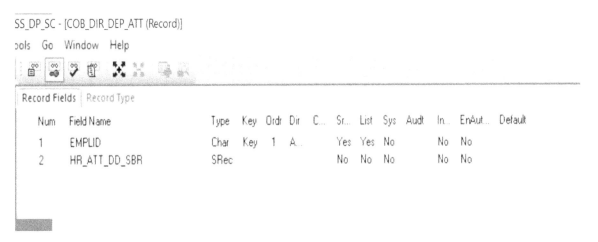

When opened, the HR ATT DD SBR is shown as above. The Sequence Number field is a key field of the sub record. Build this record after creating it.

118

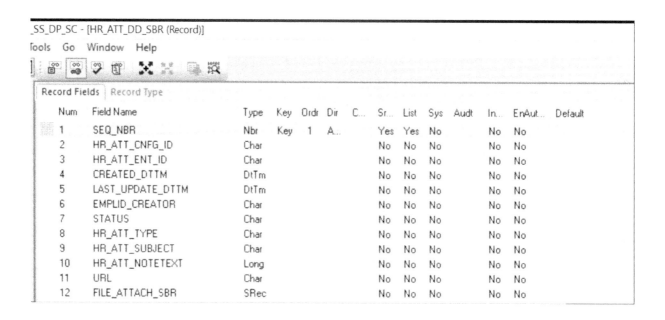

Step 2. Add the HR_ATT_FL_SBF subpage to the Fluid Self Service Direct Deposit page.

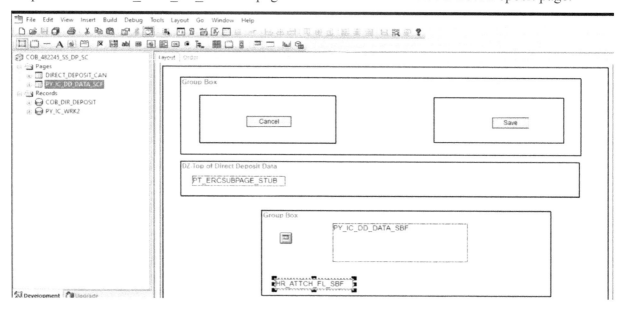

Step 3. Create a new authorization entry.

Navigate to Set Up HCM Common Definitions Attachments, and then go to the Define Authorization Entries page.

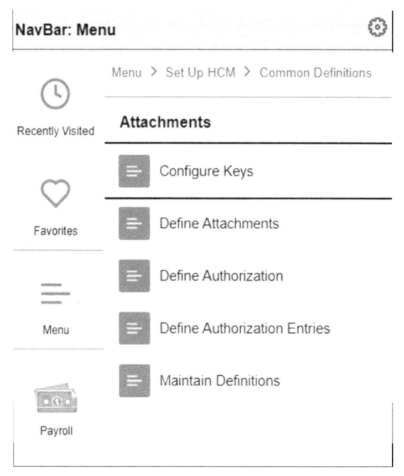

Add a new authorization entry:

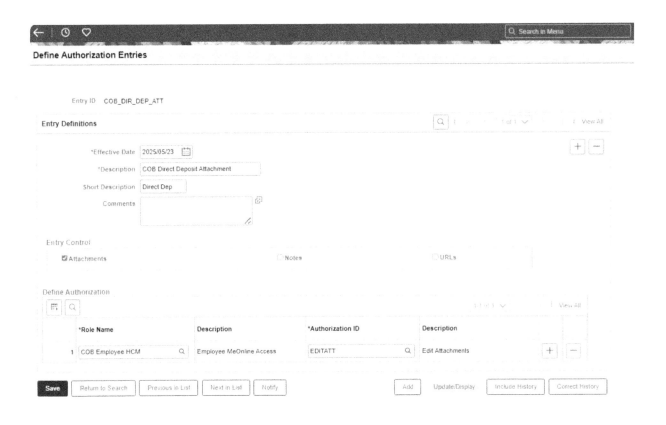

Step 4. Create a new attachment.

Go to the Define Attachments page and add a new attachment.

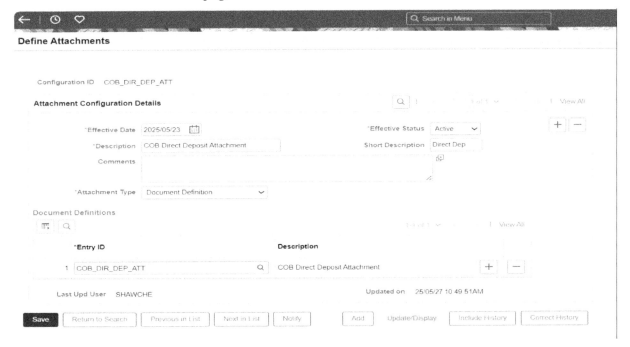

Step 5. Configure keys.

Go to the Configure Keys page and add a new row with the module as the object owner id and the functional area as the sub id.

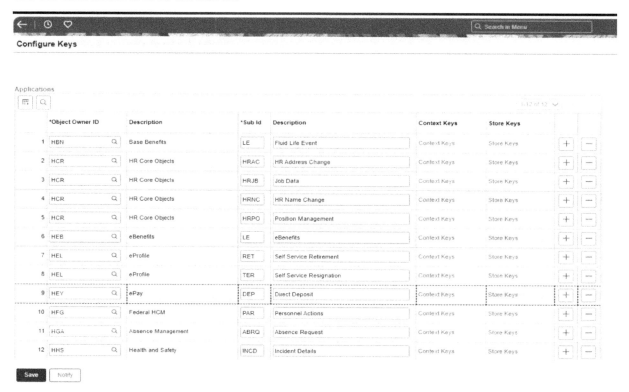

Step 6. Click the Context Keys link and Configure the Context Keys. The Key Prompt table should be set to the base record of the fluid page which the attachments are added to. In this case, it is the Direct Deposit Distribution table.

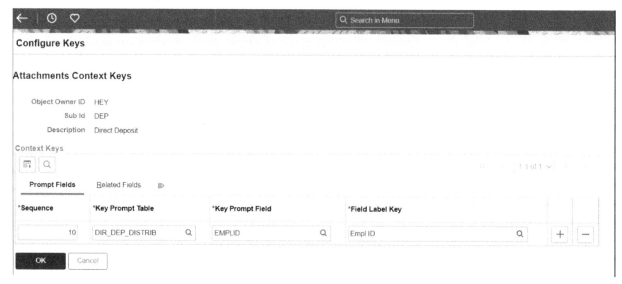

Step 7. Click the Configure Store Keys link and configure the Store Keys. Add the primary key field of the custom attachment record. In this case, it is the EMPLID field.

Step 8. Create a new definition.

Go to the Maintain Definitions page and create a new definition.

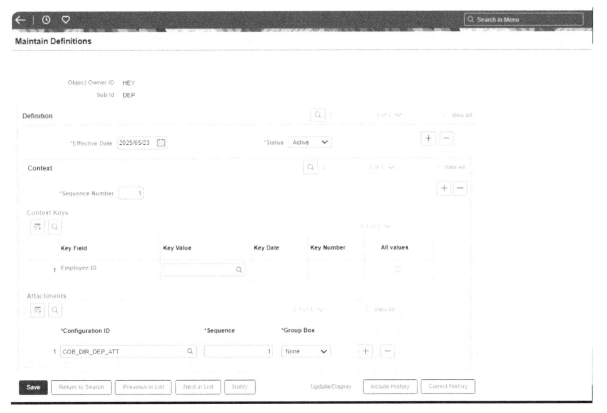

Step 9. Add the following PeopleCode to the Employee Self Service Direct Deposit.
Edit Account PageActivate Event:

```
import PY_DD_SELFSERVICE:*;
import HR_ATTACHMENT_FLU:Attachment_Fluid;


/*Initialize parameters for calling attachment constructor*/
Component HR_ATTACHMENT_FLU:Attachment_Fluid &call_attachment;


Local array of string &CKeys = CreateArray(" "); /*This array would
contain the Context
key values*/


Local array of string &Store_Keys_Array = CreateArray(%EmployeeId);
/*This array would
contain the Store key values*/ /*Initialize component rowsets*/
&Lvl1 = GetLevel0()(1).GetRowset(Scroll.HR_ATT_KEYS_S);
&RS_DocDefns = GetLevel0()(1).GetRowset(Scroll.HR_ATTACH_FLU);
/*Calling attachment constructor*/
&call_attachment = create HR_ATTACHMENT_FLU:Attachment_Fluid("HEY",
"DEP",
"COB_DIR_DEP_ATT",  %Date,  &CKeys,  %UserId,  %Component,  "",
&Store_Keys_Array, False);
```

Step 10. Add the following PeopleCode to the FieldChange event of the Save button field on
the Edit Account page:

```
import HR_ATTACHMENT_FLU:Attachment_Fluid;
Component HR_ATTACHMENT_FLU:Attachment_Fluid &call_attachment;
&call_attachment.Attachment_SaveProcessing();
```

Step 11. Add the following PeopleCode to Employee Pay Data. Request Direct Deposit page
PageActivate event:

```
import HR_ATTACHMENT_FLU:Attachment_Fluid;
```

Step 12. Add a grid to show the attachments at the bottom of the Request Direct Deposit page, and add the Employee ID, Sequence Number and View Attachment fields to it.

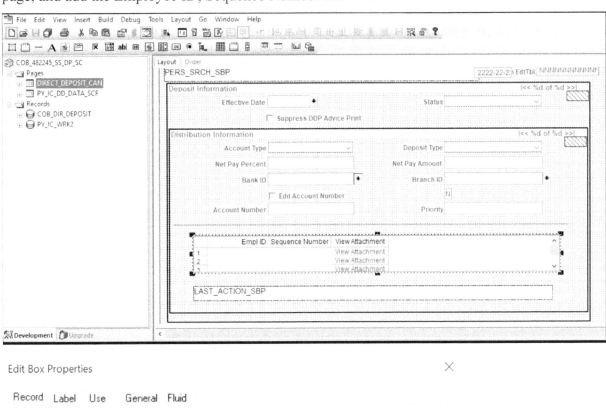

Edit Box Properties   ×

Record   Label   Use   General   Fluid

Field

Record Name: COB_DIR_DEP_ATT   ∨

Field Name: EMPLID   ∨

Style: *** Use Default Style ***   ∨   Fill Character: ☐

Size   Alignment
◉ Average   ◉ Auto
○ Maximum   ○ Left
○ Custom   ○ Right

Family Name   Display Name

Display Options
☐ Display Zero   ☐ Display Century
☐ Password   ☐ Currency Symbol
☑ Show Prompt Button ☐ 1000 Separator
☐ Auto Fill   ☐ Auto Decimal
☐ Display Time Zone   ☐ Enable Spell Check
   Input Only

Edit Box Properties   ✕

Record   Label   Use   General   Fluid

Field

Record Name: COB_DIR_DEP_ATT   ∨

Field Name: SEQ_NBR   ∨

Style: *** Use Default Style ***   ∨   Fill Character: ☐

Size   Alignment

○ Average   ◉ Auto

○ Maximum   ○ Left

◉ Custom   ○ Right

Family Name   Display Name

Display Options

☐ Display Zero   ☐ Display Century

☐ Password   ☐ Currency Symbol

☑ Show Prompt Button   ☐ 1000 Separator

☐ Auto Fill   ☐ Auto Decimal

☐ Display Time Zone   ☐ Enable Spell Check

   Input Only

Push Button/Hyperlink Properties   ✕

Type   Label   Use   General   Fluid

Type   External Link

◉ Push Button ○ Hyperlink ○ Action Widget   Static   Dynamic

Destination: PeopleCode Command   ∨   URL ID

Record Name: HR_ATTACH_WRK   ∨   URL Encoded by Application

Field Name: FF_VIEW_ATTCHMNT ∨   Internal Link

Style: *** Use Default Style *** ∨   Portal   Use Current

Actions   Node   LOCAL_NODE

Action Type   Menu

Related Control   Component

Process   Market

Type   Page

Name   Action

Secondary Page   ☐ Use data from current page in search

Page

Action Widget Settings   Related Content Event

Use Default JavaScript   ☐ Display in Related Action Menu

Custom Java Script   ☐ Show in Page

Display Single Action   Action

Menu as   Widget

Step 13. Add the following PeopleCode to the View Attachment field RowInit event:

```
If %Page = Page.DIRECT_DEPOSIT_CAN Then
```

127

```
    If COB_DIR_DEP_ATT.SEQ_NBR.Value = 0 Or
        COB_DIR_DEP_ATT.STATUS.Value = "D" Then
     HR_ATTACH_WRK.FF_VIEW_ATTCHMNT.Enabled = False;
    End-If;
End-If;
```

Step 14. Add the following PeopleCode to the View Attachment FieldChange event:

```
If %Page = Page.DIRECT_DEPOSIT_CAN Then
    If COB_DIR_DEP_ATT.SEQ_NBR.Value <> 0 Then
        view_attachment(&URL_ID,
COB_DIR_DEP_ATT.ATTACHSYSFILENAME.Value,
COB_DIR_DEP_ATT.ATTACHSYSFILENAME.Value, 2, &RETCODE);
    End-If;
End-if;
```

After all of the above steps have been completed, the build and development work is done and you can perform the unit testing.

Go to HCM Employee Self Service > Payroll > Direct Deposit > Edit Account page.

You should see an Attachment section at the bottom of the page and also an Add Attachment button.

Click the Add Attachment button and upload a file.

You should see a row inserted into the attachment grid at the bottom:

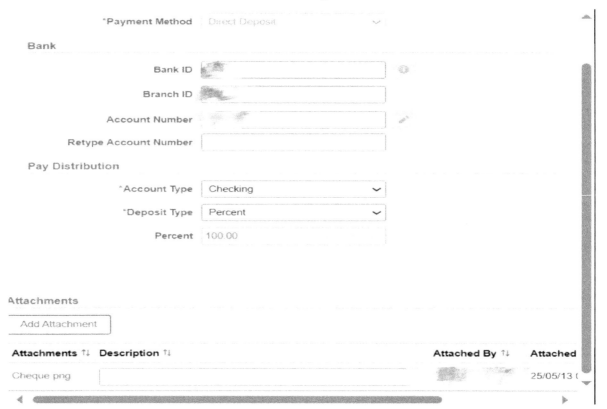

If you go to Payroll > for North America > Employee Pay Data > Request Direct Deposit page and enter the Employee ID for which the attachments were uploaded, you will see the attachments listed.

Click the View Attachment button of an attachment, and you should be able to view the attachment. The following is an example:

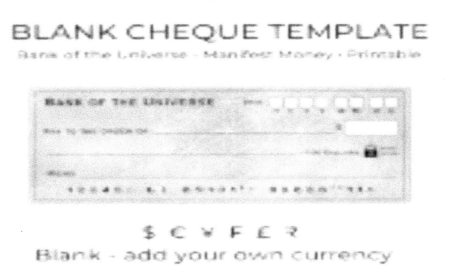

If you query the custom attachment table through a SQL client, you should see the attachments that have been created in the custom attachment table shown as below:

130

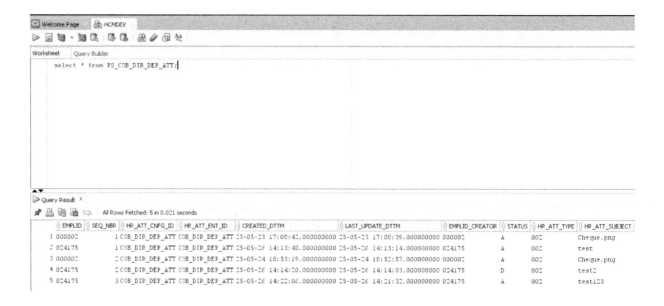

If you want to migrate the attachment configuration from one environment to another using a DMS script, you can use this DMS export script as an example:

```
--HR_ATT_ENT_TBL
EXPORT HR_ATT_ENT_TBL
where HR_ATT_ENT_ID = 'COB_DIR_DEP_ATT';


--HR_ATT_ENT_ROL
EXPORT HR_ATT_ENT_ROL
where HR_ATT_ENT_ID = 'COB_DIR_DEP_ATT';


--HR_ATT_CNFG_TBL
EXPORT HR_ATT_CNFG_TBL
where HR_ATT_CNFG_ID = 'COB_DIR_DEP_ATT';


--HR_ATT_CNFG_DD
EXPORT HR_ATT_CNFG_DD
where HR_ATT_CNFG_ID = 'COB_DIR_DEP_ATT';


--HR_ATT_DEFN_TBL
EXPORT HR_ATT_DEFN_TBL
where OBJECTOWNERID = 'HEY' and HR_ATT_SUB_ID = 'DEP';
```

```
--HR_ATT_DFN_ATCH
EXPORT HR_ATT_DFN_ATCH
where OBJECTOWNERID = 'HEY' and HR_ATT_SUB_ID = 'DEP';


--HR_ATT_DFN_KEYS
EXPORT HR_ATT_DFN_KEYS
where OBJECTOWNERID = 'HEY' and HR_ATT_SUB_ID = 'DEP';


--HR_ATT_DFN_KYS2
EXPORT HR_ATT_DFN_KYS2
where OBJECTOWNERID = 'HEY' and HR_ATT_SUB_ID = 'DEP';


--HR_ATT_DFN_KEYS_TBL
EXPORT HR_ATT_KEYS_TBL
where OBJECTOWNERID = 'HEY' and HR_ATT_SUB_ID = 'DEP';


--HR_ATT_DFN_KEYS_C
EXPORT HR_ATT_KEYS_C
where OBJECTOWNERID = 'HEY' and HR_ATT_SUB_ID = 'DEP';


--HR_ATT_DFN_KEYS_S
EXPORT HR_ATT_KEYS_S
where OBJECTOWNERID = 'HEY' and HR_ATT_SUB_ID = 'DEP';
```

Please note:

1. The Attachment Framework is available in all products but only available within the certain PUM releases onward.

2. Only the Document Definition type is supported by the Fluid Attachment Framework.

137. **Error:** Wrong grid layout on a Fluid page

Cause: Putting a classic grid on a Fluid page will result in wrong grid layout.

Solution:

Replace the classic grid layout with a Fluid grid layout. Use a Fluid supported grid layout instead, such as Flex Grid Layout.

- Open the page in question
- Access the Grid Properties
- Go to the Use tab
- Under the Grid Style section, select Flex Grid Layout
- Save

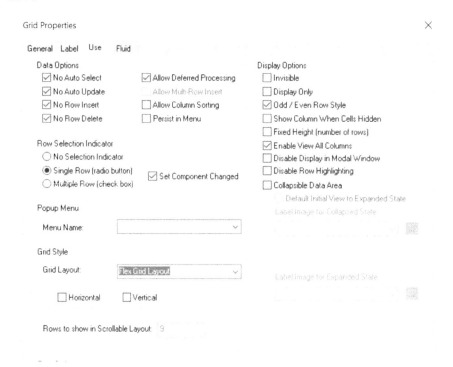

138. **Error:** Pagelet {Pagelet Name} is missing from the EMPLOYEE portal for homepage tab name {Fluid Homepage Name} (95,6500)

Cause: When the delete of the Fluid page or tile from a Fluid Homepage happens, the system does not immediately update this information for the parent Fluid Homepage. This triggers the error.

Solution: The system will eventually update the Fluid Homepage. However, if you want to remove the error immediately:

Make a minor change to the description of the content reference. For example, put a dot (.) in the long description field and then save. Log out and log back in and the error will be gone.

Sometimes a minor update to the long description will not update the definition. If the solution 1 doesn't resolve the error, try making a change in the Long Description, then click on the Security & Tile Content tabs and save.

It has also been seen that removing the pagelet (if not required) from the portal or recreating the missing pagelet after an upgrade in the content provider has resolved the issue.

Location to locate pagelet: PeopleTools -> Portal -> Structure and Content -> Portal objects -> Pagelets.

FTP/SFTP

139. To change the access privilege of a folder or a file from an FTP client in Unix, you can right click on the folder/file and choose the CHMOD command.

140. Make sure to upload your scripts and data files in Ascii mode, not in binary mode.

141. Though FTP can be used directly by giving the URL as a string to the PeopleCode method, other protocols (FTPS, SFTP, HTTP and HTTPS) require the URL to be passed as a URL identifier only. When a URL identifier is created, the URL properties link on the page gets enabled. Users need to provide the URL properties specific to the protocol they are using on this "URL properties" page. The URL properties differ based on the protocol chosen. Once URL Identifier is ready, it can be used in any of the file attachment PeopleCode methods just like the existing way.

Password and Public Key authentication are the authentication methods supported for sftp.
For password authentication:
Create a URL Identifier and provide Authentication Type, User ID and Password as URL properties. Password needs to be encrypted before using it. Use the "Password Encryption" Utility provided on the URL properties page for that.

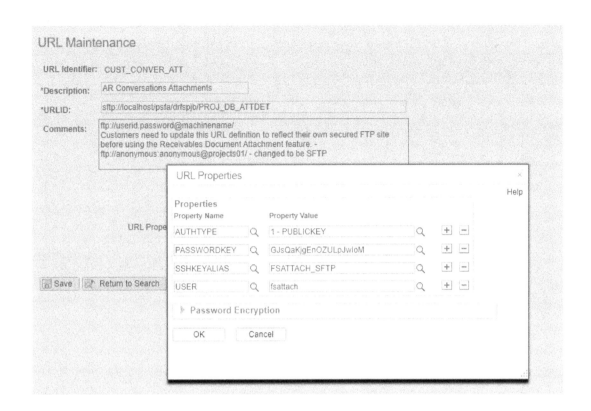

142. How to use the PeopleTools Test Utilities page to test attachments through FTP/SFTP? Select PeopleTools, then select Utilities, then select Debug, then select PeopleTools Test Utilities to access the PeopleTools Test Utilities page.

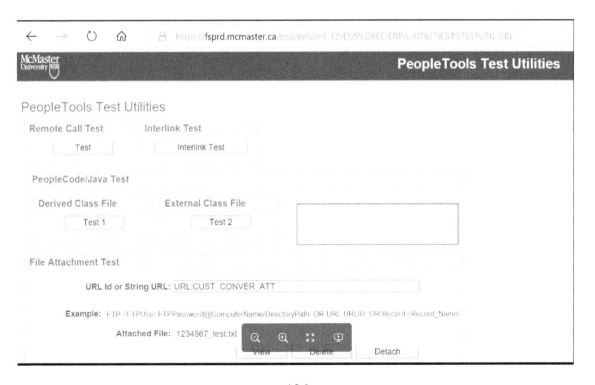

INTEGRATION BROKER

143. What is the difference between a synchronous integration and an asynchronous integration?

In synchronous integrations, all processing stops until a response is received. In asynchronous integrations, each request is placed in a queue and is processed as soon as the system can accommodate the request.

144. To successfully receive an IB message from a sender, on the receiving end, you need to ensure

- PeopleSoft Gateway is active
- PeopleSoft Pub/Sub services are running
- PeopleSoft Listener/ Target Connectors are running
- Queue is active

145. What are the default user ID and password to open the Integration Broker gateway setup properties file?

The default user ID is *administrator* and the default password is *password*. To open the Integration Broker gateway setup properties file. The password can be changed. You may need to ask your system administrator for the appropriate credentials if the default values do not work.

146. How to perform Integration Broker logging?

Integration Broker logging can be very useful for troubleshooting messaging issues. It can be enabled through:

PeopleTools -> Integration Broker -> Configuration -> Gateways.

Open your local Gateway (usually called LOCAL) and click on the Gateway Setup Properties link. Once you login, click on the Advanced Properties Page link. This will open the integration Gateway properties file and allow you to edit it. (The default userid is *administrator*, and the default password is *password*)

Scroll through the integration Gateway properties file until you find the logging section. The following line is what sets the logging level:

ig.log.level=2

The logging levels are:

Level	Value
-100	Suppress any logging
-1	Language Exception
1	Standard Gateway Exception
2	Errors and Warnings
3	Important information, errors and warnings
4	Standard and important information, errors and warnings
5	Low importance, standard, and important information, errors and warnings

The default log level of 2 should be sufficient for troubleshooting. Remember, with logging, less is more. It is easier to dig deeper once you have found the relevant issue rather than creating a haystack of log output.

Ask your PS admin to get the integration broker log files from the server when you need to look at them. There should be two files, msgLog.html (message log file) and errorLog.html (error log file).

The location of the msgLog.html is

<PIA_HOME> \webserv\<DOMAIN>\applications\peoplesoft\PSIGW.war \WEB_INF\msgLog.html.

The location of the errorLog.html is

<PIA_HOME \webserv

\<DOMAIN>\applications\peoplesoft\PSIGW.war\WEB-INF \errorLog.html.

147. How to perform a full sync of a table between PeopleSoft databases?

The following steps are the steps required to do a full sync of a table from one PeopleSoft database to another where there is no delivered messages or process to do so. This could be custom records or records which Oracle has not delivered syncs for.

Publication Steps:

1. Create Message

2. Create Service

3. Setup one routing from your publishing node to your subscribing node

4. Configure full data publish rule

    There is a delivered process that you can run which will dynamically look at the message object and find any parent child records/tables and gather the data for us and package it up into a service operation. This means you do NOT have to write a custom process just to sync this one record and any child records.

    Enterprise Components -> Integration Definitions -> Full Data Publish Rules

5. You can then schedule the delivered application engine to run.

    Enterprise Components -> Integration Definitions -> Initiate Process -> Full Data Publish

    The Application Engine EOP_PUBLISHT process will run and dynamically gather and publish all the data in the table in the underlying message definition of the submitted service operations

    Note the full sync process is not considered done until the publication integration broker publishes to the subscriber and the subscriber integration broker handlers complete successfully. This application engine just creates the service operation "operation instances". The operations then have to publish and get subscribed to. The application engine does not wait around for that or even have a "window" into that integration broker activity. Therefore, the application will run to "success" and you cannot trust the data is actually published until you verify that is published in the integration broker and the subscription contracts in the subscription side completed.

    Subscription Steps:

The subscription side as very similar setup in regards to the publishing service operation. The only difference is that you need to create a handler to run some generic code that can work for any full sync message you setup.

1. Create Message
2. Create Service
3. Create Service Operation Handler
4. Setup Service Operation Routings

Note you need to grant security to the service operations on the publishing side to the user who is going to run the publishing process and the service operations on the subscription side to the user who is going to receive the messages on the subscription side.

148. How to publish a web service?

In PeopleSoft, a web service is a method of communication that allows different applications to interact with each other over the web. PeopleSoft supports both SOAP (Simple Object Access Protocol) and REST (Representational State Transfer) web services.

You should follow the next steps to publish a web service

1) Go to PeopleTools -> Integration Broker -> Web Services -> Provide Web Service and publish a web service with the following steps.

Provide Web Service Wizard   Step 1 of 4

Select Services

Enter search criteria and click Search. Select one or more services you would like to provide.

Search Criteria

Service Name	begins with ∨	TWC_CALC
Description	begins with ∨	
Object Owner ID	equals ∨	∨
	☐ REST Service	

Search

Search Results	Find | View All |	First ◄ 1 of 1 ► Last
Service	**Description**	
☑ TWC_CALC_APP_FEE	Calculate Application Fee	

☑ Select All   ☐ Clear All

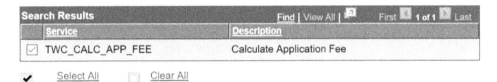

Provide Web Service Wizard   Step 2 of 4

< Previous   Next >

Select Service Operations

Select one or more operations for each service

Service TWC_CALC_APP_FEE   Description Calculate Application Fee
        Use Service Alias in WSDL   Service Alias
        Use Secure Target Location   ☐ Generate WSDL 2.0

Operations			Find | View All |	First 1 of 1 Last	
Service Operation	**Description**	**Operation Type**	**Request Message**	**Response Message**	**Fault Message**
☑ TWC_CALC_APP_FEE.V1	Calculate Application Fee	Synchronous	TWC_CALC_APP_FEE_REQ.V1	TWC_CALC_APP_FEE_RES.V1	

☑ Select All   ☐ Clear All

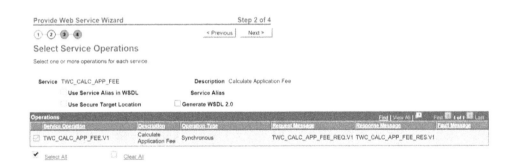

Provide Web Service Wizard   Step 3 of 4

< Previous   Next >

View WSDL

View the generated WSDL for each service.

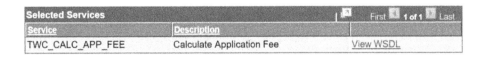

Selected Services		First ◄ 1 of 1 ► Last
Service	**Description**	
TWC_CALC_APP_FEE	Calculate Application Fee	View WSDL

①─②─③─④   < Previous | Finish

Specify Publishing Options

The WSDL for the selected services will be published to the PeopleSoft WSDL Repository.

☐ **Publish to UDDI**

☑ **WSDL Repository**

Provide Web Service Wizard

Confirm Results

View the WSDL Generation Log to confirm the results of the wizard.

WSDL Generation Log:

Service: TWC_CALC_APP_FEE has been exported.

Inserted WSDL: TWC_CALC_APP_FEE.1 in the repository

Generated WSDL URL:
http://fitst6.tarion.com//PSIGW/PeopleSoftServiceListeningConnector/TWC_CALC_APP_FEE.1.wsdl

Provide Another Service | Generate SOAP Template

2) Copy the url from the box above to a new browser window and see if it is working. If it is, the web service is working.

Note when using the Provide Web Service wizard, leave the Generate WSDL 2.0 checkbox unchecked.

149. How to create a CI-based web service?

The first step is to create a component interface for the component. You should check if one already exists by opening your component and performing a Find Definition References in application designer.

The next step is to provide security to the component interface through a relevant permission list that you have. This means editing the permission list and assigning component interface security to your component interface.

Make sure that you

- Press edit and give full access to the component interface methods

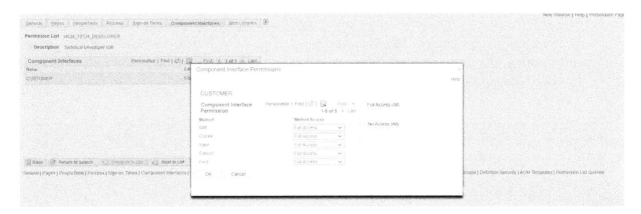

The CI-Based Services component is located at:

PeopleTools -> Integration Broker -> Web Services- > CI-Based Services

Select your component interface and press the Review CI Status button.

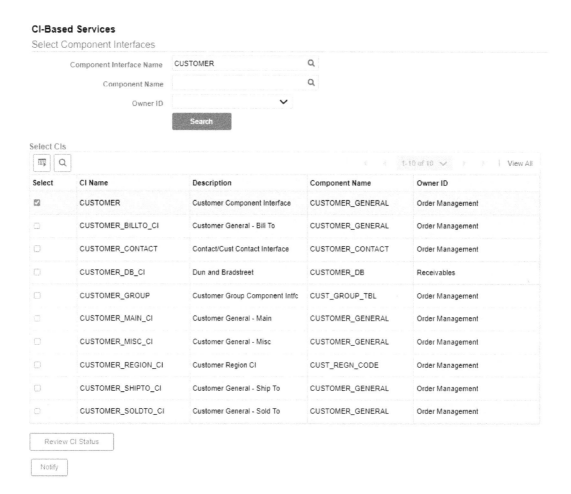

Next step you need to select the component interface methods that you want service operations created for. These are essentially going to be the methods that can be accessed through the web service. In this case, the get, create, find, update and updatedata methods have been selected.

The service created will be your component interface name prefixed with CI_. Service operations will be created using the service name and suffix relating to the method and version of the service operation.

CI-Based Services
Review Status

| Status | | | | | | | Find | First | ◄ 1 of 1 ► | Last |

    CI Name CUSTOMER   **Description** Customer Component Interface

    Service CI_CUSTOMER   **Status** Service does not exist and will be created.

Choose Method

Select	Action	Method	Service Operation	Status
☑	Create Operation.	Get		Does not exist.
☑	Create Operation.	Create		Does not exist.
☑	Create Operation.	Find		Does not exist.
☑	Create Operation.	Update		Does not exist.
☑	Create Operation.	Updatedata		Does not exist.

☑ Select All ☐ Deselect All

[Display Selected Actions]   Return to Select CIs

Click Display Selected Actions

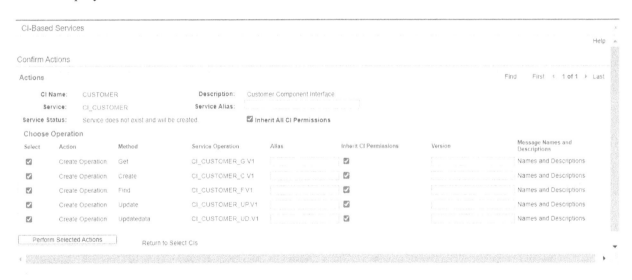

Finally press the Perform Selected Actions button to create the service and service operations.

CI-Based Services

Review Status

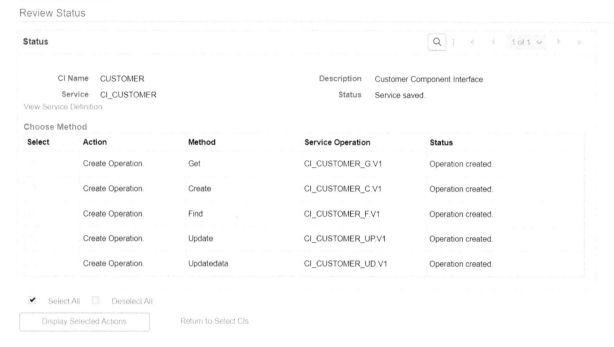

After creating the CI based service and service operations for each of the methods, you need to use the Provide Web Service wizard to generate the web service in PeopleSoft. This includes the following steps

- Creates the relevant request, response, and fault messages for your (synchronous) service operations
- Creates the WSDL (web service description language) for your service.
- Publishes your WSDL to the PeopleSoft WSDL repository (and optionally to a UDDI server)
- Refer to the video that I created with the title of How to publish a web service

150. How to exclude a service operation from user security and test the service operation with the Node's Default user?

There is a feature that lets you exclude the user security from the service operation and use the Node's Default User instead. To enable this, navigate to PeopleTools -> Integration Broker -> Configuration -> Service Configuration.

Select the "Exclude PSFT Auth Token" tab. On this page, you can select specific service operations to exclude from user security.

151. How to check the status of an incoming or an outgoing message via SQL?

You can use the following SQLs to check the statuses of incoming subscription and outgoing publication messages via SQL.

```
--SUBSCRIPTION MESSAGES
SELECT * FROM PSIBSUBCON_VW
WHERE IB_OPERATIONNAME = '';

--PUBLICATION MESSAGES
SELECT * FROM PSIBPUBCON_VW
WHERE IB_OPERATIONNAME = '';
```

The values for PUBSTATUS or PUBCONSTATUS fields in the views are the same. They are as follows,

```
 0 = Error
 1 = New
 2 = Started
 3 = Working
 4 = Done
 5 = Retry
 6 = Time
 7 = Edited
 8 = Canceled
 9 = Hold
10 = Submitted
11 = DoneNoAck
```

152. How to change the maximum size of IB messages?

You can change the maximum size of IB messages at

PeopleTools -> Utilities -> Administration -> PeopleTools Options

By default, it is 10M bytes.

153. You can use the Handler Tester to test the handler application class of a Service Operation and use the Service Operation Tester to invoke and test a Service Operation.

You can use the Handler Tester and the Service Operation Tester without setting up routing and without impacting other developer activity on the system.

The navigation paths of the Handler Tester and the Service Operation Tester are PeopleTools -> Integration Broker -> Service Utilities.

154. How to configure and publish a synchronous web service after migrating a PS project containing the web service from one environment to another?

1) Grant access to the required permission lists to the Service Operation.

2) Get the WSDL URL from the source environment and replace the source environment name with the target environment name. If there is no error when opening the URL and the page would look like as follows, the WSDL URL for the target environment is valid, and there is no need to do anything.

155. How to set up a JMS node for integrating with a third-party Java-based application?

Setting up a JMS (Java Message Service) node for integrating with a third-party Java-based application in PeopleSoft involves several steps. Here's a general guide to help you get started:

1). Configure the JMS Provider

- Install and configure your JMS provider (e.g., Apache ActiveMQ, IBM MQ). Ensure it is running and accessible.
- Create queues or topics as needed for your integration.
- Ensure messages can be sent out and received

2). Set Up PeopleSoft Integration Broker

- Log in to PeopleSoft and navigate to the Integration Broker setup.
- Configure the Integration Gateway:

- Go to PeopleTools > Integration Broker > Configuration > Gateways.
- Add a new gateway or configure an existing one.
- Ensure the gateway is active and properly configured.

3). Create a JMS Node
- Define a new node:
    - Navigate to PeopleTools > Integration Broker > Integration Setup > Nodes.
    - Add a new node for your JMS provider.
    - Set the node type to JMS.
- Configure the node:
    - Provide the necessary connection details (e.g., JNDI provider URL, connection factory, queue/topic names).
    - Ensure the node is active.

Here is an example of how to set up a new JMS node.

4). Set Up JMS Connectors

- Configure JMS connectors:

    - Navigate to PeopleTools > Integration Broker > Configuration > Connectors.

    - Add or configure a JMS connector.

    - Specify the connection details and properties required by your JMS provider.

Here is an example of how to set up a new JMS connector.

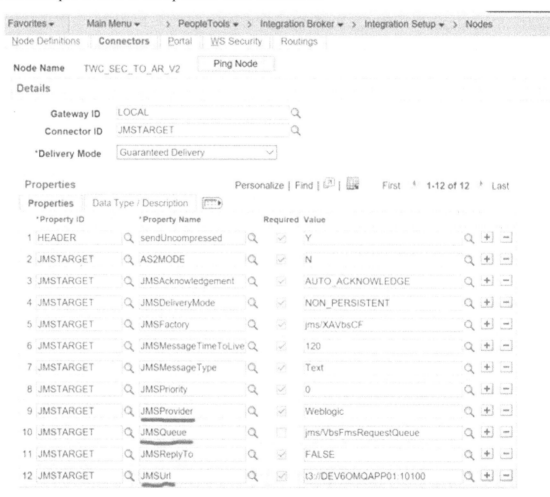

The most important properties that need to be configured are JMSProvider, JMSQueue, and JRSUrl.

5). Create and Configure Messages

- Define messages:

    - Go to PeopleTools > Integration Broker > Integration Setup > Messages.

- Create new messages or use existing ones.
- Ensure the messages are active and properly structured.

6). Create routings:

- Navigate to PeopleTools > Integration Broker > Integration Setup > Routings.
- Create routings to route your messages to and from the JMS node.

7). Testing and Validation

- Test the integration:
  - Send test messages between PeopleSoft and the JMS provider.
  - Verify that messages are being sent and received correctly.
- Monitor and troubleshoot:
  - Use the monitoring tools within PeopleSoft and the JMS provider to check the status of messages and troubleshoot any issues.

A few important Notes

1) After setting up a new JMS node, you need to add a new JMS queue to the local Gateway Setup Properties file, bounce app server, web server, and clear cache. You may need to bounce the servers of the message sender, f.i., the MQ server, before bouncing the PeopleSoft servers.

2) You need to have a JMS queue entry for a request message in the Gateway Setup Properties file. You don't need to create a JMS queue for a response message in the file.

3) You can put more than one queue in the URL of a node in one JMS queue entry in the Gateway Properties File.

4) You need to ensure the message header from the third-party system has been set up correctly; verify the message name, version, queue, etc. on the third-party message server.

Here is an example of the message header of a JMS message sent from a MQ server,

```
FmsRequestQueue.MessageName=XXX_REG_TO_AR.V1
FmsRequestQueue.RequestingNode=XXX_REG_TO_AR
FmsRequestQueue.JMSProvider=Weblogic
FmsRequestQueue.MessageType=async
FmsRequestQueue.version=V1
FmsRequestQueue.JMSMessageType=Text
FmsRequestQueue.Password=password
```

156. How to integrate your PeopleSoft system with a third-party system using synchronous service operation and rowset-based messaging?

The communication between a third-party system and PeopleSoft will take place with the provided WSDL (Web Service Definition Language), which will connect to the Web Service, which resides in Peoplesoft Web Server. The WSDL will have all the information, including the input/output parameters, length, type, etc., in its XML format.

In the following example, a new service operation is created to

1. Receive the message and extract the file from it

2. Place it in specific Landing zone directory, based on a mapping table

3. Send a response with status 0 on success, 1 on failure

You need to create a PS-Project with the following:

New Application Package

New Application Class

Application class implementing PS_PT: Integration: IRequestHandler has to be used in the application package.

New Messages

1. Rowset-Based Request message from Third Party

2. Rowset-Based Response message to send from your system

3.

New Service Definition

New Service Operation Definitions

1. Create a New Service Operations Definition with Service Definition in it.

2. Add the Request/Response message in the subsequent section.

Message Information

Type	Request	
Message.Version	MCM_FILE_EXCH V1	🔍 View Message
Type	Response	
Message.Version	MCM_FILE_EXCH_RESP V1	🔍 View Message

Save   Return to Service   Add Version

General | Handlers | Routings

3. Routing Status should be Any to Local.

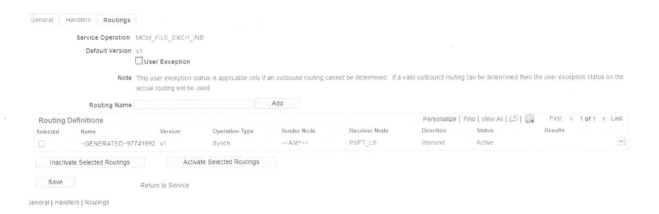

4. In the Handler tab part, enter the name of the Handler. Type: OnRequest; Implementation: Application Class; Status: Active. Assign your Application Package here.

Handler Details

Handler Name	REQUESTHDLR
Handler Type	On Request
Description	File Exchange Inbound Sync
Comments	1. Receives the Message and extracts the file from it. 2. Places it in specific LZ directory, based on MCM_INTF_FL_MAP table 3. Sends a response with status 0 on success, 1 on failure
Handler Owner	

Application Class

*Package Name	MCM_INTF_COMMON
*Path	:
Class ID	FileExchInbSync
Method	OnRequest

OK   Cancel

After this, you can create your own WSDL, which you provide to the third party to interact with your system using the Provide Web service wizard.

The Application Package code for the handler will look like this:

```
import PS_PT:Integration:IRequestHandler;

class           FileExchInbSync           implements
PS_PT:Integration:IRequestHandler
   method InboundSyncRequestHandler();
   method OnRequest(&Inp_Msg As Message) Returns Message;
   method OnNotify(&_MSG As Message)
end-class;


/* constructor */
```

157

```
method InboundSyncRequestHandler
end-method;

method OnRequest
   /+ &Inp_Msg as Message +/
   /+ Returns Message +/
   /+                                        Extends/implements
PS_PT:Integration:IRequestHandler.OnRequest +/


   If &Inp_Msg.Name = "MCM_FILE_EXCH" Then
      /* Read file */
      Local    XmlNode    &BodyNode,    &RootNode,    &EnvNode,
&childNode1,    &childNode2,    &childNode3,    &childNode4,
&FldTypeNode, &FldTypeNode1, &FldTypeNode2;
      Local string &PrgID, &Filename, &OutPath, &File_Sts,
&SoapStrFinal,    &EncryptionID,    &Msg,    &ProcessName,
&Direction;
      Local            Record            &Rec           =
&Inp_Msg.GetRowset()(1).GetRecord(Record.MCM_INTF_FL_WRK);
      Local object &Crypt;
      Local boolean &DecryptFailed;
      Local           Message           &Resp_Msg          =
CreateMessage(Operation.MCM_FILE_EXCH_INB,
%IntBroker_Response);
      Local           Record           &Resp_Rec          =
&Resp_Msg.GetRowset()(1).GetRecord(Record.MCM_INTF_RP_WRK)
;


      SQLExec("SELECT FILENAME, PRCSNAME, IB_DIRECTION FROM
PS_MCM_INTF_FL_MAP    WHERE    MCM_SYSTEM_ID    =    :1",
&Rec.MCM_SYSTEM_ID.Value,    &Filename,    &ProcessName,
&Direction);
```

```
If All(&ProcessName, &Direction) Then

    /* Assemble &OutPath */
    If None(&Filename) Then
        &Filename = &Rec.MCM_INTF_FILENAME1.Value;
    End-If;
    If &Direction = "I" Then
        &OutPath  = GetURL(URL.MCM_INTF_FILE_ZONE)  |
&ProcessName | "/IN/" | &Filename;
    Else
        &OutPath  = GetURL(URL.MCM_INTF_FILE_ZONE)  |
&ProcessName | "/OUT/" | &Filename;
    End-If;

    /* Decrypt file */
    &Crypt = CreateObject("Crypt");
    &Crypt.Open("MCM_BASE64_DECODE");
    &Crypt.UpdateData(&Rec.MCM_FLAT_FILE.Value);
    &Msg = &Crypt.Result;
    If None(&Msg) Then
        &DecryptFailed = True;
    Else
        &DecryptFailed = False;
    End-If;

    /* Respond */
    If &DecryptFailed Then
        &Resp_Rec.RESPONSE.Value = "1";
        &Resp_Rec.DESCR.Value = "Decrypt failed";
    Else
        Local File &Out_File = GetFile(&OutPath, "W",
%FilePath_Absolute);
```

159

```
                &Out_File.WriteString(&Msg);
                &Out_File.Close();

                If  FileExists(&OutPath,  %FilePath_Absolute)
Then
                   &Resp_Rec.RESPONSE.Value = "0";
                   &Resp_Rec.DESCR.Value    =    "Transaction
successful";
                Else
                   &Resp_Rec.RESPONSE.Value = "1";
                   &Resp_Rec.DESCR.Value    =    "File    creation
failed";
                End-If;
             End-If;
          Else
             &Resp_Rec.RESPONSE.Value = "1";
             &Resp_Rec.DESCR.Value    =    "Invalid    mapping
instructions";
          End-If;
       End-If;

    Return &Resp_Msg;

end-method;

method OnNotify
   /+ &_MSG as Message +/
   Local Rowset &RS;
   Local Record &Rec;
   Local string &Filename, &OutPath, &Msg, &ProcessName,
&Direction;
   Local object &Crypt;
```

160

```
Local boolean &DecryptFailed;

&RS = &_MSG.GetRowset();
&Rec = &RS(1).GetRecord(1);

SQLExec("SELECT FILENAME, PRCSNAME, IB_DIRECTION FROM
PS_MCM_INTF_FL_MAP   WHERE   MCM_SYSTEM_ID   =   :1",
&Rec.MCM_SYSTEM_ID.Value,   &Filename,   &ProcessName,
&Direction);
If All(&ProcessName, &Direction) Then

    /* Assemble &OutPath */
    /*
    If None(&Filename) Then
        rem here we use the filename as configured;
        &Filename = &Rec.MCM_INTF_FILENAME1.Value;
    End-If;
    */
    If All(&Rec.MCM_INTF_FILENAME1.Value) Then
        rem we use the filename as passed from the
datastream;
        &Filename = &Rec.MCM_INTF_FILENAME1.Value;
    End-If;

    If &Direction = "I" Then
        &OutPath  =  GetURL(URL.MCM_INTF_FILE_ZONE)  |
&ProcessName | "/IN/" | &Filename;
    Else
        &OutPath  =  GetURL(URL.MCM_INTF_FILE_ZONE)  |
&ProcessName | "/OUT/" | &Filename;
    End-If;
```

```
/* Decrypt file */
&Crypt = CreateObject("Crypt");
&Crypt.Open("MCM_BASE64_DECODE");
&Crypt.UpdateData(&Rec.MCM_FLAT_FILE.Value);
&Msg = &Crypt.Result;
If None(&Msg) Then
    &DecryptFailed = True;
Else
    &DecryptFailed = False;
End-If;


/* Respond */
If &DecryptFailed Then
Else
    Local  File  &Out_File  =  GetFile(&OutPath,  "W",
%FilePath_Absolute);
    &Out_File.WriteString(&Msg);
    &Out_File.Close();
    If FileExists(&OutPath, %FilePath_Absolute) Then
        rem good;
    Else
        rem error;
    End-If;
    End-If;
Else
    rem mapping error;
End-If;

end-method;
```

Here is the application package code for another example which processes data stored in a table in the message instead of a file.

```
/*Import the PS_PT Application Package*/
import PS_PT:Integration:IRequestHandler;
/*Class definition and usage of imported method*/
class CLASS_NAME implements
PS_PT:Integration:IRequestHandler
method InboundSyncRequestHandler();
/* Onrequest method declation for Synchronous
Communication*/
method onRequest(&MSG As Message) Returns Message;
/* On Error -String reply */
method onError(&MSG As Message) Returns string;
end-class;
method InboundSyncRequestHandler
end-method;
method onRequest
/+ &MSG as Message +/
/+ Returns Message +/
/+ Extends/implements
PS_PT:Integration:IRequestHandler.OnRequest +/
/*Variable Declation */
Local string &r_EMPLID, &temp1, &temp2, &temp11,
&temp22, &temp10, &temp20, &EXISTS, &X, &Flag;
Local Rowset &requestRowset, &responseRowset;
Local Record &requestRecord, &responseRecord;
/* Get the data from incoming message */
&requestMessage = GetMessage();
&requestRecord = CreateRecord(Record.
REQUESTRECORDNAME);
&requestRowset = &requestMessage.GetRowset();
&r_EMPLID = &requestRowset.GetRow(1).GetRecord(Record.
REQUESTRECORDNAME).EMPLID.Value;
```

```
&r_DATE1 = &requestRowset.GetRow(1).GetRecord(Record.
REQUESTRECORDNAME).DATE1.Value;
/*Inserting into response record*/
rem &responseRecord = CreateRecord(Record.
REQUESTRECORDNAME);
&responseRowset = CreateRowset(Record.
REQUESTRECORDNAME);
/* Do your own code to retrive the data from the fields
or assign it to any other places in system or record*/
/*Send Acknowledgement to the third Party */
&responseRowset.GetRow(1).GetRecord(Record.RESPONDERECOR
DNAME).LAST_NAME.Value = &w_LAST_NAME;
&responseRowset.GetRow(1).GetRecord(Record.
RESPONDERECORDNAME).FIRST_NAME.Value = &w_FIRST_NAME;
/* create the response message */
&responseMessage =
CreateMessage(Operation.SERVICEOPERATIONNAME,
%IntBroker_Response);
/* initiates a message object */
&responseMessage.CopyRowset(&responseRowset);
Return (&responseMessage);
end-method;
```

157. How to create a REST web service and test it?

1) Create documents for request and response.
2) Create request and response messages based on the above created documents.
3) Create REST service.
4) Create GET service operations.
5) Give security to Service Operations.
6) Create handler application class and assign it to the service operation.
7) Test the REST web service.

Create documents for request and response.

Navigate to PeopleTools → Documents → Documents Builder

Add a new value

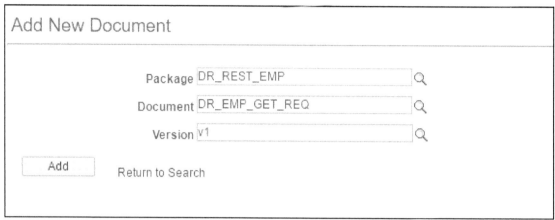

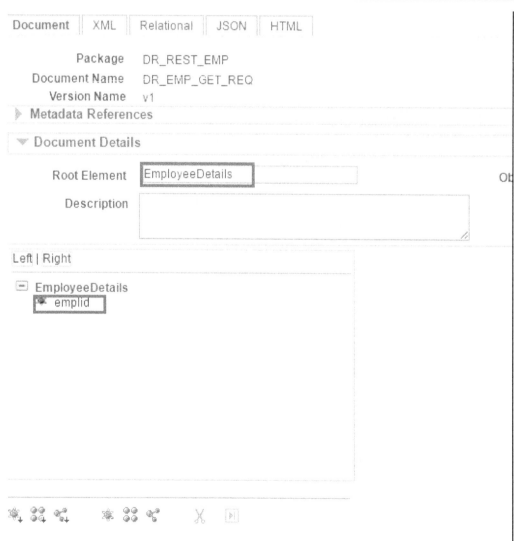

Similarly create a document for response also.

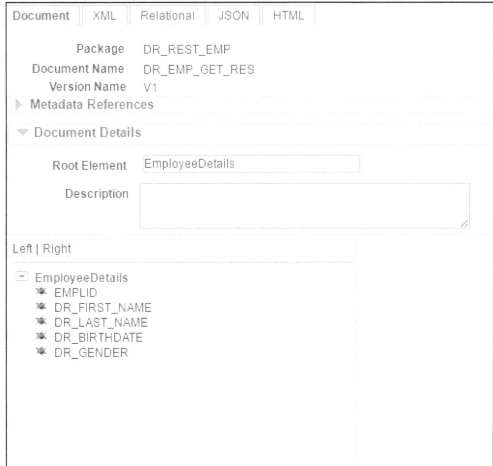

Note if you are creating a document where you have to include the fields of a record then you can go to PeopleTools → Document → Document Utilities → Create Document from Record

Create messages

Navigate to PeopleTools → Integration Broker → Integration Setup → Messages

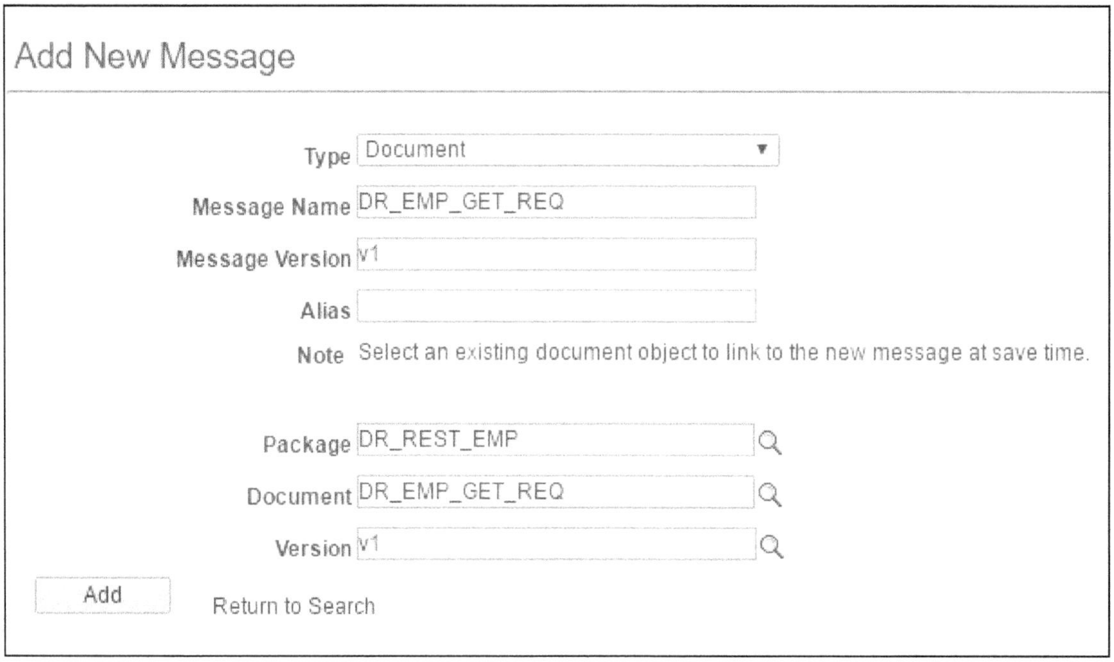

Add New Message

Type	Document ▼
Message Name	DR_EMP_GET_REQ
Message Version	v1
Alias	
Note	Select an existing document object to link to the new message at save time.
Package	DR_REST_EMP 🔍
Document	DR_EMP_GET_REQ 🔍
Version	v1 🔍

Add   Return to Search

Click on Add

Create a message for response

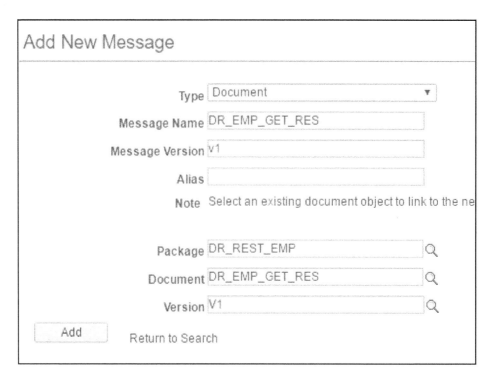

Add New Message

Type	Document ▼
Message Name	DR_EMP_GET_RES
Message Version	V1
Alias	
Note	Select an existing document object to link to the ne
Package	DR_REST_EMP 🔍
Document	DR_EMP_GET_RES 🔍
Version	V1 🔍

[Add]   Return to Search

Click on Add

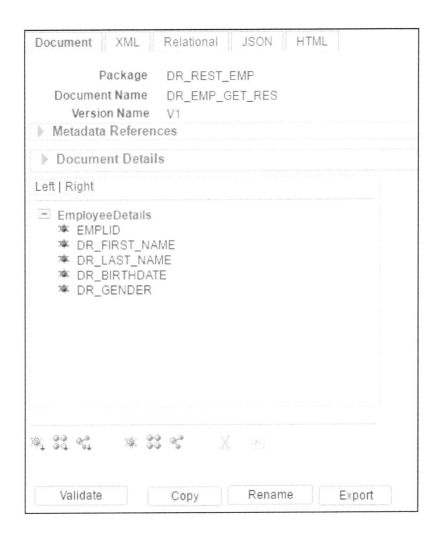

Create REST service

Navigate to PeopleTools → Integration Broker → Integration Setup → Services

Add New Service

Service: DR_EMP_REST   🔍
              ☑ REST Service
Add   Return to Search

Click Add

Services

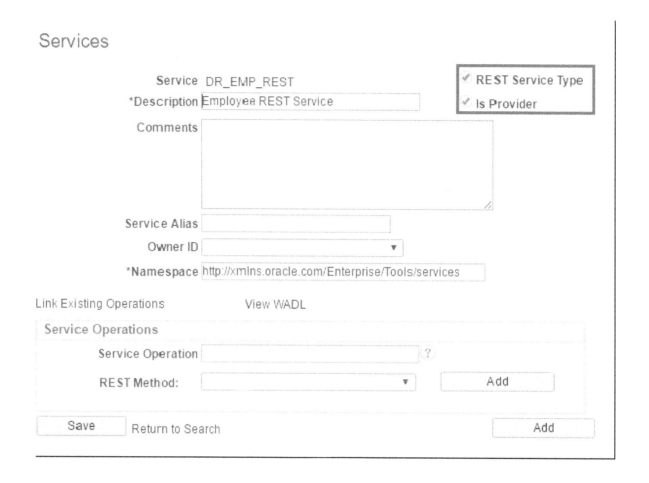

Service DR_EMP_REST

*Description Employee REST Service

☑ REST Service Type
☑ Is Provider

Comments

Service Alias

Owner ID

*Namespace http://xmlns.oracle.com/Enterprise/Tools/services

Link Existing Operations   View WADL

Service Operations

Service Operation   ?

REST Method: ▼   Add

Save   Return to Search   Add

Create Service Operation

Open the above service and create a service operation.

Services

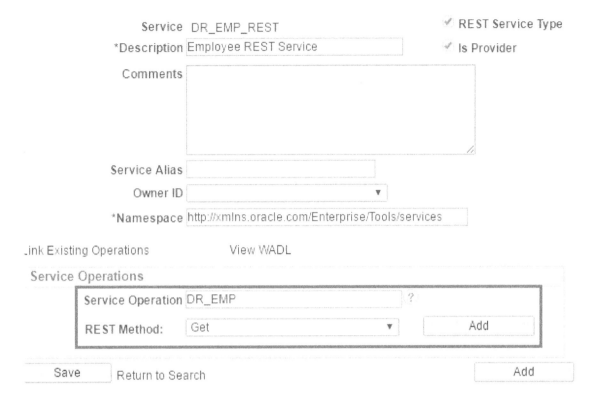

Click on Add

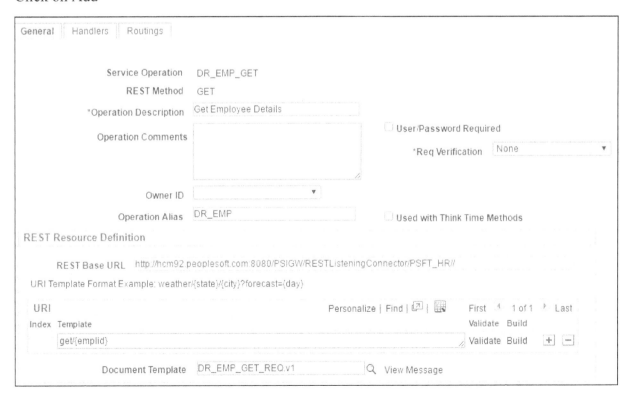

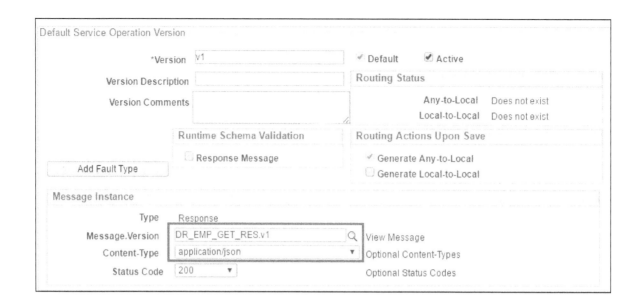

Give security to Service Operation

Create handler application class and assign it to the service operation.

Create an application class to read the employee id from the incoming request and to send back the employee details.

Here is the sample code of an application class which gets an Employee ID and returns his or her First Name, Last Name, Birth Date and Gender.

```
import PS_PT: Integration: IRequestHandler;

method OnRequest (&message As Message) Returns Message;

class DREmployee Details implements PS_PT: Integration:
IRequestHandler method OnError (&request As Message) Returns
string; rem property string OnErrorContentType;

rem property integer OnErrorHttpResponseCode;

end-class;

method OnRequest

/+ &message as Message +/

/+ Returns Message +/ /+ Extends/implements PS_PT:
Integration: IRequestHandler.OnRequest +/

Local Document &doc, &resp_doc;

Local Compound &com, &resp_com;

Local Message &response;

Local string &emplid;

Local Record &rec;

Local SQL &sql;
/* Get the URI request document */

&doc = &message.GetURIDocument();

&com = &doc.DocumentElement;

&response = CreateMessage (Operation.DR_EMP_GET,
%IntBroker_Response);

&resp_doc = &response.GetDocument();

&resp_com = &resp_doc.DocumentElement;

/* Get the employee id from the request */

&emplid=&com.GetPropertyByName ("emplid").value;

&rec = CreateRecord (Record.DR_EMPL_TBL);
```

```
If &response.HTTPMethod = %IntBroker_HTTP_GET Then

   /* Fetch the details for the employee id */

   sql = CreateSQL ("$selectall (:1) where emplid=:2", Record.
   DR_EMPL_TBL, &emplid);

   While sql.Fetch (&rec)

        &resp_com.GetPropertyByName ("EMPLID").value =
        &rec.EMPLID.Value;

        &resp_com.GetPropertyByName ("DR_FIRST_NAME").value =
        &rec.DR_FIRST_NAME.Value;

        &resp_com.GetPropertyByName ("DR_LAST_NAME").value =
        rec.DR_LAST_NAME.Value;

        &resp_com.GetPropertyByName ("DR_BIRTHDATE").value =
        &rec.DR_BIRTHDATE.Value;

        &resp_com.GetPropertyByName ("DR_GENDER").value =
        &rec. DR_GENDER.Value;

   End-While;

End-If;

/* Return the response */

Return &response;

end-method;


method OnError

/+&request as Message +/

/+Returns String +/

/+Extends/implements PS_PT:Integration:IRequestHandler.OnError
+/

rem Enter error handling code here;

Return "";

end-method;
```

Now use this as handler in the service operation.

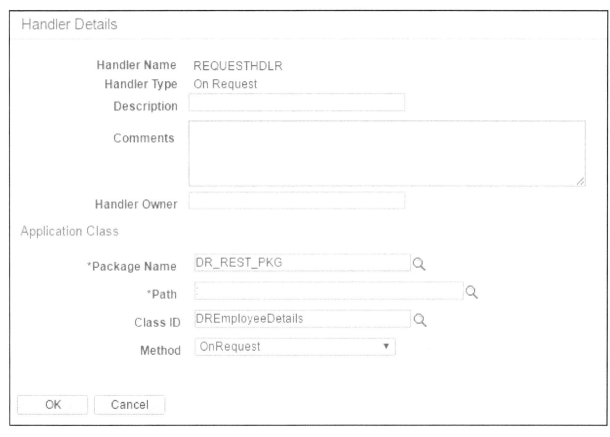

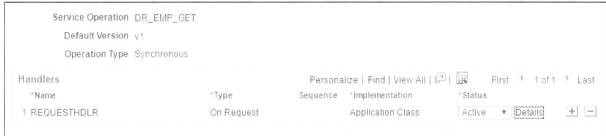

Test the service operation

Open sendmaster or any other web service testing tool

Get the url by clicking validate link

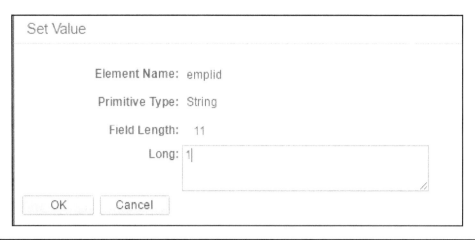

Click on Generate URL

Use this url in sendmaster.

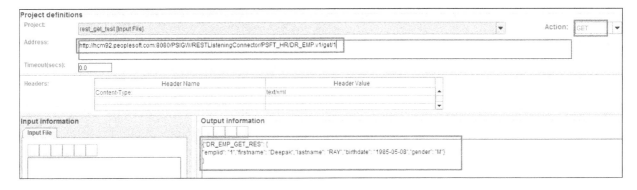

Similarly change the employee id to 2 and test

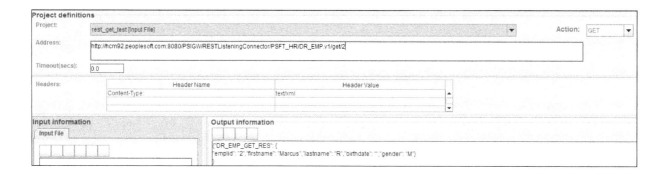

158. How to schedule to run the full data publish process with PeopleCode?

Here is an example,

```
Local ProcessRequest&RQST;

&RQST = CreateProcessRequest();

&RQST.RunControlID = "TEST";

&RQST.ProcessType = "Application Engine";

&RQST.ProcessName = "EOP_PUBLISHT";

&RQST.RunDateTime = %Datetime;

&RQST.Schedule(); */
```

159. How to copy an entire component, a header/line page rowset, or only the changed rows of data from a component into a message object?

CopyRowset copies the data, including rows that haven't been modified. If you want to copy only data that has changed in some way, you should use the CopyRowsetDelta method.

The following example copies an entire component into a message object.

```
&Msg = %IntBroker.GetMessage();

&Rowset = &Msg.GetRowset()

&Component_Rowset = GetLevel0();

&Msg.CopyRowset(&Component_Rowset);
```

The following example copies a header/line page rowset into a header/line message object.

```
&Msg = %IntBroker.GetMessage();
    &Rowset= &Msg.GetRowset();
    &Component_Rowset = GetLevel0();
    &Msg.CopyRowset(&Component_Rowset,
RECORD.PO_HDR_VW, RECORD.PO_HDR, RECORD.PO_LINE_VW,
RECORD.PO_LINE);
```

The following example copies all the changed rows of data from a component into a message object.

```
    &Component_Rowset = GetLevel0();
    &Msg.CopyRowsetDelta(&Component_Rowset);
```

160. How to publish a message for incremental sync?

You can refer to the following code example.

```
&MSG = CreateMessage(Operation.XXX_ALTACCT_XREF_SYNC);
If &MSG.IsOperationActive Then
    Local Record &REC;
    /* Copy the delta changes in the account and alt
    account mapping scroll into the message */
    &MSG.CopyRowsetDelta(GetLevel0()(1).GetRowset(Scr
    oll.ACC_XREF_SET_VW).GetRow(1).GetRowset(Scroll.A
    CC_XREF_VW), Record.ACC_XREF_VW,
    Record.ALTACCT_XREF);
    /* Set the ALTACCT_SETID field value as it is not
    in the mapping scroll */
    &REC = &MSG.GetRowset()(1).ALTACCT_XREF;
```

```
        &REC.ALTACCT_SETID.Value = "SHARE";
        /*Resequence Audit Actions*/
        ReSeqAuditAction(&MSG);
        /* Publish the message */
        %IntBroker.Publish(&MSG);
End-If;
&MSG = CreateMessage(Operation.XXX_BOOK_CODE_SYNC);
If &MSG.IsOperationActive
Then
&MSG.CopyRowsetDelta(GetLevel0()(1).GetRowset(Scroll.B
OOK_CODE_TBL));
  If All(&MSG.GetRowset()(1).BOOK_CODE_TBL.SETID.Value)
  Then
        /*Resequence Audit Actions*/
        ReSeqAuditAction(&MSG);
        %IntBroker.Publish(&MSG);
  End-If;
End-If;
```

161. How to subscribe a message for full sync?

   Here is a code example,

```
import PS_PT:Integration:INotificationHandler;
class XXX_FullSync implements
PS_PT:Integration:INotificationHandler
method XXX_FullSync();
 method OnNotify(&_MSG As Message);
 end-class;
 Declare Function Subscribe_FullReplication PeopleCode
 FUNCLIB_EOEIP.SUBSCRIBE_MSG_PC FieldFormula;
 /* constructor */
```

```
method XXX_FullSync
end-method;
method OnNotify
/+ &_MSG as Message +/
/+
Extends/implements
PS_PT:Integration:INotificationHandler.OnNotify +/
/* Variable Declaration */
Local Message &MSG;
&MSG = &_MSG;
Subscribe_FullReplication(&MSG);
end-method;
```

162. How to subscribe a message for incremental sync?

Here is a code example,

```
import PS_PT:Integration:INotificationHandler;
class XXX_BUIncrSync implements
PS_PT:Integration:INotificationHandler
method XXX_BUIncrSync();
method OnNotify(&_MSG As Message);
end-class;
Declare Function Subscribe_IncrReplication PeopleCode
FUNCLIB_EOEIP.SUBSCRIBE_MSG_PC FieldFormula;
Declare Function add_setid PeopleCode
FUNCLIB_UTIL.FIELDNAME FieldFormula;
/* constructor */
method XXX_BUIncrSync
end-method;
method OnNotify
/+ &_MSG as Message +/
```

```
/+ Extends/implements
PS_PT:Integration:INotificationHandler.OnNotify +/
/* Variable Declaration */
Local Message &MSG;
Local Rowset &RS;
Local string &BUSINESS_UNIT, &DOC_SEQ, &DESCR,
&DESCRSHORT, &DEFAULT_SETID, &TEMP;
&MSG = &_MSG;
&RS = &MSG.GetRowset();
&BUSINESS_UNIT =
&RS(1).BUS_UNIT_TBL_GL.BUSINESS_UNIT.Value;
      &DOC_SEQ = &RS(1).BUS_UNIT_TBL_GL.DOC_SEQ.Value;
      /*** call incremental subscription function ***/
      Subscribe_IncrReplication(&MSG);
      end-method;
```

163. How to create and publish a rowset based message using PeopleCode?

Here is a code example,

```
&msgDemand = CreateMessage(Message.XXX_DMND_STAT_V1);
If &msgDemand.IsActive Then
&rsDemandToVBS = CreateRowset(Record.XXX_DMND_STAT);
&recDemandToVBS =
&rsDemandToVBS.GetRow(1).GetRecord(Record.XXX_DMND_STAT);
&recDemandToVBS.XXX_SECURITY_NBR.Value  =
Value(&strSecNbr);
&recDemandToVBS.SEQNUM.Value = Value(&strSeqNum);
&recDemandToVBS.DEPOSIT_ID.Value = &strDepositId;
&recDemandToVBS.ACCOUNTING_DT.Value = &dAcctDt;
&recDemandToVBS.AMOUNT.Value = &nbrAmount;
  &recDemandToVBS.XXX_INTEREST_AMT.Value =
Value(&strInterest);
```

```
If &recDemandToVBS.XXX_INTEREST_AMT.Value
>&recDemandToVBS.AMOUNT.Value Then
&recDemandToVBS.XXX_INTEREST_AMT.Value
= &recDemandToVBS.AMOUNT.Value
End-If;
&recDemandToVBS.ROW_ADDED_OPRID.Value = &strCollector;
&recDemandToVBS.ROW_ADDED_DTTM.Value = %Datetime;
&rsMessageRowset = &msgDemand.GetRowset();
&rsDemandToVBS.CopyTo(&rsMessageRowset);
For &i = 1 To &rsMessageRowset.ActiveRowCount
&rsMessageRowset.GetRow(&i).PSCAMA.AUDIT_ACTN.Value  =
"A";
End-For;
&msgDemand.Publish();
```

164. How to create and publish a non rowset based message?

Here is a code example,

```
Local XmlDoc &xmlResponseDoc;
Local XmlNode &xmlSecurityIdNode, &xmlSecurityIdTextNode,
&xmlSequenceNumberNode, &xmlSequenceNumberTextNode,
&xmlDepositIdNode, &xmlDepositIdTextNode,
&xmlDepositDateNode, &xmlDepositDateTextNode, &xmlAmountNode,
&xmlAmountTextNode, &xmlInterestNode, &xmlInterestTextNode,
&xmlCollectorNode, &xmlCollectorTextNode;
&xmlResponseDoc = CreateXmlDoc("<?xml
version='1.0'?><createDrawdownResponse/>");
&xmlSecurityIdNode =
&xmlResponseDoc.DocumentElement.AddElement("securityId");
&xmlSecurityIdTextNode =
&xmlSecurityIdNode.AddText(&strSecNbr);
```

```
&xmlSequenceNumberNode =
&xmlResponseDoc.DocumentElement.AddElement("sequenceNumber");
&xmlSequenceNumberTextNode =
&xmlStatusNode.AddText(&strSeqNum);
&xmlDepositIdNode =
&xmlResponseDoc.DocumentElement.AddElement("depositId");
&xmlDepositIdTextNode =
&xmlStatusNode.AddText(&strDepositId);
&xmlDepositDateNode =
&xmlResponseDoc.DocumentElement.AddElement("depositDate");
&xmlDepositDateTextNode = &xmlStatusNode.AddText(&dAcctDt);
&xmlAmountNode =
&xmlResponseDoc.DocumentElement.AddElement("amount");
&xmlAmountTextNode = &xmlStatusNode.AddText(&nbrAmount);
&xmlInterestNode =
&xmlResponseDoc.DocumentElement.AddElement("interest");
&xmlInterestTextNode = &xmlStatusNode.AddText(&strInterest);
&xmlCollectorNode =
&xmlResponseDoc.DocumentElement.AddElement("collector");
&xmlCollectorTexttNode =
&xmlStatusNode.AddText(&strCollector);
&msgDemand.SetXmlDoc(&xmlResponseDoc);
/* Send XML reponse document to VBS through IB */
%IntBroker.Publish(&msgDemand);
```

165. How to subscribe and consume a rowset based message using PeopleCode?

The following example shows how to load an incoming rowset-based message into a record, parse out the message data, construct an output string and log the output string into a page record,

Here is an example,

```
Method OnNotify
/+ &_MSG as Message +/
/+Extends/implements
PS_PT:Integration:INotificationHandler.+/
/+ OnNotify +/
/* Variable Declaration */
Local any &outstring;
Local any &i;
Local any &CRLF;
Local Message &MSG;
Local Rowset &rs, &rs1;
Local Record &FLIGHTDATA, &REC;
Local XmlDoc&xmldoc;
Local string &return_string_value;
Local boolean&return_bool_value;
&CRLF = Char(13) | Char(10);
&MSG = &_MSG;
&rs = &MSG.GetRowset();
&REC = &rs(1).QE_FLIGHTDATA;
&FLIGHTDATA = CreateRecord(Record.QE_FLIGHTDATA);
&REC.CopyFieldsTo(&FLIGHTDATA);

    /* Parse out Message Data */
&acnumber_value = &FLIGHTDATA.QE_ACNUMBER.Value;
&msi_sensor_value = &FLIGHTDATA.QE_MSI_SENSOR.Value;
&ofp_value = &FLIGHTDATA.QE_OFP.Value;
```

```
&actype_value = &FLIGHTDATA.QE_ACTYPE.Value;

&callsign_value = &FLIGHTDATA.QE_CALLSIGN.Value;

&squadron_value = &FLIGHTDATA.QE_SQUADRON.Value;

&comm1_value = &FLIGHTDATA.QE_COMM1.Value;

&comm2_value = &FLIGHTDATA.QE_COMM2.Value;

&ecm_value = &FLIGHTDATA.QE_ECM.Value;

&outstring = "Send Async FLight test";


    /* Construct Output String */
&outstring = &outstring | &acnumber_value | &CRLF |
&msi_sensor_value |
&CRLF | &ofp_value | &CRLF | &actype_value | &CRLF |
&callsign_value |
&CRLF | &squadron_value | &CRLF | &comm1_value | &CRLF |
&comm2_value |
&CRLF | &ecm_value;


/* Log Output String into page record */
&FLIGHTDATA.GetField(Field.DESCRLONG).Value = &outstring;
SQLExec("DELETE FROM PS_QE_FLIGHTDATA");
&FLIGHTDATA.Insert();
end-method;
```

166. How to subscribe and consume a non rowset based message using PeopleCode?

Here is a code example,

```
Local Message &MSG;
Local XmlDoc&xmlDoc;
```

```
Local XmlNode&xmlnRoot;

Local array of XmlNode&xmlNode_tc_array, &xmlNode_sn_array,
&xmlNode_vb_array, &xmlNode_amt_array, &xmlNode_dt_array;

Local string &sTransactionCode, &sSecurityNbr, &sCompanyId,
&sOprId, &sErrorDescr, &strSubject, &strText;

Local SQL &SQLInsert, &SQLInsert1;

Local date &dReceivedDt, &dIntDt;

Local integer &i;

Local number &nIntAmt;

Local boolean&bError, &bNotProcessed;

Local Record &recTarget, &recTarget1;

&MSG = &_MSG;

/*** Read Request ***/

&xmlDoc = &MSG.GetXmlDoc();

&xmlnRoot = &xmlDoc.DocumentElement;

&xmlNode_tc_array
= &xmlnRoot.GetElementsByTagName("TRANSACTION_CODE");

&xmlNode_sn_array
= &xmlnRoot.GetElementsByTagName("XXX_SECURITY_NBR");

&xmlNode_vb_array =
&xmlnRoot.GetElementsByTagName("COMPANYID");

&xmlNode_amt_array
= &xmlnRoot.GetElementsByTagName("XXX_DAILY_INTEREST_AMT");

&xmlNode_dt_array
= &xmlnRoot.GetElementsByTagName("XXX_DAILY_INTEREST_DATE");

&bNotProcessed = False;

If &xmlNode_tc_array.Len> 0 Then

      For &i = 1 To &xmlNode_tc_array.Len

            rem &sCompanyId = &xmlNode.NodeValue;
```

188

```
            &sSecurityNbr = &xmlNode_sn_array [&i].NodeValue;

            &sCompanyId = &xmlNode_vb_array [&i].NodeValue;

            &nIntAmt = Value(&xmlNode_amt_array

            [&i].NodeValue);

            &dIntDt = Date(&xmlNode_dt_array [&i].NodeValue);

      End-For;

   End-If;
```

A sample XML message the code above is used for processing is as follows,

```
<?xml version="1.0"?>

<createSecurityInterestJournalRequest>

<TRANSACTION_CODE>INT</TRANSACTION_CODE>

<XXX_SECURITY_NBR>38333</XXX_SECURITY_NBR>

<COMPANYID>B45102</COMPANYID>

<XXX_DAILY_INTEREST_AMT>0.2055</XXX_DAILY_INTEREST_AMT>

<XXX_DAILY_INTEREST_DATE>2019-01-15</XXX_DAILY_INTEREST_DATE>

<TRANSACTION_CODE>INT</TRANSACTION_CODE>

<XXX_SECURITY_NBR>38334</XXX_SECURITY_NBR>

<COMPANYID>B45104</COMPANYID>

<XXX_DAILY_INTEREST_AMT>0.2055</XXX_DAILY_INTEREST_AMT>

<XXX_DAILY_INTEREST_DATE>2019-01-15</XXX_DAILY_INTEREST_DATE>

</createSecurityInterestJournalRequest>
```

167. How to use SQL to update the status of an IB message from DONE to NEW so that the message can be reprocessed?

The status of a message can be changed through the following SQL,

Here is the SQL to update the status of a subscription message.

```
UPDATE PSAPMSGSUBCON
SET SUBCONSTATUS = 1, -- Corresponds to 'NEW' or 'PENDING'
status
STATUSSTRING = 'NEW', -- Or 'PENDING' depending on desired
status string
RETRYCOUNT = 0 -- Reset retry count if applicable
WHERE QUEUENAME = {QueusName} and QUEUESEQID = {QueueSeqId};
```

Here is the SQL to update the status of a publication message.

```
UPDATE PSAPMSGPUBHDR
SET PUBSTATUS = 1,
STATUSSTRING = 'NEW'
RETRYCOUNT = 0
where QUEUENAME = {QueusName} and QUEUESEQID = {QueueSeqId};
```

168. How to create an Application Engine program that can log and auto re-submit the error and timeout IB messages?

There are 8 steps to create an Application Engine program that can log and auto re-submit the error and timeout IB messages.

Step 1 - Create IB log table

	Num	Field Name	Type	Len	Format	Short Name	Long Name
	1	IBTRANSACTIONID	Char	36	Mixed	Transaction ID	Transaction ID
	2	IB_SEGMENTINDEX	Nbr	4		Segment Index	IB Segment Index
	3	PROCESS_INSTANCE	Nbr	10		Instance	Process Instance
	4	PUBNODE	Char	30	Upper	Pub Node	Publishing Node
	5	SUBNODE	Char	30	Upper	SubNode	Subscribing Node
	6	IB_MESSAGE	Char	1	Upper	Message	You do not have ac..
	7	QUEUENAME	Char	30	Upper	QUEUENAME	Queue Name
	8	IB_OPERATIONNAME	Char	30	Upper	Operation	Service Operation
	9	STATUSSTRING	Char	5	Upper	Status String	Status String
	10	DATETIME_STAMP	DtTm	26		DateTime	DateTime Stamp
	11	EMAIL_NOTIFICATION	Char	1	Upper	Email Notify	Email Notify for Statu..

Step 2 - Get default local node

```
%Select(IB_MSGNODENAME)
     SELECT MSGNODENAME
     FROM PSMSGNODEDEFN
     WHERE LOCALDEFAULTFLG = 'Y'
```

Step 3 - Log publication error messages

```
INSERT INTO PS_XXX_IB_MON_LOG (
SELECT A.IBTRANSACTIONID
, A.IB_SEGMENTINDEX
, %Bind(PROCESS_INSTANCE)
, A.PUBNODE
, A.SUBNODE
, 'P'
, A.QUEUENAME
, A.IB_OPERATIONNAME
, A.STATUSSTRING
, SYSDATE
, 'N'
  FROM PSAPMSGPUBCON A
WHERE A.PUBCONSTATUS = '0')
```

Step 4 - Log publication timeout messages

```
INSERT INTO PS_XXX_IB_MON_LOG (
 SELECT A.IBTRANSACTIONID
, A.IB_SEGMENTINDEX
, %Bind(PROCESS_INSTANCE)
, A.PUBNODE
, A.SUBNODE
, 'P'
, A.QUEUENAME
```

```
, A.IB_OPERATIONNAME

, A.STATUSSTRING

, SYSDATE

, 'N'

  FROM PSAPMSGPUBCON A

WHERE A.PUBCONSTATUS = '6')
```

Step 5 - Log subscription error messages
```
INSERT INTO PS_XXX_IB_MON_LOG (

 SELECT A.IBTRANSACTIONID

, A.IB_SEGMENTINDEX

, %Bind(PROCESS_INSTANCE)

, A.PUBNODE

, %Bind(IB_MSGNODENAME)

, 'S'

, A.QUEUENAME

, A.IB_OPERATIONNAME

, A.STATUSSTRING

, SYSDATE

, 'N'

  FROM PSAPMSGSUBCON A

WHERE A.SUBCONSTATUS = '0')
```

Step 6 - Log subscription timeout messages
```
INSERT INTO PS_XXX_IB_MON_LOG (

 SELECT A.IBTRANSACTIONID

, A.IB_SEGMENTINDEX

, %Bind(PROCESS_INSTANCE)

, A.PUBNODE

, %Bind(IB_MSGNODENAME)

, 'S'

, A.QUEUENAME
```

```
, A.IB_OPERATIONNAME
, A.STATUSSTRING
, SYSDATE
, 'N'
  FROM PSAPMSGSUBCON A
 WHERE A.SUBCONSTATUS = '6')
```

Step 7 - Re-submit the error messages and timed-out messages and send out an email notification after 4 attempts are failed

```
Local Record &XXX_IB_MON_LOG, &XXX_IB_MON_WRK;
Local SQL &IB_SQL, &EMAIL_SQL;
Local number &EmailsSent, &ErrorCount, &MailReturn;
Local string &MailTo, &MailSubject, &MailText, &MailFrom,
&MailSep, &ErrorText;


&XXX_IB_MON_LOG = CreateRecord(Record.XXX_IB_MON_LOG);
&IB_SQL = CreateSQL("%SELECTALL(:1) WHERE PROCESS_INSTANCE =
:2", &XXX_IB_MON_LOG, XXX_IB_MON_AET.PROCESS_INSTANCE);


/* Loop through errors created in this process instance */
While &IB_SQL.Fetch(&XXX_IB_MON_LOG)

   /* Fetch the actual message for the IB issue */
   &ErrorText = "Issue description not found.";
   SQLExec("SELECT  MESSAGE_PARM  FROM  PSIBERRP  A  WHERE
A.IBTRANSACTIONID = :1 AND A.SEQNO = (SELECT MAX(B.SEQNO) FROM
PSIBERR  B  WHERE  B.IBTRANSACTIONID = A.IBTRANSACTIONID  AND
B.MESSAGE_SET_NBR                  <>                  0)",
&XXX_IB_MON_LOG.IBTRANSACTIONID.Value, &ErrorText);


   &ErrorCount = 0;
```

```
SQLExec("SELECT   COUNT(*)   FROM   PS_XXX_IB_MON_LOG   WHERE
IBTRANSACTIONID = :1", &XXX_IB_MON_LOG.IBTRANSACTIONID.Value,
&ErrorCount);


/* If the error has less then 4 rows then re-submit the IB
message for processing.
     If there are more than 4 rows then notification is
required. */


If &ErrorCount < 5 Then


   If &XXX_IB_MON_LOG.IB_MESSAGE.Value = "P" Then
      If                                              Not
(%IntBroker.ReSubmit(&XXX_IB_MON_LOG.IBTRANSACTIONID.Value,
&XXX_IB_MON_LOG.QUEUENAME.Value,          %IntBroker_PUB,
&XXX_IB_MON_LOG.IB_SEGMENTINDEX.Value)) Then
         MessageBox(0, "", 158, 2354, "Unable to resubmit
transaction %1", &XXX_IB_MON_LOG.IBTRANSACTIONID.Value);
         Exit;
      End-If;
   Else
      If                                              Not
(%IntBroker.ReSubmit(&XXX_IB_MON_LOG.IBTRANSACTIONID.Value,
&XXX_IB_MON_LOG.QUEUENAME.Value,          %IntBroker_SUB,
&XXX_IB_MON_LOG.IB_SEGMENTINDEX.Value)) Then
         MessageBox(0, "", 158, 2354, "Unable to resubmit
transaction %1", &XXX_IB_MON_LOG.IBTRANSACTIONID.Value);
         Exit;
      End-If;
   End-If;
   MessageBox(0, "", 21000, 3, "Resubmit IB transaction %1
status %2 : %3 at %4", &XXX_IB_MON_LOG.IBTRANSACTIONID.Value,
```

```
&XXX_IB_MON_LOG.STATUSSTRING.Value,                    &ErrorText,
Substring(&XXX_IB_MON_LOG.DATETIME_STAMP.Value, 1, 20));


    Else /* Three attempts to re-submit have failed - check to
see if notrification is required. */


        /* Check if an email has already been sent for this IB
transaction */
        &EmailsSent = 0;
        SQLExec("SELECT  COUNT(*)  FROM  PS_XXX_IB_MON_LOG  WHERE
IBTRANSACTIONID  =  :1  AND  EMAIL_NOTIFICATION  =  'Y'",
&XXX_IB_MON_LOG.IBTRANSACTIONID.Value, &EmailsSent);


        If &EmailsSent = 0 Then
            /* Build  the  recipient  list  base  on  the  role
XXX_IB_MONITOR */
            &XXX_IB_MON_WRK                                  =
CreateRecord(Record.XXX_IB_MON_WRK);
            &EMAIL_SQL  =  CreateSQL("SELECT  A.EMAILID  FROM
PSOPRDEFN  A,  PSROLEUSER  B  WHERE  A.OPRID  =  B.ROLEUSER  AND
B.ROLENAME = 'XXX_IB_MONITOR'");
            &MailTo = "";
            While &EMAIL_SQL.Fetch(&XXX_IB_MON_WRK)
                &MailTo = &MailTo | &XXX_IB_MON_WRK.EMAILID.Value
| ";";
            End-While;


            &MailSubject = MsgGetExplainText(21000, 2, "IB Monitor
Error Notification", %DbName, XXX_IB_MON_AET.IB_MSGNODENAME);
            &MailText = MsgGetExplainText(21000, 1, "Error on IB
transaction",          &XXX_IB_MON_LOG.IBTRANSACTIONID.Value,
&XXX_IB_MON_LOG.STATUSSTRING.Value,
```

195

```
&XXX_IB_MON_LOG.PUBNODE.Value,  &XXX_IB_MON_LOG.SUBNODE.Value,
&XXX_IB_MON_LOG.QUEUENAME.Value,
&XXX_IB_MON_LOG.IB_OPERATIONNAME.Value, &ErrorText);
        &MailFrom = %DbName | "@XXXaster.ca";
        &MailSep = ";";
        &MailReturn   =   SendMail(0,   &MailTo,   "",   "",
&MailSubject, &MailText, "", "", &MailFrom, &MailSep, "", "",
"");
        If &MailReturn <> 0 Then
        MessageBox(0,   "",   21000,   5,   "Failed   email
notification - Return code from SendMail = %1", &MailReturn);
        XXX_IB_MON_AET.AE_APPSTATUS = 1;
        Else
        MessageBox(0, "", 21000, 4, "Error Notification of
IB   transaction   %1   has   been   sent   to   %2",
&XXX_IB_MON_LOG.IBTRANSACTIONID.Value, &MailTo);
        &XXX_IB_MON_LOG.EMAIL_NOTIFICATION.Value = "Y";
        &XXX_IB_MON_LOG.Update();
        End-If;
    Else /* Log that a previous message was sent */
        MessageBox(0,   "",   21000,   6,   "Notification   was
previously   sent   for   IB   transaction   %1",
&XXX_IB_MON_LOG.IBTRANSACTIONID.Value, &MailTo);
    End-If;

  End-If; /* &ErrorCount < 4 loop */

End-While;
```

Step 8 - Schedule to run to the process periodically

Schedule to run the process via process scheduler periodically (for example, every 15 minutes) If an error or timeout message still fails after 4 resubmit attempts, an email notification will be sent to the user who has the IB monitor role.

169. **Error**: User not authorized to invoke Service Operation

    Cause: The Service Operation's security may not set up properly.

    Solution: Update the Service Operation's security to grant access to a permission list that user 'XXX' has.

170. **Error**: "Message name not in message data" error in inbound service operation

    Cause: Message name is not the same as the service operation name.

    Solution: Change the message name to be the same as the service operation name.

171. **Error**: Cannot find a service operation in IB Monitor

    Cause:

    1) User does not have the security to access the service operation.

    2) an IB monitor criteria has filtered out the service operation.

172. **Error**: Messages are processed in an unexpected order

    Cause: The message queue may have been partitioned.

173. **Error**: Message instance stays in WORKING status

    Cause:

    1)The Message Handler has crashed.

    2)The Message Handler working on the message is "blocked"

    3)Cancel the message and regenerate it

    4)Bounce the server and clear cache

174. **Error**: Publication contract stuck in NEW status

Cause:

1)Publication Dispatcher has crashed or has been brought down.

2)Queue paused.

3)Node paused.

4)Previous message in an ordered queue had a status of ERROR or TIMEOUT.

5)Domain is inactive.

6)Bounce the server and clear cache

175. **Error**: Publication contract stuck in WORKING status

Cause:

1) The publication handler processing the contract is on another machine and either the machine or the domain is down. Processing should continue when the pub/sub system on the other machine comes back up.

2) Receiving Node URL is incorrect in the integrationGateway.properties file.

176. **Error**: Publication contract stuck in TIMEOUT status

Cause:

1)An exception occurred on the target application server; look in the APPSRV.LOG file for details.

2)The reply is incorrectly routed; check Gateway to get the correct machine address of the target node.

3)Bad XML syntax.

177.**Error**: Publication contract stuck in ERROR status

Cause:

1)Receiving node user profile not authorized to service operation.

2)Inbound routing is not set up on the receiving system.

3)Service operation is not active on the receiving system.

4)Service operation has not been granted security access on the receiving system.

5)The source node is not defined in the target database.

6)Handler PeopleCode is bad.

7)Remote application server is down.

8)Receiving Node is not defined in the integrationGateway.properties file.

9)Receiving PeopleSoft node has not been added to single signon.

10) Service operation version on target is not active.

178. **Error**: Subscription contract is not created

   Cause: Service operation may be in-active.

179. **Error**: Subscription contract stuck in NEW status

   Cause:

   1)The Subscription Dispatcher has crashed or has been brought down.

   2)Queue, Node or System paused.

   3)Message Definition not Active.

   4)Previous message had a status of ERROR, or TIMEOUT.

   5)The Subscription contract is not at the top of the queue. All Subscription Contracts with the same Queue/ Sub Queue and subscription owner are in the same queue.

   6)Bounce the server and clear cache.

180. **Error**: Subscription contract stuck in WORKING status

   Cause:

   1) The Message Handler has crashed or has been brought down.

   2) Also look for any errors in App Server Log.

   3) Bounce the server and clear cache.

181. **Error**: Subscription contract stuck in ERROR status

Cause:

1) Subscription PeopleCode errors.

2) Application data errors.

182. **Error**: Subscription contract stuck in TIMEOUT status

Cause:

1)Subscription PeopleCode errors.

2)If the message works sometimes, and sometimes does not this may be a problem with the application server configuration. Tune up your application server min/max values or reconfigure your domain to a medium or large domain. Also, try changing the recycle count for these services from 0 to 25,000 or 10,000 may eliminate this problem.

183. **Error**: Service operation instance stuck in STARTED Status

Cause:

1) All message handlers crashed or were brought down; processing will resume when message handlers come back up.

2) The message dispatcher processing the message is on another machine, and either the machine or the application server domain is down.

3) Application server domain was created using the developer template. Recreate using small, medium or large.

184. **Error**: UserName is not defined in database

Cause:

1)The Default User ID set for the ANONYMOUS Node may not have a valid username.

2)The user account is active (e.g. not locked out)

185. **Error**: User unable to view detail of an XML message

Cause: User may not have the security to do so.

186. Error: Message appears to have been consumed from the source but not loaded into the target PeopleSoft environment

    Cause:

    1) Service opcration routing may be missing in the target environment.

    2) Security may not be granted to the service operation.

187. Error: Duplicated messages are shown in the IB monitor

    Cause: Multiple active service operation routings with the same source and target nodes may exist.

188. Error: Message rowset not getting populated into the destination tables

    Cause: The message handler PeopleCode may not work properly

189. Error: User 'XXX' not authorized to invoke Service Operation

    Cause:

    1) User on the publishing side doesn't have security.

    2) User on the receiving side doesn't have security.

190. Error: MsgProcessor Process Routing Failed: Failed to create contracts

    Cause: Service operation routing may have been set up incorrectly.

191. Error: Unable to find a routing corresponding to the incoming request message

    Cause:

    1)Node authentication may be wrong; reset the node password or change to None.

    2)Message name does not match the external service operation name.

192. Error: Unable to ping a node

Cause:

1) The web server for the Gateway is down.

2) The Gateway is not configured properly.

3) The app server for the node is down.

4) Verify if the url is correct.

193. **Error**: "Invalid queue/topic name" when pinging a third-party application node?

    Cause: The third party application message queue, f.i., a JMS queue, has not been added into the IB Gateway setup properties file, or, the settings are not correct

    Solution: Make sure the third-party message queue has been added in the Gateway setup properties file and verify the settings of the JMS Provider, including the JMS Factory, the JMS queue, the URL and the port are correct.

    The IB Gateway setup properties file is located at

    PeopleTools -> Integration Broker -> Configuration -> Gateways

    If there is a change on any of these settings, you need to bounce the PeopleSoft servers. You may need to have the servers of the third-party system to be bounced as well.

    Check the IB error log on the server to get more details of the error.

194. **Error**: Application class not found in the service operation handler configuration

    Solution: It could be caused by migration, check if all the objects of the service operation in the source environment have been included in the PS project and re-migrate the project.

195. **Error**: No consumer attached to the queue on the third-party server

    Solution: Check the Gateway property file and make sure the configurations are correct, bounce the server, and then bounce the third-party server.

196. **Error**: A consumer was attached to the queue of the third-party server but not anymore

    Solution: Bounce the PS server and clear cache.

197. **Error**: Incorrect number of consumers in a clustered environment

    Solution: Bounce the third-party server first and then bounce the PS server and clear cache.

198. **Error**: There is a consumer attached to the queue on the third-party server but messages do not flow through to PS

    Solution:

    1) Check the message header if it is the first time testing the message.

    2) Bounce the PS server if it has been working before.

    3) Send more test messages.

199. **Error**: A message appears to have been consumed from the third-party server but it is not picked up in PeopleSoft

    Solution:

    1) Check if the routing is missing for the service operation. Check if the required permission lists have been granted to the service operation. Check if the messages are in the message table in the database.

    2) Check if there is a message in a working status, if so, change the status of the message to new

    3) Bounce the server and clear cache

200. **Error**: A message appears to have been consumed from the sending party, but it is not showing up in the IB Monitor. The error message in the IB error log is "RequestingNode and Message name are required properties. These should be present, either in JMSMessageHeaders, XML content, or integrationgateway.properties file"

    Solution:

    1) Check the IB error log for details.

    2) Asking the sending party to verify that the message name and the requesting node are specified correctly for the message.

201. **Error**: "RequestMessageListener:Connection manager thrownExternalApplicationException(StatusCode = 20)"

Solution: Check the IB error log for details.

202. **Error**: Some messages flow through, but other messages don't flow through in a clustered environment with 2 nodes. There is a login failure error message for 'VP1@JavaClient' in the IB error log

Solution: The encrypted password for the IB user VP1 may have been corrupted.

You may need a re-encrypt password. You can use the PS Cipher utility to do it.

203. **Error**: A message stuck in NEW Status

Solution: If there is a message stuck in NEW status, check if there is any prior message that is in timeout, hold, or error status.   That message is holding the messages. Try to resubmit that message. If it still fails, cancel that message, and other messages may start flowing.

Note if the queue is an ordered queue, in case of any issue with a message earlier, all other messages will be stuck in NEW status.

Check if there is any message in Working status if it is an ordered queue;

Find the 'Working' message in PSAPMSGPUBHDR and PSAPMSGSUBCON table and update its status to Canceled.

```
UPDATE PSAPMSGSUBCON SET SUBCONSTATUS = 8, STATUSSTRING =
'CNCLD' where QUEUENAME = 'XXX_SEC_TO_AR_V2' and
IBTRANSACTIONID = '7882ef06-fd8a-11e8-8d42-ad0556a801eb';
```

204. **Error**: "NamingException, name not found. Unable to resolve 'jms.XAVbsCF'. Resolved 'jms'javax.naming.NameNotFoundException: Unable to resolve 'jms.XAVbsCF'. Resolved 'jms'; remaining name 'XAVbsCF'" error in the IB error log

Solution: The URL in the Gateway properties file may be wrong; it may be pointing to a wrong server

205. **Error** Msg: MsgProccesorProcess_RoutingFailed: Failed to create contracts

Cause: The routing of the service operation may be wrong.

Solution: You may need to delete the routing and re-create it. Review the application server log for more details.

206. **Error**: Integration Synchronous Handler: No destination node can be determined for the request on node (NodeName).

Cause: This issue could be caused by an incorrect routing setup.

If it occurs when publishing a web service, retrieving WSDL and/or Schema, it could be the routing for GETWSDL and/or the GETSCHEMA web service not set up correctly.

Solution: Make sure the Sender Node is the default local node and the Receiver Node is correct.

In the second case, inactivate the routings for GETWSDL or GETSCHEMA that doesn't have GetWSDL as an alias and save the routing.

207. **Error**: "Invalid parameter 1 for function CreateRecord. (2,116)
IB_MONITOR.TREECTLEVENT.FieldChange Name:insertsubfields PCPC:6407 Statem ent:101
Called from:
IB_MONITOR.TREECTLEVENT.FieldChange Name:initinsertsubpart Statement:166
Called from:IB_MESSAGE_BUILDER.GBL.PostBuild" when trying to open a message after migration

Cause: The base record of the message may not exist in the target database

Solution: Migrate the base record to the target database and build it

208. **Error**: Message data is not getting populated into the target tables

Cause: The code of the application class in the Message Handler may not work properly.

Solution: Check the Message Handler PeopleCode

209. **Error**: Email notifications do not come through

    Cause: Events and Notification framework makes use of IB definitions to generate and routealerts. Email notification queue or service operation may not be running.

    Solution: Check whether the below definitions are activated/running:

    Queue - EOEN_MSG_CHNL   Service Operation - EOEN_MSG

210. **Error**: "Destination node does not match the local node" error when viewing a web service after publishing

    Cause:

    1) The node name that is being used as a target by a messaging service operation is not its default local node of the target system.

    2) In the gateway properties, the target node is missing, misspelled, or its Jolt URL (//{host}:{port}) is pointing to the wrong app sever domain.

    Solution: You need to make sure the node in the web service URL (Service Configuration ->Setup Target Location) is the name of actual Local Node

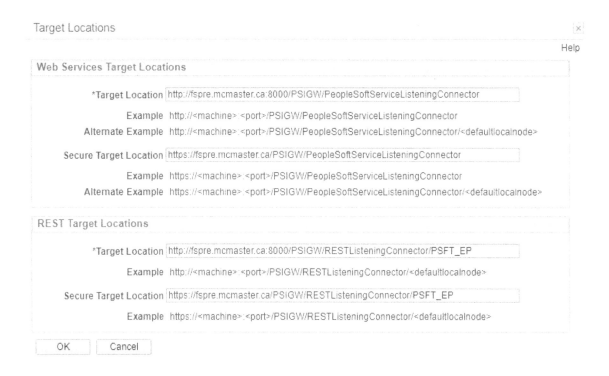

Also check Gateway Properties Setup for the node; the target node may not have been setup properly in the Gateway properties.

211. **Error**: "Message cannot be changed. Message referenced in runtime tables"

Solution: The status "Message cannot be changed. Message referenced in runtime tables" is resolved by running AppMsgPurgeAll.dms, or if purging is not an option, by archiving messages with APPMSGARCH . If there are not too many of the message specified, you can archive/delete the messages individually from the Service Operation Monitor.

1. For running AppMsgPurge*.dms, refer to the following PeopleBook section: Integration Broker -> Integration Broker Service Operations Monitor -> Purging Runtime Monitor Tables. The AppMsgPurgeAll.dms script will delete all messages in active message tables as well as archive tables regardless of the status of the messages. There are other variations of this DataMover script, AppMsgPurgeLive.dms (delete all messages in active message tables only) and AppMsgPurgeArchive.dms (delete all messages in archive message tables only). They are explained in more detail in the above-referenced PeopleBook section.

OR

207

2. To run the Application Engine archiving process APPMSGARCH, go to Integration Broker -> Service Operations Monitor->Running Batch Service Operation Archiving Processes. This will archive the DONE and/or CANCEL messages in the runtime tables to the archive tables if the queue was set up as archive. Else the messages are deleted.

OR

3. From the Service Operation Monitor (PeopleTools->Integration Broker->Service Operation Monitor->Monitoring->asynchronous Service Operations)

Select the Message in question. Click on Details.

Click on Archive (if the queue was set to archive) or Click on Delete.

Confirm the Archive or Delete. Repeat for all the messages for which the schema needs to be deleted/modified. Once the runtime tables have been cleared, then delete the schema

- Navigate to PeopleTools->Integration Broker->Integration Broker->Messages.
- Search for message in question.
- Click on the Schema tab.
- Click on the Delete Schema button.
- Save.

MIGRATION

212. Don't forget to include field translate values for a field that has translate values when translate values have been added or changed. Insert the field object to the project and select Translate Values in Related Definitions.

213. Don't forget to include Process definition, message catalog, and file reference objects in the project when needed.

214. Don't forget to build tables and views in the project after migration if there are any.

215. Message catalog and file reference objects can't be migrated through copy project to file and copy file to project migration.

216. Ensure the upgrade and the done flags are set correctly for all the objects before migration Ensure the upgradeflags are not set to None for the objects to be migrated.

217. A project can't be migrated directly between different PeopleTools versions. It can only be migrated through copy project to file and copy file to project.

218. You can verify if an object has been migrated to the target database by checking if it exists in PeopleSoft object definition tables, such as PSQRYDEFN.

219. Page access setup in a permission list can be migrated from one environment to another by adding the permission list in the project for migration.

220. Check to ensure descriptions of all projects, components, and records have been created and are correct before migration to Production.

221. To migrate secondary indexes on a record, use Insert Definitions into Project and choose Indexes from the list of definition types.

222. Ensure you include all the new and modified PeopleCode objects to a project, especially when migrating changes to an Application Engine program and an Application Package.

    When migrating an Application Engine program, make sure to include all affected sections, steps, PeopleCode, and SQL objects in the project to migrate.

223. To migrate portal objects through a project, including all portal registry structures, include folders, content references and registry definitions, and check all 3 entries (including Children, HTML, Templates) and migrate all of them to the target database.

224. If you just modify a SQL in an Application Engine program to migrate the change, you don't need to include the Application Engine program in the PS project. Just including the SQL object in the project is good enough.

225. Carefully check the project build log and ensure all the records and views are built successfully and there is no error in the log after migration.

    Check the detail of a migration error in Application Designer output window by clicking the object which has got error during migration.

226. Ensure you have included all the new and modified PeopleCode objects to a project, especially when migrating the changes to an Application Engine program and an Application Package.

227. If the changes to an object doesn't show up in the Application Designer in the target database after migration, i.e., Application Engine programs doesn't get updated, you may need to clear PS cache for the database.

228. If the content reference of a new page doesn't show up in the target environment, first do a compare of the source and the target on the project, if all the objects have been migrated, ask PS admin to bounce the app server and clear cache.

229. If a new menu item doesn't show up from the navigation menu, or doesn't display correctly after migration, clear cache on app server and web server and recycle the servers.

230. It is recommended to clear cache on the app server, the web server, and the process scheduler before running the Portal Sync process.

231. If a page is blank after migration, it is possible that there is some issue with its search record. You can try to update the search record of the page and save it, and then check if the page is working.

232. If you have created a content reference by registering a component, and you would like to delete it, but you couldn't find from the Portal Structure and Content because you had specified a wrong folder to place the content reference within, you can delete the content reference from behind the scenes and re-create it by doing registration of the component again.

    To delete a content reference from behind the scenes, delete it from the portal object table PSPRSMDEFN; to delete a permission list assigned to it, delete it from the portal object permission list table PSPRSMPERM.

233. Always check if there is any testing or debugging code left in the code and make sure to remove it when migrating the code from the development/testing environment to the production environment.

234. What is the difference between PeopleSoft Vanilla and Keep Customizations when selecting a Target Orientation in Compare and Reports and how to use the setting?

The Target Orientation window will be set for objects that were last modified by the customer in one database and last modified by PeopleSoft in the other database.

If you select the PeopleSoft Vanilla orientation, the Upgrade checkboxes will be set so as to preserve PeopleSoft's changes. If you select the Keep Customizations option, the checkboxes will be set so that your changes are preserved.

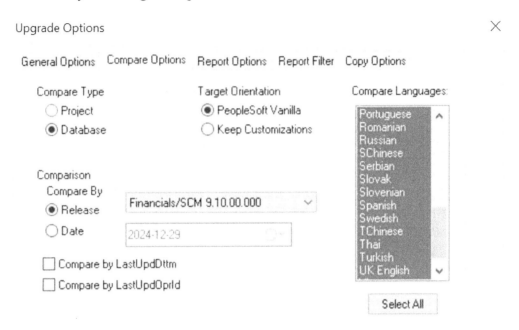

This setting is useful when a PeopleSoft Admin performing database compare between a vanilla database and a custom database during the upgrade process. Typically, a vanilla database is selected as the source and a custom database is selected as the target, and the PeopleSoft Vanilla option is selected as the Target Orientation. A compare report is generated and provided to a PeopleSoft developer. The PS Admin would then apply the change package to the target database, and then the PeopleSoft developer would do the retrofit work in the target database based on the compare report.

235. What is PHIRE?

PHIRE is an Application Change Management (ACM) solution built using PeopleTools that helps organizations better control and manage changes that are necessary for PeopleSoft and other large enterprise applications. PHIRE enables PeopleTools object versioning and automates the migrations of Application Designer projects and files.

236. What are the differences between the migration Tools PHIRE and Quest Stat?

PHIRE: easy to use, no dedicated Admin

Quest Stat: quite complex, separate server, dedicated Admin

237. You can update the upgrade flags for all objects in a PS-Project using the following SQL,

```
UPDATE PSPROJECTITEM
SET UPGRADEACTION = 0, TAKEACTION = 1, COPYDONE = 0
WHERE PROJECTNAME = 'PROJECT_NAME';
```

The SQL update statement above provides a quick way to mark all fields in the project for an upgrade. This should not be relied on up too extensively, as the compare report is still useful for other reasons (such as checking for differences between databases). However, if you're copying a large project to file, a quick-and-dirty update will save a bit of time.

Before running the update statement, make sure you save and close your project in Application Designer.

238. How to migrate Approval Workflow Engine (AWE) configurations?

If your AWE transaction is completely new and you want to migrate it to production, then no backup is required because your transaction is absent on production, but if you have some changes on AWE Configuration, specially Approval Process Setup then it is a good idea to take backup of current copy using this script.

Make sure to update the scripts with appropriate WHERE clauses, using the Keys on respective tables to export the data that should be migrated.

Here are the data mover scripts that migrate Approval Workflow Transactions from one environment to another.

AWE Transaction Configuration Data Mover export script is as follows,

213

```
SET OUTPUT D:\awe_dms_data\AWE_EXP.dat;

SET LOG E:\awe_dms_data\AWE_EXP_EXPORT.log;

-- Export Transaction Registry and Configuration

EXPORT PS_EOAW_ADMMON_CFG WHERE EOAWPRCS_ID IN ('');

EXPORT PS_EOAW_MONDIS_DTL WHERE EOAWPRCS_ID IN ('');

EXPORT PS_EOAW_MONDIS_HDR WHERE EOAWPRCS_ID IN ('');

EXPORT PS_EOAW_USRMON_CFG WHERE EOAWPRCS_ID IN ('');

EXPORT PS_EOAW_USRMON_LNG WHERE EOAWPRCS_ID IN ('');

EXPORT PS_EOAW_TXN WHERE EOAWPRCS_ID IN ('');

EXPORT PS_EOAW_TXN_CFG WHERE EOAWPRCS_ID IN ('');

EXPORT PS_EOAW_TXN_LBL WHERE EOAWPRCS_ID IN ('');

Export PS_EOAW_TXN_LNG WHERE EOAWPRCS_ID IN ('');

EXPORT PS_EOAW_TXN_LVL WHERE EOAWPRCS_ID IN ('');

--Export Transaction Notifications

EXPORT PS_EOAW_NOTIFY WHERE EOAWPRCS_ID IN ('');

EXPORT PS_EOAW_NOTIFYDEF WHERE EOAWPRCS_ID IN ('');

EXPORT PS_EOAW_NOT_USER WHERE EOAWPRCS_ID IN ('');

EXPORT PS_EOAW_NOT_USRDEF WHERE EOAWPRCS_ID IN ('');

-- Export User Lists and Approver User List

EXPORT PS_EOAWUSER_LIST WHERE EOAWUSER_LIST_ID IN ('');

EXPORT PS_EOAWUSER_LIST WHERE EOAWUSER_LIST_ID IN ('');

EXPORT PS_EOAWUSER_LIST WHERE EOAWUSER_LIST_ID IN ('');

EXPORT PS_EOAWUSER_LIST WHERE EOAWUSER_LIST_ID IN ('');

EXPORT PS_EOAWUSER_LNG WHERE EOAWUSER_LIST_ID IN ('');

EXPORT PS_EOAWUSER_LNG WHERE EOAWUSER_LIST_ID IN ('');

EXPORT PS_EOAWUSER_LNG WHERE EOAWUSER_LIST_ID IN ('');

EXPORT PS_EOAWUSER_LNG WHERE EOAWUSER_LIST_ID IN ('');

-- Export Process Stage Path Step Definitions
```

```
EXPORT PS_EOAW_IDS WHERE EOAWCOUNTERNAME IN ('ZZ_EXP_XREF');
EXPORT PS_EOAW_PATH WHERE EOAWPRCS_ID IN ('');
EXPORT PS_EOAW_PATH_LNG WHERE EOAWPRCS_ID IN ('');
EXPORT PS_EOAW_PRCS WHERE EOAWPRCS_ID IN ('');
EXPORT PS_EOAW_PRCS_LNG WHERE EOAWPRCS_ID IN ('');
EXPORT PS_EOAW_STAGE WHERE EOAWPRCS_ID IN ('');
EXPORT PS_EOAW_STEP WHERE EOAWPRCS_ID IN ('');
EXPORT PS_EOAW_STEP_LNG WHERE EOAWPRCS_ID IN ('');
EXPORT PS_EOAW_STG_LNG WHERE EOAWPRCS_ID IN ('');
EXPORT PS_EOAW_TIMEOUT WHERE EOAWPRCS_ID IN ('');
EXPORT PS_EOAW_TIMEOUTDEF WHERE EOAWPRCS_ID IN ('');
EXPORT PS_EOAW_AUTH WHERE EOAWPRCS_ID IN ('');
EXPORT PS_EOAW_AUTH_DTL WHERE EOAWPRCS_ID IN ('');
-- Export Criteria Related Definitions
EXPORT PS_EOAWCRTA WHERE EOAWCRTA_ID LIKE ('');
-- EXPORT PS_EOAWCRTA WHERE EOAWCRTA_ID LIKE ('%ZZ_EXP%2014-
09-16%'); -- With Effective Date Criteria
EXPORT PS_EOAWCRTA_LNG WHERE EOAWCRTA_ID LIKE ('%ZZ_EXP%');
-- EXPORT PS_EOAWCRTA_LNG WHERE EOAWCRTA_ID LIKE
('%ZZ_EXP%2014-09-16%'); -- With Effective Date Criteria
EXPORT PS_EOAWCRTA_REC WHERE EOAWCRTA_ID LIKE ('%ZZ_EXP%');
-- EXPORT PS_EOAWCRTA_REC WHERE EOAWCRTA_ID LIKE
('%ZZ_EXP%2014-09-16%'); -- With Effective Date Criteria
EXPORT PS_EOAWCRTA_RECLNG WHERE EOAWCRTA_ID LIKE
('%ZZ_EXP%');
-- EXPORT PS_EOAWCRTA_RECLNG WHERE EOAWCRTA_ID LIKE
('%ZZ_EXP%2014-09-16%'); -- With Effective Date Criteria
EXPORT PS_EOAWCRTA_VAL WHERE EOAWCRTA_ID LIKE ('%ZZ_EXP%');
```

```
-- EXPORT PS_EOAWCRTA_VAL WHERE EOAWCRTA_ID LIKE
('%ZZ_EXP%2014-09-16%'); -- With Effective Date Criteria
-- Export NEM (Notification and Escalations)
EXPORT PS_EOAWNEM;
EXPORT PS_EOAWNEM_EMAIL;
EXPORT PS_EOAWNEM_EVENTS;
-- Export EMC (Email Collaboration)
EXPORT PS_EOAWEMCLTLN_LNG;
EXPORT PS_EOAWEMC_LYT_HDR;
EXPORT PS_EOAWEMC_LYT_LIN;
EXPORT PS_EOAWEMC_MSGHDR;
EXPORT PS_EOAWFIELD_LIST;
EXPORT PS_EOAWFRMINPT_HDR;
EXPORT PS_EOAWFRMINPT_LIN;
EXPORT PS_EOAWXLAT_SYMBOL;
Export EOAW HTML Email Approvals
EXPORT PS_EOAW_EML_CFG_DT WHERE EOAWPRCS_ID IN (' ');
EXPORT PS_EOAW_EML_CFG_LN WHERE EOAWPRCS_ID IN (' ');
EXPORT PS_EOAW_EML_TMPL WHERE EOAWPRCS_ID IN (' ');
-- Export Workflow Generic Template
EXPORT PS_WL_TEMPLATE_GEN WHERE WL_TEMPLATE_ID LIKE '';
EXPORT PS_WL_TEMPL_GEN_TK WHERE WL_TEMPLATE_ID LIKE ";
-- Export Workflow Transaction Setup Tables
EXPORT PS_EO_TRANSACTIONS WHERE TRANSACTION_NAME IN ('`);
EXPORT PS_HCM_EO_TXN WHERE TRANSACTION_NAME IN ('`);
-- Export Self Services Tables for Workflow Config with CI
Setup
EXPORT PS_WF_HR_TRANS WHERE TRANSACTION_NAME IN ('`);
```

216

```
EXPORT PS_WF_HR_TRANS_NOT WHERE TRANSACTION_NAME IN ('');
EXPORT PS_SS_TRANS_CI_DTL WHERE TRANSACTION_NAME IN ('');
```

AWE Transaction Configuration Data Mover import script is as follows,

```
SET INPUT D:\awe_dms_data\AWE_EXP.dat;
SET LOG E:\awe_dms_data\AWE_EXP_IMPORT.log;
SET UPDATE_DUPS;
IMPORT *;
```

For import you should use UPDATE_DUPS because it will automatically update the duplicate values with only one value, and thus avoid the Unique Constraint Violation Error.

239. How to migrate Page and Field configurations?

You can use the DMS scripts to migrate Page and Field Configurations.All below tables should be included in the migrations,

- PS_EOCC_CONFIG_HDR
- PS_EOCC_CONFIG_SEQ
- PS_EOCC_CONFIG_CRT
- PS_EOCC_CONFIG_FLD
- PS_EOCC_CONFIG_PNL
- PS_EOCC_SEQ_EXLST
- PS_EOCC_SEQ_USRLST
- PS_EOCC_USER_LST
- PS_EOCC_EX_USR_LST
- PS_ EOCC_CONFIG_LOG

Note only pull the rows of thosespecific componentsthat changes have been made from these tables in the Export script.

240. How to migrate Navigation Collections?

A navigation collection provides a way of building your own custom 'group' of components, without having to rely on what the system has given you in advance. By setting up a navigation collection, you can gather together a series of commonly-accessed components and put them all in the one place. A navigation collection can be defined through the front end of the system. No technical assistance is required. If you wish to migrate your collection to another database however, you may need a technical person to assist with this process.

1)   Make sure the link is added to the navigation collection in Portal Utilities -> Navigation Collections

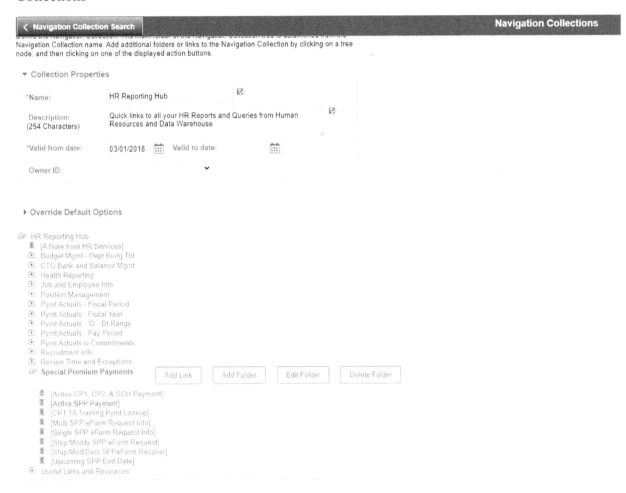

2)   Delete any objects in the target database which are duplicates of the intended migration. This eliminates any orphans or conflicts.

3)   In Application Designer on the source database, create a new project and insert the modified Navigation Collection. In order to find the appropriate object name use %COLLECTION_NAME% in the object name when inserting the definitions in the project.

218

4) Include the Children of the Navigation Collection in the project.

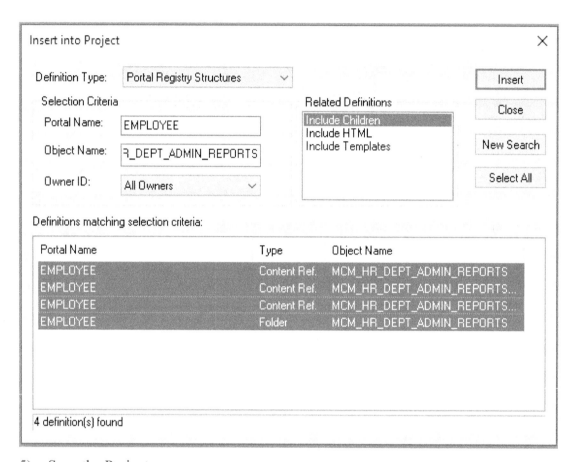

5) Save the Project

6) Migrate the project to the target database.

7) In the target database, bounce the AppServer& Webserver, and clear cache on them. Also clear cache on the end-user browser.

8) Navigate to the new Content Reference within the target system's Structure and Content (PeopleTools -> Portal -> Structure and Content).

9) On the security tab of the Content Reference, make sure the proper access has granted within the target database.

10) Make sure the proper access has been granted to any parent folders of the Content Reference within the target database

11) In PeopleTools -> Portal -> Portal Utilities -> Sync Collection Security, choose the EMPLOYEE portal and the appropriate Navigation Collection name which was migrated and run the process.

Synchronize Collection Security

The Synchronize Collection Security process updates the security on the published Navigation Collection pages. Select a Collection Name to only synchronize the published pages for that collection. Leave the Collection Name blank to synchronize all the published pages in the specified Portal Name. The process adds the security objects of the folders and links, in the collection definition, to the published pages that are marked as 'Allow Collection Sync'. It removes security objects from the published pages marked as 'Public'.

Run Control ID   TEST1   Report Manager   Process Monitor   [Run]

Request Parameters

*Portal Name:	EMPLOYEE 🔍	Employee-facing registry content
Collection Name:	MCM_HR_DEPT_ADMIN_REPORTS 🔍	HR Reporting Hub

[Save] [Notify]   [Add] [Update/Display]

12) Test the new Navigation Collection.

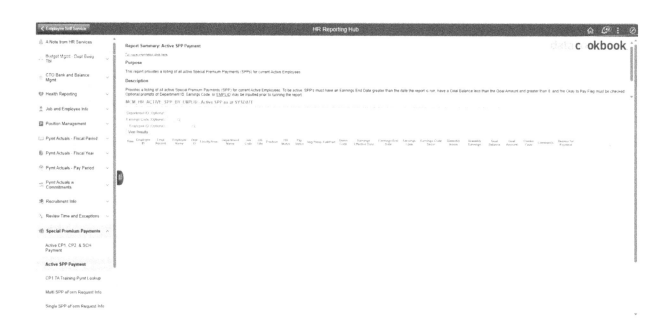

241. How to migrate Event Mappings?

Since the Event Mapping Framework is simply an extension of the 'Related Content Service' functionality, the procedure to migrate the configuration is also the same as migrating 'Related Content'.

221

For those who are new to Related Content and/or Event Mapping Framework, here are the steps that will help with the migration.

Step 1: Insert 'Related Content Definition' into the Project

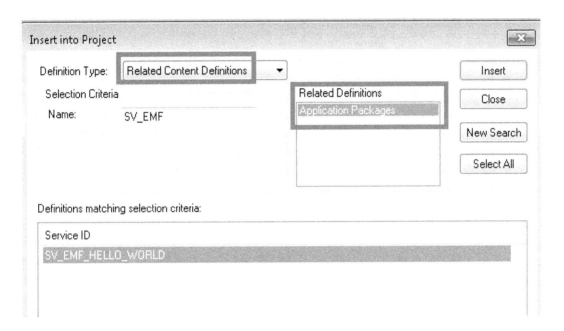

This will take care of migrating the 'Related Content Definition' and associated Application Class. Note: You must highlight 'Application Packages' under the 'Related Definitions' before inserting the Related Content Service ID into the project.

Step 2: Insert 'Related Content Service' into the Project

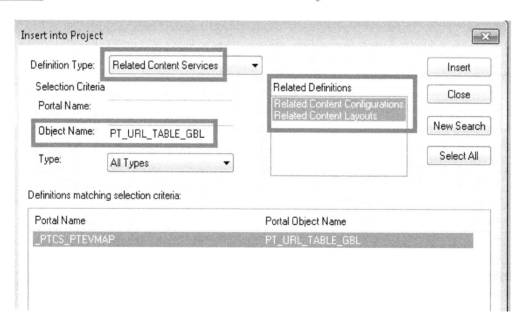

Insert the 'Related Content Service' by entering the 'Portal Object Name' of the associated 'Content Reference'. This will take care of migrating the 'Event Mapping' Configuration.

Step 3: Save and Migrate the Project

To migrate the project from the source to the target environment, save it first and then transfer it. If there are any changes to an event mapping and the portal registry has been run, you must remove all the existing event mapping objects that were inserted into the PS project before and then re-insert them for re-migration

242. How to migrate Fluid objects?

1) For generic Fluid pages and homepages, and in general Fluid structure & content entries, you can migrate those as with any other "Portal Registry Structures" definitions via Application Designer. They are treated the same as classic Content References in that regard. Same goes for the Fluid components. What makes a component Fluid or classic is a parameter in the component. They are treated the same during migration as you would with classic components.

2) All of these items are Portal Registry structure items:

a. Tiles: PeopleTools -> Portal -> Structure and Content -> Fluid Structure Content -> Fluid Pages

Navigation Collections: PeopleTools -> Portal -> Structure and Content -> Portal Objects -> Navigation Collections

Homepages: PeopleTools -> Portal -> Structure and Content -> Fluid Structure Content -> Fluid Homepages

Security: There is a security tab for all the items mentioned above

3) To migrate these objects in Application Designer, you will do the following:

4) Insert definitions into Project

I. Click to choose Definition Type: Portal Registry Structure

II. Object Name: <insert the objects that you want to migrate>

III. Click to highlight all items under "Related Definitions". This includes:

a. Include Children

b. Include HTML

c. Include Templates

IV. Once you have inserted all objects into the project

V. Save the project

VI. Migrate the object using Tools -> Copy Project -> To Database

5) For tiles created by Tile Wizard though, you'd also need to migrate the Tile Wizard data which has to be done with the Data Migration WorkBench tool.

I. PTPPB_GROUPLET is the delivered data set definition to migrate Tile Wizard data.

II. Navigation: PeopleTools -> Lifecycle Tools -> Migrate Data -> Data Migration WorkBench

6) For Fluid Dashboard migration:

Use Data Migration Workbench. Make sure to add the parent portal object of the Dashboard results in the dashboard definition arriving in the target environment.

243. **Error**: "Tablespace Doesn't Exist" when migrating a project to an environment from another environment

Cause: By default, a migration only migrates the objects in a tablespace, not the tablespace definition itself. In this case, the migration is complaining because a tablespace with the same name as the source tablespace does not exist.

Solution: Change tablespace in Tools -> Data Administration -> Set Tablespace

NVISION

244. Where to add the Developer Tab into Excel?

    Go to Options -> Customize Ribbon

245. To view the SQL that is used in a nVision report, you can check on 'Show Report SQL' in nVision -> Options, and then run the report.

246. Variables can be used in any cell except Column A or Row 1.

247. To do a clean run of a nVision report, you should kill all Excel sessions and psnvs.exe sessions under the Processes tab in the Windows Task Manager.

248. You can use Alt-F11 to open a Visual Basic window to view the VBA code in the modules; use ALT-F11 to close the VB window.

249. When performing VBA code debugging, you use F8 to step through, use Cntl-Break to stop, and use F5 to continue.

250. The most common error made by users when using scopes is not updating the filename variable in the report request.

251. You can apply the style sheets to layouts and drilldown layouts. Style sheets can be modified also.

252. Instead of navigating to nVISION / Layout Definition, you can double click anywhere on your .xnv file and see the Layout Definitionmenu.

253. Unchecking 'Data from requesting business unit only' option on a report request allows you to retrieve data from all business units. It can be used in the cases of multiple business units reporting and drilling down reports.

254. If you don't see a newly created query on the list of the nVision layout definition, try to log out and then log back in.

255. If you can't check the 'Copy formulas to nPloded cells' box in the layout definition, just type '%,C' value for the column, and it will set the column to have the feature.

256. How to enable nVision report drill down in Excel?

　　1) In Excel, click on the File tab.

　　2) Click on the Options link.

　　3) Click on the Add-ins link in the left hand column

　　4) At the bottom of the open window, next to the option for Manage, choose Excel Add-ins, and click Go.

　　5) Click on the Browse button.

　　6) Under your local C: drive or where you have nVision installed, click on the nVision folder.

　　7) Click on the DrillToPIA file.

　　8) Click on the box to add the DrillToPIA option to Excel

　　9) Now close out of Excel and then reopen Excel to see the Add-Ins tab for running drill down reports

257. You can only drill down from a nVision report with a matrix layout; you can't drill down from a nVision report with a query-based tabular layout.

258. If there are several sheets in a nVision layout, with one of them is used to extract data, and another one contains the summary of the extracted data, make sure the data extract sheet is the active sheet when the layout is saved. Or else the report may not run properly.

259. To run drilldown from an Excel report output file, you need to close the nVision Window. Otherwise, the error of 'drill down layout not found' may show.

260. You can run multiple level drilldown by specifying the drilldown levels for the layout of a drilldown, or, including the intermediate level.

261. nVision drill down can be done anywhere from a nVision Excel output file, even in an Email attachment.

262. You can enable or disable nPlosion at the row orcolumn level in Layout Options.

263. If you disable nPlosion for a nVision report on its report definition, nPlosion will be disabled at both column and row level.

264. How to perform nVision report output formatting with nPlosion?
    1)   From Excel(nVision) standard menu toolbar select the Format submenu;
    2)   From Format submenu select Style;
    3)   Create your own style and name it;
    4)   From nVision menu select the Layout Options;
    5)   From Layout Options, select the nPlode Rows or nPlodecolumns;
    6)   From the nPlode (rows or columns) tab, type in the style you just created;
    7)   Save the layout and re-run your report;

265. To change the subroutine a nVision report calls, go to Formulas -> Name Manager ->NvsInstanceHook and change the subroutine name to what you want to call.

266. If there is a row/column/cell which doesn't return correct values, and you can't figure out the cause of it, you can delete all the other rows and columns, and save the layout into a different one, and turn on SQL for the layout, run it, and then check the SQL used for the row/column/cell.

267. If some cells in a row in a nVision report don't return data from the database as it is supposed to, one possible reason could be that the cells are on the summarizing row of a group. Remove the grouping from the row should resolve the issue.

268. **Error**: "calendar 01 not defined or invalid as 1900-01-01" error message

    Cause: Main As Of Date is wrong

    Solution: You should choose a recent date or today's date; don't use the default 1900-01-01 date.

269. **Error**: nVision report output file is blocked from downloading by IE

    Solution:

    1) Check the popup blocker setting of the browser, it should allow access to the website of the server.

    2) Check security.

    3) Try log off Windows and log back in.

PEOPLEBOOKS

270. What is the URL of the Oracle PeopleBooks website?

https://docs.oracle.com/en/applications/peoplesoft/index.html

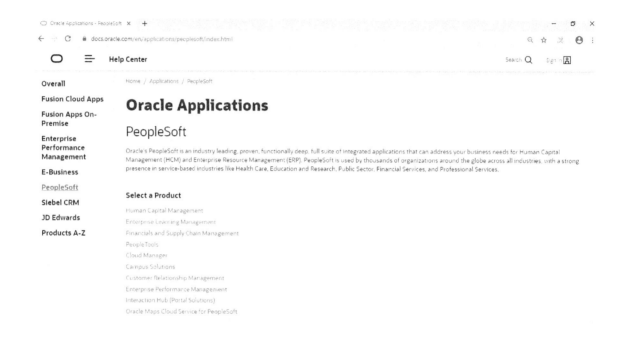

271. PeopleBook Keyword Search Syntax

- back "up" - The word back plus stemmed variations, followed by the word up only. For example: back up, backing up and backs up;

- sql and sqr - Topics containing both sql and sqr.

- list or report - Topics containing list or report

PEOPLECODE

272. PeopleCode can be commented out using REM, REMARK, /*....*/, <*.....*>.

273. How to increment an id field and then convert it to 8-character string?

```
&request_id_new = NumberToString("%08", Integer(&request_id)
    + 1);
```

274. What is the difference of global variables and component variables?

```
Global string &Str;
```

Use the Global statement to declare PeopleCode global variables. A global variable, once declared in any PeopleCode program, remains in scope throughout the PeopleSoft session. The variable must be declared with the Global statement in any PeopleCode program in which it is used.

```
Component string &Str;
```

A variable declared as a component variable remains defined and holds the value as long as any page in the component in which the variable is declared remains active.

Note you can create a drived record and use a field in it instead of using global variables or component variables, so that you don't have to declare the on the top of each PeopleCode event that use them.

275. What is the execution order of PeopleCode events?
The execution order of PeopleCode events is as follows,

SEARCHINIT, SEARCHSAVE, ROWSELECT, PREBUILD, FIELDDEFAULT, FIELD FORMULA, ROWINIT, POSTBUILD, PAGEACTIVATE, FIELDEDIT, FIELDCHANGE, POP_UP, ROWINSERT, ROWDELETE, SAVEEDIT, SAVEPRECHANGE, WORKFLOW, SAVEPOSTCHANGE

276. What events fire after clicking the Save button?

    After you click on the Save button, the following events fire

    1) SaveEdit

    2) SavePrechange

    3) WorkFlow

    4) After database update is done, SavePostchange is fired.

277. When adding new PeopleCode or changing existing PeopleCode to a record field; always check whether if the record is used somewhere else by doing a definition reference search. If it is used by some other page, a PeopleCode page check or component check criteria may be needed to make sure the newly added PeopleCode only applies to the specific page or the specific component. This applies to the derived/work records as well.

278. You cannot hide a static text field by specifying its properties or using PeopleCode, but you can hide it by adding a group box to surround it and hide the group box field using PeopleCode.

279. %This when used in application class constructor code refers to the object currently being constructed.

280. You can use the CommitWork() function to commit transactions within one piece of record PeopleCode or Application Engine PeopleCode, including database updates and component interface update, etc.

281. How to check if the value of a field on a page has been changed by user?

233

To check if a field value has been changed on a page, you can use the IsChanged property of the field.

```
If EX_ADV_LINE.MONETARY_AMOUNT.IsChanged Then
      ......
End-If;
```

You can also check if a field value has been changed by comparing the original value and the new value of the field.

Here is an example,

```
If REQ_HDR.BUSINESS_UNIT.OriginalValue <>
REQ_HDR.BUSINESS_UNIT.Value Or
          REQ_HDR.REQUESTOR_ID.OriginalValue <>
REQ_HDR.REQUESTOR_ID.Value Or
          REQ_HDR.REQ_NAME.OriginalValue <>
REQ_HDR.REQ_NAME.Value Or
          REQ_HDR.REQ_ID.OriginalValue <>
REQ_HDR.REQ_ID.Value Or
          REQ_HDR.PRIORITY_FLG.OriginalValue <>
REQ_HDR.PRIORITY_FLG.Value Or
          REQ_HDR.CURRENCY_CD.OriginalValue <>
REQ_HDR.CURRENCY_CD.Value Then
      ......
End-If;
```

OriginalValue is the value of the field pulled from the database if the field hasn't been saved.

To check if a field value has been changed in a grid or scroll, you can use the following PeopleCode as two examples.

```
For &i = 1 To &dist_data.ActiveRowCount
         If &dist_data.GetRow(&i).EX_SHEET_DIST.IsChanged
Then
              currency_and_rates(&i);
         End-If;
End-For;


For &i = 1 To &rs.ActiveRowCount
     If All(&rs(&i).RS_FR_SUP_UTIL.UTIL_PCT.Value) Then
         If &rs(&i).RS_FR_SUP_UTIL.UTIL_PCT.OriginalValue <>
&rs(&i).RS_FR_SUP_UTIL.UTIL_PCT.Value Then

                   ......

         End-If;
      End-If;
   End-For;
```

282. How to select all fields from a table and ensure only one single row is returned based on the key field values using %SelectByKey and %SelectByKeyEffdt?

%SelectByKey is shorthand for selecting all fields in a specified table based on the key field values. It's used in PeopleCode or Application Engine to read data into memory.

The pseudocode looks like this:

```
Select %List(Select_List, :num correlation_id) from
%Table(:num) correlation_id where %KeyEqual(:num,
correlation_id)
```

Here is an example:

```
&recTMP = CreateRecord(Record.ACCT_CD_TBL_TMP);
```

```
&recTMP.PROCESS_INSTANCE.Value                              =
    TL_CF_AET.PROCESS_INSTANCE.Value;

&recTMP.CF_VLDTN_STATUS.Value = "00";

&SelectTMP = CreateSQL("%SelectByKey(:1)");

&SelectTMP.Execute(&recTMP);


While &SelectTMP.Fetch(&recTMP)
    /* Process row content ... /*
End-While;
```

Here is another example.

```
Local           Record          &profileTBL           =
    CreateRecord(Record.PROFILE_TBL);

&profileTBL.SETID.Value = &SetId;

&profileTBL.PROFILE_ID.Value = &ProfileId;

 SQLExec("%SelectByKey(:1)", &profileTBL, &profileTBL);

    &profileTBL.CopyFieldsTo(&intfcPhyA);
```

%SelectByKeyEffdt is shorthand for selecting all fields in the specified table, ensuring that only one row is returned based on the effective date value.

The pseudocode looks like this:

```
Select %List(Select_List, :num1) from %Table(:num1) A where
%KeyEqualNoEffDt(:num1 A) and %EffDtCheck(:num1 B, A, :num2)
```

Here is an example:

236

```
Local Record &rec = CreateRecord(Record.VNDR_NAME_HST);

&rec.SETID.Value = &SETID;

&rec.VENDOR_ID.Value = &VENDOR_ID;

If &rec.SelectByKeyEffDt(&INVOICE_DT) Then

    &hVENDOR_NAME_SHORT = &rec.VENDOR_NAME_SHORT.Value;

    &hNAME1 = &rec.NAME1.Value;

    &hNAME2 = &rec.NAME2.Value;

 End-If;
```

Here is another example.

```
 REM Get Profile Book;
 Local          Record          &ProfileDetTbl          =
 CreateRecord(Record.PROFILE_DET_TBL);
 &ProfileDetTbl.SETID.Value = &ProfileSetID;
 &ProfileDetTbl.PROFILE_ID.Value = &HeaderProfileID;
 &ProfileDetTbl.BOOK.Value = &rec.BOOK.Value;


 SQLExec("%SelectByKeyEffDt(:1,    :2)",    &ProfileDetTbl,
 %Date, &ProfileDetTbl);
 REM MessageBox(0, "", 0, 0, " 2 &ProfileDetTbl.BOOK.Value
 = " | &ProfileDetTbl.BOOK.Value);
 If None(&ProfileDetTbl.BOOK.Value) Or
        &ProfileDetTbl.BOOK.Value = " " Then


    &errorTxt = MsgGet(8850, 163, "%1 Book not defined for
 this Profile %2", &rec.BOOK.Value, &HeaderProfileID);
    &bError = True;
    &amSeqNum = &amSeqNum + 1;
```

```
        InsertIntoErrorLog(&rec, &amSeqNum, &errorTxt);
    Else
        &ProfileDetTbl.CopyFieldsTo(&rec);
    End-If;
```

283. You can avoid confusion when using meta-SQL such as %Datein and %Dateout if you keep in mind that the "in" functions are used in the WHERE subclause of a SQL query and "out" functions are used in the SELECT (main) clause of the query. F.i. %DateIn('2015-04-01').

284. The Value() function converts a string representing a number to the number; The String() function converts any non-string data type (except Object) to a string.

285. The Hide() function remains for backward compatibility only. Use the Visible field class property instead.

286. You can use the FieldChanged(FieldName) function to check if the value of a field has been changed.

287. You can use the FindFiles() function to know dynamically which files are in a given folder.

```
    file_names = FindFiles(&file_loc, %FilePath_Absolute);
```

288. In order check whether a user has a role, you can use the IsUserInRole() function.

```
If IsUserInRole("ROLENAME") then
  < do something >
else
  < do something else >
End-if;
```

289. You can skip a search record prompt by using the SetSearchDialogBehavior function in SearchInit event.

```
SetSearchDialogBehavior(0) -skip if possible
SetSearchDialogBehavior(1) -force display
```

290. You can assign a date value using the Date function.

```
(RECORD_NAME).FROM_DT = Date(19010101);
```

291. How to set the value of a field to default value?

```
SetDefault(RECORD.DATE_FIELD);
```
or,
```
RECORD.DATE_FIELD.SetDefault();
```

292. How to set the value of a date variable or a date field to Null?

You can use the Date() function to assign a null value to a date variable. See the example below.

```
Local Date &dMyDate;
&dMyDate = Date(0);
```

To set the value of a date field to null,

```
RECORD.DATE_FIELD.Value = "";
```

293. %DateDiff(from_date,to_date) gives date difference in days and %DateTimeDiff(from_datetime,to_datetime) gives date difference in

minutes"abs(days(to_date) - days(from_date))" can also be used. This also takes Leap Years into consideration.

294. You can use the AddToDate function to add years, months, or days to a date variable.

```
AddToDate(XXX_DECONS_AET.ASOFDATE, 0, 0, 1);
```

295. How to create a string with a repeated charactor or a substring?

The 'Rept' function simply repeats the supplied string a certain number of times:

```
&string = Rept("a", 5);
```

This will produce 'aaaaa'.

The string passed to the 'Rept' function need not be a single character:

```
&string = Rept("abc", 3);
```

This will produce the string 'abcabcabc'.

296. How to perform left padding or right padding on a string?

By using the 'Rept' function in combination with the 'Len' function – to return a string length – you can now perform anlpad-like function. The following example left-pads a string with the '0' character to a maximum of ten places:

```
If Len(&string) < 10 Then
&string = Rept("0", 10 - Len(&string)) | &string;
End-If;
```

Here is the equivalent 'rpad' version:

```
If Len(&string) < 10 Then
&string = &string | Rept("0", 10 - Len(&string));
End-If;
```

296. How to copy field values between different records?

You can use CopyFieldsTo() function. This delivered function only works between two like named records. If you have two record objects based on the same record you could do something like this.

```
&Record1.copyfieldsTo(&record2);
```

However, if &record1 and &record2 are not based on the same record this is not supported. It is very easy to write a function that will copy like name fields between records that are not based on the same underlying record object.

Here is the code.

```
Function copyLikeFieldNames (&FromRec As Record, &ToRec As
Record)
local integer &i, &j;
For &1 = 1 To &FromRec.fieldcount
   &FromFld = &FromRec.getfield(&1);
   For &j = 1 To &ToRec.fieldcount
      If &ToRec.getfield(&j).NAME = &FromFld.name Then
          &ToRec.getfield(&j).value = &FromFld.value;
          Break;
       End-If;
    End-For;
End-For;
End-Function;
```

297. What is the difference between the DoSave() function and the DoSaveNow() function?

Use the DoSave() function to save the current page. DoSave() defers processing to the end of the current PeopleCode program event, as distinct from DoSaveNow, which causes save processing (including SaveEdit, SavePreChange, SavePostChange, and Workflow PeopleCode) to be executed immediately.

Think you have written PeopleCode at an event

```
PeopleCode Stmt 1
PeopleCode Stmt 2
PeopleCode Stmt 3
DoSave() / DoSaveNow()
PeopleCode Stmt 4
PeopleCode Stmt 5
PeopleCode Stmt 6
```

In the case of DoSave(), PeopleCode Stmt 1 to PeopleCode Stmt 6 will execute then save processing will trigger

And in case of DoSaveNow() PeopleCode Stmt 1 to PeopleCode Stmt 3 will execute, then save processing will trigger, and the rest PeopleCode Stmt 4 to PeopleCode Stmt 6 will execute after save.

DoSave can be used only in FieldEdit, FieldChange, or MenuItemSelected PeopleCode. DoSaveNow can only be called from a FieldEdit or FieldChange event.

298. What are the differences between the Transfer(), TransferPage() and DoModalComponent() function?

TransferPage() can take the user from one page to the other page within a component.

Its syntax is:

```
TransferPage (Page.PageName);
```

The Transfer() function is used for transferring the user from component A to component B. All control is passed to component B; component A is closed completely. Transfer() can take the user from one page to the other page of different component.

Its syntax is:

```
Transfer (new_Instance, MenuName."Menuname",
Barname."Barname",    ItemName."Componentname",
Page."pagename", action [, keylist] [, Autosearch]);
```

new_instance: can be true or false, true means it will create a new window for called page, false means reuse the existing window.

To figure out the MenuName, Barname, Componentname, query the PSAUTHITEM table.

```
Select * from PSAUTHITEM    where MENUNAME =
'XXX_EMP_PAGES_MNU' And PNLITEMNAME = 'XXX_EMPDEPT_PNL'
```

Action: A –Add   U-update   L-Update/display   C-Correction   E-Data Entry.

Auto search: To pass search key values for the called page.

```
&rec = CreateRecord(Record.XXX_DEPT_TBL);
&rec.XXX_DEPTNO.value = "10";
Transfer (True, MenuName."XXX_EMP_PAGES_MNU",
BarName."MENUITEM1", ItemName."XXX_EMPDEPT_CMP",
Page."XXX_EMPDEPT_PNL", "A", &rec);
```

Another similar function is the DoModalComponent() function. This is used to open a secondary component in a modal window while still keeping the original component held in memory. The secondary component must be completed and dismissed before the user can resume working on the original component. The Transfer() function, on the other hand, works as a one-way street.

299. What is the difference between the Transfer() function and the TransferExact() function? When the Transfer() function attempts to do the search based on the passed parameters, it will do a 'LIKE' search on all the string parameters. If, however, you prefer the system to do an exact match on the passed parameters, which will always be quicker than a 'LIKE' search, then use the TransferExact() function instead. As long as you have provided the function with all the necessary values, 'TransferExact' will deliver a faster response time.

300. Variables used by the Transfer() function can be set by specifying each individually or by specifying in a record object that is pre-populated with the search values.

Here is an example of using the Transfer() function with individual fields specified for the search,

```
Transfer(True, MenuName.SA_LEARNER_SERVICES,
BarName.FINANCES, ItemName.SSF_SS_MISC_PUR,
Page.SSF_SS_BU_SELECT, &Action_UpdateDisplay,
&guid, &oper, &ver, &trxtype);
```

Here is an example of a record object being used to set the search record fields:

```
&searchRec = CreateRecord(Record.RECORD_NAME);
&searchRec.EMPLID.Value = ¤tEmplID;
&searchRec.ACAD_CAREER.Value = ¤tCareer;
Transfer(True,MenuName.SA_LEARNER_SERVICES, BarName.FINANCES,
ItemName.SSF_SS_MISC_PUR, Page.SSF_SS_BU_SELECT,
&Action_UpdateDisplay, &searchRec);
```

301. How to pass a variable to a new window opened by the TransferExact() function and the DoModalComponent() function?

To pass a variable to a window opened by the TransferExact function, use the %Request.GetParameter("CUST_ID") function to retrieve the variable in the PreBuild event PeopleCode. A code example is as follows,

```
&strCustomerID = %Request.GetParameter("CUST_ID");
If All(&strCustomerID) Then
    XXX_BP_WRK.CUST_ID = &strCustomerID;
End-If;
```

To pass a variable to a window opened by the DoModalComponent function, put the variable in a shared record.

302. How to retrieve the data in an unknown table using the CreateArrayAny() function?

The CreateArrayAny() function allows us to define an array consisting of any number of object types. Better still, the array can contain a combination of values. Strings, numbers, booleans, and dates can all be stored in the same array.

The CreateArrayAny() function allows us to select all fields from the unknown table at run-time.

Here is a code example.

```
Local integer &i;
Local string &sql_text = "select * from external_table";
Local SQL &Select_SQL = CreateSQL(&sql_text);
Local array &FieldArray = CreateArrayAny();
While &Select_SQL.Fetch(&FieldArray)
For &i = 1 To &FieldArray.Len
        &logFile.WriteLine("Field Number " | &i |
```

245

```
            " contains value " | &FieldArray [&i]);
End-For;
End-While;
```

303. How to save the results from a SQL query to a file using the CreateArrayAny() function?
You can refer to the following code example.

```
/* Create the output file and write in the header */
&filePath = "/XXX/" | Lower(%DbName) |
"/outbound/ABC_Extracts/";
&file = GetFile(&filePath | "ABC_ACTUALS_" |
XXX_ABC_XT_AET.FISCAL_YEAR | "_P1_to_P" |
XXX_ABC_XT_AET.ACCOUNTING_PERIOD | "_" |
XXX_ABC_XT_AET.PROCESS_INSTANCE | ".csv", "w", "a",
%FilePath_Absolute);
&file.writeline("Legacy GL Account,Account Code,Account
Name,Customer Segment Code,Product Code,Transit
Code,Department Code,Business Unit Code,Location
Code,Ledger,Currency,YTD Amount");
/* Use the SQL.OUTPUT object and traverse through it,
printing to the csv file */
Local SQL &SQL;
&SQL
= GetSQL(SQL.XXX_ABC_XTRACT, XXX_ABC_XT_AET.FISCAL_YEAR,
XXX_ABC_XT_AET.ACCOUNTING_PERIOD, "LOCAL");
&arr = CreateArrayAny();
/* Number of fields the SQL statement will return */
Local number &FieldSize;
&FieldSize = 12;
```

```
While (&SQL.Fetch(&arr))

For &i = 1 To &FieldSize

&OutputString = &OutputString | &arr [&i] | ",";

End-For;

&OutputString = Substring(&OutputString, 1,

Len(&OutputString) - 1);

&file.writeline(&OutputString);

&OutputString = "";

End-While;
```

304. If there is nothing on the screen which needs to be saved, DoSave() won't be effective, and therefore the SavePreChange and the SavePostChange event won't be fired. A temp record can be used to trigger saving.

305. In a file layout in the Delimited format, the start position of any field doesn't really matter; but for a file layout in the Fixed format, the start position of any field has to be the actual start position of the field.

306. You can embed a hyperlink in a message catalog entry. f.i.

```
<a href="http://www.oracle.com" target="_blank">click
here</a>
```

The parameter target="_blank" tells the browser to open a new window or a new tab when that link is clicked.

307. How to call a secondary page from a main page?
    There are two ways to call a secondary page from a main page
      1) Set the destination as Secondary Page in PushButton properties and specify the name of the secondary page

Note every push button should be associated with a field of that page record.

2) Set the destination as PeopleCode Command in Pushbutton properties and use the Domodal() function

The DoModal() function displays a secondary page. Secondary pages are modal, meaning that the user must dismiss the secondary page before continuing work in the page from which the secondary page was called. To use Domodal() function set the Destination as 'PeopleCodeCommand' in Pushbutton properties as shown below.

Note DoModal is also used to call Standard page. You can use more than one DoModal function in single event PeopleCode to call more than one secondary page.

The syntax of the DoModal function is as follows,

```
DoModal(PAGE.pagename, title, xpos, ypos, [level,
scrollpath, target_row])
```

Any variable declared as a component variable will still be defined after using a DoModal function.

Any PeopleCode event that fires as a result of a ScrollSelect, ScrollSelectNew, RowScrollSelect or RowScrollSelectNew function call.

DoModal() returns a number that indicates how the secondary page was terminated. A secondary page can be terminated by the user clicking a built-in OK or Cancel button, or by a call to the EndModal function in a PeopleCode program. In either case, the return value of DoModal is one of the following:

1 if the user clicked OK in the secondary page, or if 1 was passed in the EndModal function call that terminated the secondary page.

0 if the user clicked Cancel in the secondary page, or if 0 was passed in the EndModal function call that terminated the secondary page.

A code example is as follows,

```
DoModal(PAGE.XXX_DTL, MsgGetText(1000, 167,
"EducationDetails - %1", EDUCATN.DEGREE), - 1, - 1,
1, RECORD.EDUCATN, CurrentRowNumber());
```

EndModal()

The EndModal() function closes a currently open secondary page. It is required only for secondary pages that do not have OK and Cancel buttons. If the secondary page has OK and Cancel buttons, then the function for exiting the page is built in and no PeopleCode is required.

The following statement acts as an OK button:

```
EndModal(1);
```

The following statement acts as a Cancel button:

```
EndModal(0);
```

IsModal()

The IsModal() function returns True if executed from PeopleCode running in a modal secondary page and False if executed elsewhere. This function is useful in separating secondary page-specific logic from general PeopleCode logic.

308. How to set an edit table for a record field at run-time?

You can use the SetRecFieldEditTable() function to set an edit table at run-time.

The syntax is

SetRecFieldEditTable(Record.*RecordName*, Field.*FieldName*, *EditTable* [, *TableEditType*])

Here is an example.

```
&ret =
SetRecFieldEditTable
(RECORD.AbsHist,Field.OrgId,RECORD.EmplId_Tbl,%EditTableType_
Prompt);

If (&ret = %MDA_Success) Then
 MessageBox(0, "", 0, 0,"SetRecFieldEditTable succeeded");
Else
 MessageBox(0, "", 0, 0,"SetRecFieldEditTable failed");
End-If;
```

309. Use the SetRecFieldKey function to specify whether a field on a record is a key field or not.

```
SetRecFieldKey(Record.RecordName, Field.FieldName, Key)
```

Because performing this operation changes records, you must subsequently rebuild the record (alter tables).

310. How to perform quick and dirty bulk delete of records with the same key value?

To delete records from a set of tables, all with the same key value (eg for a certain Employee ID), you can run the code below,

```
/* Select matching records with a prefix of XX_STG */
&RecordsToDelete_RS = CreateRowset(Record.PSRECDEFN);
&RecordsToDelete_RS.Fill("where RECNAME like 'XX_STG%' and
RECTYPE = 0");

For &i = 1 To &RecordsToDelete_RS.ActiveRowCount
&RecordsToDelete_Rec =
&RecordsToDelete_RS.GetRow(&i).PSRECDEFN;
```

```
&sql_delete = "delete from ps_" |
&RecordsToDelete_Rec.RECNAME.Value | " where EMPLID = :1";
SQLExec(&sql_delete, "1234567");
End-For;
```

To delete the records based on a project definition, you can run the code below,

```
/* Select matching records from the XXXXX project */
&RecordsToDelete_RS = CreateRowset(Record.PSPROJECTITEM);
&RecordsToDelete_RS.Fill("where OBJECTTYPE = 0 and
PROJECTNAME = 'XXXXX' and exists (select 'x' from PSRECDEFN A
where A.RECNAME = FILL.OBJECTVALUE1 and A.RECTYPE = 0)");

For &i = 1 To &RecordsToDelete_RS.ActiveRowCount
  &RecordsToDelete_Rec =
  &RecordsToDelete_RS.GetRow(&i).PSPROJECTITEM;

  &sql_delete = "delete from ps_" |
  &RecordsToDelete_Rec.OBJECTVALUE1.Value | " where EMPLID =
  :1";
  SQLExec(&sql_delete, "1234567");
End-For;
```

311. You can use GetSQL and SQL.Fetch to loop through the distinct value combinations from a query and process each combination.

```
&sql = GetSQL("SELECT DISTINCT A.BUSINESS_UNIT,
A.JOURNAL_DATE, A.LEDGER_GROUP, TO_CHAR(A.JOURNAL_DATE,
'YYYY-MM-DD') AS JRNL_DT_STR FROM PS_XXX_GLM_JNLVLD A WHERE
A.PROCESS_INSTANCE = :1", XXX_JNL_EX_AET.PROCESS_INSTANCE);
```

```
While &SQL.Fetch(&BU, &JOURNAL_DATE, &LEDGER_GROUP,
&JRNL_DT_STR)….
End-While;
```

312. How to keep a small set of data in working memory without having to create a temporary table in the database?

You can use two-dimensional array to do it. You don't need to ask DBA to create a physical table. A two-dimensional array can also be accessed much quicker than a standard SQL table.

F.i, in order to create a two-dimensional array for the following table,

000049	Y
000093	Y
000136	N
000249	N
000303	Y

You can write the code as below,

```
Local array of string &singleEmp;
Local array of array of string &allEmp;

/* Set up employees */
&singleEmp = CreateArray("");
&singleEmp [1] = "000049";
&singleEmp [2] = "Y";
&allEmp = CreateArray(&singleEmp);

&singleEmp = CreateArray("");
&singleEmp [1] = "000093";
&singleEmp [2] = "Y";
&allEmp.Push(&singleEmp);

&singleEmp = CreateArray("");
```

```
&singleEmp [1] = "000136";
&singleEmp [2] = "N";
&allEmp.Push(&singleEmp);


&singleEmp = CreateArray("");
&singleEmp [1] = "000249";
&singleEmp [2] = "N";
&allEmp.Push(&singleEmp);


&singleEmp = CreateArray("");
&singleEmp [1] = "000303";
&singleEmp [2] = "Y";
&allEmp.Push(&singleEmp);


/* Check for array length */
&array_len =&allEmp.Len;


/* Search for employee */
&pos =&allEmp.Find("000249");


/* Update status */
If &pos <> 0 Then
   &allEmp [&pos, 2] = "Y";
End-If;


/* See the entire array */
&all_string =&allEmp.Join(", ");
MessageBox(0, "", 0, 0,&all_string);
```

The result appears as follows

```
((000045, Y),(000089, Y),(000132, N), (000245,Y), (000299,Y))
```

313. You can create a SQL object first and use it later. An example of using a SQL object is as follows,

```
Local SQL &SQL_CUST_UPD;

&SQL_CUST_UPD = GetSQL(SQL.XXX_SUBCUST_UPD_AE);

&SQL_CUST_UPD.Execute(&STATUS, &NULL, &NULL, &NULL, &NULL,
&XP_ID, &SETID);
```

314. How to check if there are any rows returned from SQLExec("Select")?

```
If %SqlRows = 0 Then

    ......

End-If;
```

315. What is the difference between SQLEXEC and CREATESQL?

SQLExec means it bypasses the component buffer and it is directly contacts database to retrieve data. But it retrieves the data row by row and not possible for bulk insert.

But in the case of CreateSQL you are able to insert the data in bulk.

SQLExec commands with Insert, Update & Delete are only allowed in SavePreChange, SavePostChange, and Workflow event PeopleCode.

316. You can use Insert Into {TABLE} Select from {TABLE} in a SQLExec statement; the two tables can be the same; however, binding with variables can only be used in the where clause, and not field values in the SQL select statement, where the string concatenation should be used instead.

Here is a code example,

```
SQLExec("INSERT INTO PS_XXX_GC_PROMO SELECT SETID, '" |
&sNewCustID | "', EFFDT, XXX_GASCARD, XXX_PROMO_PGM,
PGM_FROM_DATE, PGM_TO_DATE, XXX_GASCARD_DISC, XXX_PROMO_LOAD,
XXX_TOPUP_AMT, XXX_PROMO_LOAD_DT, XXX_REVERSE_AMT,
REVERSAL_DATE FROM PS_XXX_GC_PROMO P1 WHERE P1.SETID = :1 AND
P1.CUST_ID = :2 AND P1.XXX_GASCARD = :3  AND P1.PGM_FROM_DATE
= %DATEIN(:4) AND P1.XXX_PROMO_PGM LIKE 'P%'", &Setid,
&sOldCustID, XXX_GASCARD.XXX_GASCARD.Value, &dMaxFromDt);
```

317. How to select all fields from a table and ensure only distinct rows are returned?

%SelectAll is shorthand for selecting all fields in a specified table. It's used in PeopleCode or Application Engine to read data into memory.

The pseudocode looks like this:

```
SELECT(ALLFIELDS, :NUM CORRELATION_ID) FROM %TABLE(:NUM);
```
Here is an example:

```
&FETCH_SQL = CREATESQL("%SelectAll (:1) WHERE
PROCESS_INSTANCE = :2 ORDER BY PROCESS_INSTANCE,
BUSINESS_UNIT, VOUCHER_ID", &REC, &PI);
```

%SelectDistinct is shorthand for selecting all fields in the specified table, ensuring that only distinct rows are returned.

The pseudocode looks like this:

```
SELECT DISTINCT (ALLFIELDS, :NUM CORRELATION_ID)
FROM %TABLE(:NUM)
```

Here is an example:

```
&REC_PROJ_FUNDING = CreateRecord(Record.PROJ_FUNDING); /*
free standing record object */
  /* Create SQL objects */
&SQL_PROJ_FUNDING_SEL = CreateSQL("%SelectDistinct(:1)" /*
bind this later */);
  /* bind the %SelectDistinct */
&SQL_PROJ_FUNDING_SEL.Execute(&REC_PROJ_FUNDING);
While &SQL_PROJ_FUNDING_SEL.Fetch(&REC_PROJ_FUNDING);
    /* Process row content ... /*
  End-While;
```

318. How to obtain the value of a field in a grid?

```
Local Rowset &rsXXX_LMS_SDTL_VW;
&rsXXX_LMS_SDTL_VW                              =
GetLevel0()(1).GetRowset(Scroll.XXX_LMS_SDTL_VW);
&Course = &rsXXX_LMS_SDTL_VW(1).XXX_LMS_SDTL_VW.COURSE.Value;
```

319. How to obtain the value of a field of the current row in a grid?

You can use the PeopleCode function CurrentRowNumber() to get the current row number in the grid, and the code to get the value of a field of the current row is as follows,

```
GetRowset().GetRow(CurrentRowNumber()).{RecordName}.{FieldName}.Value;
```

You can also use the FetchValue() Function as follows,

256

```
&Row = CurrentRowNumber();

&Value = FetchValue({RecordName}.{FieldName}, &Row);
```

320. How to loop through all rows in a grid or a scroll and do data validation?

You can refer to the following code example.

```
&Row_Level0 = GetLevel0();

&RS_Level1 = &Row_Level0(1).GetRowset(Scroll.XXX_CREDITS);

For &I = 1 To &RS_Level1.ActiveRowCount;

&Row_Level1 = &RS_Level1.GetRow(&I);

&Rec1 = &Row_Level1.GetRecord(Record.XXX_CREDITS);

  If &Rec1.XXX_INTEREST.Value <> 0 Then

    &Rec1.ROW_NUM.Enabled = False;

  End-If;

End-For;
```

321. How to loop through the filtered rows in a grid or a scroll and do data validation?

You can refer to the following code example.

```
&rsLvl0 = GetLevel0();

&rsLv1 = &rsLvl0(1).GetRowset(Scroll.JOB_CURR_VW);

&rsLv1.Select(Record.JOB_CURR_VW, "where EMPLID = :1",
&sEmplid);

For &I = 1 To &rsLv1.ActiveRowCount

  If

  rsLv1.GetRow(&I).GetRecord(Record.XXX_SS_LMS_WRK).GetField(

  Field.SELECT_FLAG).Value = "Y" Then

      ......

  End-If;
```

```
End-For;
```

322. How to reference a rowset on a scroll on the level 2 of a page?

Here is an example,

```
&RS
=GetLevel0()(1).GetRowset(Scroll.ACC_XREF_SET_VW)(&level1_row
).GetRowset(Scroll.ACC_XREF_VW);
```

323. How to access/traverse component buffer data from level 0 to level 1, level 2 and level 3?

To obtain the level 1 rowset, traverse through the level 0 rowset first;

To obtain the level 2 rowset, traverse through the level 1 rowset first;

To obtain the level 3 rowset, traverse through the level 2 rowset first;

Here is a code example which traverses level 0 to level1 and level 2, accessing each rowset and row along the way. Level 0 has course data, level 1 has class session rows, and level 2 has class instructor rows.

```
Local Record &Lv2Record;
Local Rowset &Level1RS;
Local Rowset &Level2RS;
Local number &Level1Rowcount;
Local number &Level2Rowcount;
Local number &i1;
Local number &i2;
&Level1RS = GetLevel0()(1).GetRowset(Scroll.CRSE_SESS_DATES);
&Level1Rowcount = &Level1RS.ActiveRowCount;
/* Iterate over all the class session rows */
For &i1 = 1 To &Level1Rowcount
&Lv1Row = &Level1RS.GetRow(&i1);
```

```
   If Not &Lv1Row.IsDeleted Then

        &Level2RS = &Lv1Row.GetRowset(Scroll.CRSE_SESS_INSTR);

        /* Iterate over all the instructor/vendor rows */

        &Level2Rowcount = &Level2RS.RowCount;

        For &i2 = 1 To &Level2Rowcount

              &Lv2Row = &Level2RS.GetRow(&i2);

              If Not &Lv2Row.IsDeleted Then

                   &Lv2Record =
                   &Lv2Row.GetRecord(Record.CRSE_SESS_INSTR);

                   &Instructor_ID =
                   &Lv2Record.GetField(Field.INSTRUCTOR_ID).Val
                   ue;

              End_If;

        End-For;

   End-If;

End-For;
```

This is a demo code for traversing Level 0 to Level 3. You can modify it based on your specific requirements.

```
/*** Demo Code For Traversing Level 0 to Level 3 ***/
Local Rowset &rsLevel0, &rsLevel1, &rsLevel2, &rsLevel3;
Local Row &rowLevel0, &rowLevel1, &rowLevel2, &rowLevel3;
Local Field &fldLevel0, &fldLevel1, &fldLevel2, &fldLevel3;
Local integer &i, &j, &k;


&rsLevel0 = GetLevel0();


/** Get Level 0 Field **/
```

```
&fldLevel0                                                =
&rsLevel0.GetRow(1).GetRecord(Record.L0_REC).GetField(Field.L
0_FLD);
/** Get Level 0 Field Value **/
&Level0FldValue = &fldLevel0.Value;


&rowLevel0 = &rsLevel0.GetRow(1);
&rsLevel1 = &rowLevel0.GetRowset(Scroll.LEVEL1_RECORD);
For &i = 1 To &rsLevel1.ActiveRowCount


   /** Get Level 1 Field **/
   &fldLevel1                                             =
&rsLevel1.GetRow(&i).GetRecord(Record.L1_REC).GetField(Field.
L1_FLD);
   /** Get Level 1 Field Value **/
   &Level1FldValue = &fldLevel1.Value;


   &rowLevel1 = &rsLevel1.GetRow(&i);
   &rsLevel2 = &rowLevel1.GetRowset(Scroll.LEVEL2_RECORD);
   For &j = 1 To &rsLevel2.ActiveRowCount


      /** Get Level 2 Field **/
      &fldLevel2                                          =
&rsLevel2.GetRow(&j).GetRecord(Record.L2_REC).GetField(Field.
L2_FLD);
      /** Get Level 2 Field Value **/
      &Level2FldValue = &fldLevel2.Value;


      &rowLevel2 = &rsLevel2.GetRow(&j);
      &rsLevel3 = &rowLevel2.GetRowset(Scroll.LEVEL3_RECORD);
      For &k = 1 To &rs_level3.ActiveRowCount
```

```
/** Get Level 3 Field **/
&fldLevel3                                                =
&rsLevel3.GetRow(&k).GetRecord(Record.L3_REC).GetField(Field.
L3_FLD);

        /** Get Level 3 Field Value **/
        &Level3FldValue = &fldLevel3.Value;
        &rowLevel3 = &rsLevel3.GetRow(&k);


        /* Do Processing   **/
        /* If Any Summation Calculation */
        /* &sum = &sum + &Level3FldValue */


    End-For;
  End-For;
End-For;
```

324. How to populate a grid with selected rows from a table or view?

Populating a PeopleSoft grid with selected rows from a table or view typically involves using PeopleCode to manipulate the rowset associated with the grid.

There are two ways of fetching data from the source and populating the grid.

The first way is using CreateSQL and Fetch: You can construct a SQL statement to select the desired rows from your table or view. Then, iterate through the results using Fetch() and populate the grid row by row.

Here is a code example,

```
Local SQL &sql_data;
Local Rowset &MyGridRowset;
Local Row &NewRow;
&MyGridRowset =
GetLevel0()(1).GetRowset(Scroll.YOUR_GRID_RECORD);
```

```
&sql_data = CreateSQL("SELECT FIELD1, FIELD2 FROM
YOUR_TABLE_OR_VIEW WHERE YOUR_CRITERIA = :1",
&YourBindVariable);


While &sql_data.Fetch(&Field1_Var, &Field2_Var);

    &NewRow =
&MyGridRowset.InsertRow(&MyGridRowset.ActiveRowCount);

     /* Insert a new row */

    &NewRow.YOUR_GRID_RECORD.FIELD1.Value = &Field1_Var;

    &NewRow.YOUR_GRID_RECORD.FIELD2.Value = &Field2_Var;

End-While;
```

The second way is using ScrollSelect or Rowset.Select: If your grid is based on a record definition that directly maps to your table or view (or a dynamic view), you can use Scroll Select or Rowset Select for more efficient data population.

Here is a code example,

```
&LEVEL0 = GetLevel0();

&rsXXX_LMS_SDTL_VW

= GetLevel0()(1).GetRowset(Scroll.XXX_LMS_VW);

&rsXXX_LMS_VW.Flush();

&rsXXX_LMS_VW.Select(Record.XXX_LMS_VW,

"WHERE Course = :1 AND Session_Nbr = :2", &sCourse,

&sSessionNbr);
```

325. How to sort a grid on specific columns?

To sort a grid on some columns, you can use the following code

```
SortScroll(1, Record.TRN_WAIT_VW, TRN_WAIT_VW.COURSE, "A",
TRN_WAIT_VW.ATTENDANCE, "A", TRN_WAIT_VW.SESSION_NBR, "A",
TRN_WAIT_VW.WAIT_DT, "A", TRN_WAIT_VW.EMPLID, "A");
```

326. You can use the IsNew function or RecordNew function to check a specific row to determine whether it was added to the component buffer since the component was last saved.

Note RecordNew function remains for backward compatibility only. Use the IsNew row class property instead.

```
If &ROW.IsNew Then

       ......

End-If;
If RecordNew(Record.JOB), Then

       ......

End-If;
```

327. You can use the RecordChanged function to determine whether the data in a specific row has been modified since it was retrieved from the database either by a user or by a PeopleCode program.

```
If RecordChanged(Record.JOB) Then

       ......

End-If;
```

328. How to check if a value has been changed on a field on a page?

To check if a field value has been changed on a page, you can use the IsChanged property of the field.

```
If EX_ADV_LINE.MONETARY_AMOUNT.IsChanged Then

       ......

End-If;
```

You can also check if a field value has been changed by comparing the original value and the new value of the field.

Here is an example,

```
If REQ_HDR.BUSINESS_UNIT.OriginalValue <>
REQ_HDR.BUSINESS_UNIT.Value Or
          REQ_HDR.REQUESTOR_ID.OriginalValue <>
REQ_HDR.REQUESTOR_ID.Value Or
          REQ_HDR.REQ_NAME.OriginalValue <>
REQ_HDR.REQ_NAME.Value Or
          REQ_HDR.REQ_ID.OriginalValue <>
REQ_HDR.REQ_ID.Value Or
          REQ_HDR.PRIORITY_FLG.OriginalValue <>
REQ_HDR.PRIORITY_FLG.Value Or
          REQ_HDR.CURRENCY_CD.OriginalValue <>
REQ_HDR.CURRENCY_CD.Value Then
          ......
End-If;
```

OriginalValue is the value of the field pulled from the database if the field hasn't been saved.

To check if a field value has been changed in a grid or scroll, you can use the following PeopleCode as two examples.

```
For &i = 1 To &dist_data.ActiveRowCount
          If &dist_data.GetRow(&i).EX_SHEET_DIST.IsChanged
Then
              currency_and_rates(&i);
          End-If;
End-For;
```

```
For &i = 1 To &rs.ActiveRowCount

    If All(&rs(&i).RS_FR_SUP_UTIL.UTIL_PCT.Value) Then

        If &rs(&i).RS_FR_SUP_UTIL.UTIL_PCT.OriginalValue <>
&rs(&i).RS_FR_SUP_UTIL.UTIL_PCT.Value Then

                    ......

            End-If;

        End-If;

    End-For;
```

329. To allow row selection in a grid, you don't have to add a check box field into the grid, you can turn on the row selection indictor in the Grid Properties.

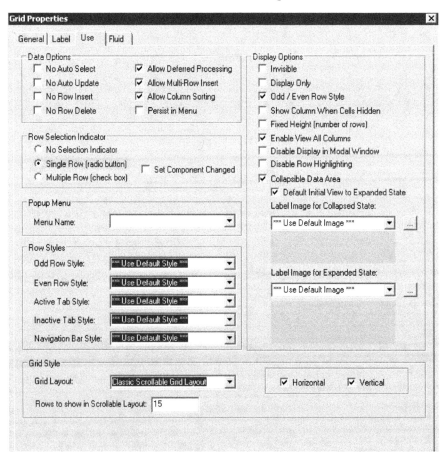

With that, you can use the following code to determine which row is selected.

265

```
If &rsLvl(&I).Selected = True Then

    ......

End-If;
```

330. How to execute a Unix command from PeopleCode?

You can execute a Unix command from PeopleCode the Exec function. The following PeopleCode renames the name of a Unix file.

```
Exec("mv <path>/file1.csv <path>/file2.csv",
%Exec_Asynchronous + %  FilePath_Absolute);
```

331. How to get the value of a component record field from the component buffer?

To get the value of a component record field from the component buffer, you can refer to the following code example,

```
&comp_pnlbuf(1).GetRecord(Record.EX_SHEET_HDR).BUSINESS_PURPO
SE.Value
```

332. How to display a confirmation dialog?

You can refer to the following code example,

```
&return = MessageBox(%MsgStyle_YesNo, "", 20001, 29, "Message
Not Found");
Evaluate &return
When = %MsgResult_Yes
    /* Ok was selected */
DoSave();
```

```
When = %MsgResult_No
        /* No was selected */
Break;
End-Evaluate;
```

333. How to set the style and the size of the font used in the text within a HTML area?

You can refer to the following code example.

```
TEST_WRK.HTMLAREA.Value = "<span class='PSTEXT'>" |
MsgGetExplainText(35001, 1, "Text") | "</span>";
```

Or

```
TEST_WRK.HTMLAREA.Value = "<div class='PAPAGEINSTRUCTIONS'>"
| Text | "</div>";
```

334. How to cause a time delay (sleep) from PeopleCode?

There is no PeopleCode to delay or sleep for some time, alternately, however, you can use the following code to cause a delay.

```
For &i=1 to 600000000
End-For;
```

This will delay for 60 seconds.

Here is a code example.

```
        /* Run the Bill Interface Transaction Loader process */
        &ProcessType1 = "Application Engine";
```

267

```
&ProcessName1 = "BIIF0001";

&PRCSRQST1 = CreateProcessRequest(&ProcessType1,
&ProcessName1);

&PRCSRQST1.RunControlID = "EForm";

&PRCSRQST1.SetOutputOption("", "", "", &ProcessName1);

&PRCSRQST1.Schedule();

/* Check the status after scheduling */

If &PRCSRQST1.Status = 0 Then

        /* Delay processing for 60 seconds */

    For &i = 1 To 60000000

      &RunStatus = " ";

    End-For;


    /* Retrieve the Invoice ID generated for the form
from the BI_HDR table */

    SQLExec("SELECT INVOICE  FROM PS_BI_HDR WHERE
PACKSLIP_NO = :1", &PackslipNo, &InvoiceID);


    /* Run the Applying VAT Default process */

    &ProcessType2 = "Application Engine";

    &ProcessName2 = "BIPVAT00";

    &PRCSRQST2 = CreateProcessRequest(&ProcessType2,
&ProcessName2);

    &PRCSRQST2.RunControlID = "EForm";

    &PRCSRQST2.SetOutputOption("", "", "",
&ProcessName2);

    &PRCSRQST2.Schedule();


  End-If;
```

In this example, The Bill Interface Transaction Loader process was scheduled to run first. One minute after the process was scheduled, the Applying VAT Default process was scheduled to run using the invoice created by the Bill Interface Transaction Loader process. It normally takes less than one minute for the first process to complete successfully. There should be enough time for the first process to complete before the second process starts running.

Or, you can use the sleep method of a java class.

```
&sleepSeconds = 60;
GetJavaClass("java.lang.Thread").sleep(&sleepSeconds        *
1000);
```

If the database is Oracle, you can use an Oracle SQL procedure.

```
SQLExec ("exec dbms_lock.sleep (60)")
```

335. How to check whether a file exists in a file system?

```
If  FileExists(&sFilePathName, %FilePath_Absolute)  Then
        ......
End-If;
```

336. How to delete a file from the file system?

```
Local JavaObject&PPSFile;
&PPSFile = CreateJavaObject("java.io.File", &sFilePathName);
&PPSFile.delete();
```

337. How to check the PeopleTools Release version in PeopleCode?

```
#If %ToolsRelease>= "8.59" #Then

    ............... .

#End-If;
```

338. How to set a new line in PeopleCode?

You need to add two special characters in ASCII code at the end of the first line. They are the carriage return and the line feed.

```
&MSG = "This is line 1" | Char(13) | Char(10);
&MSG = &MSG | "This is line 2";
```

339. How to use PeopleCode to set the cursor position to level 0 fields and level 1 fields on a page?

Here is a code example to set the cursor position to a level 0 field on a page.

```
SetCursorPos(%Page, XXX__CARS_REQ_WK.CUST_ID, 1);
Error (MsgGet(12500, 32, "You must complete the credit from
Customer ID field");
```

Here is a code example to set the cursor position to be on the current row within a scroll or a grid.

```
SetCursorPos(Page.XXX_COLL_LIT,
XXX_COLL_LIT_VW.FROM_DT, CurrentRowNumber());
```

340. How to build nested logic in PeopleCode?

```
method CheckPassCreated
If FileExists(&sFilePathName, %FilePath_Absolute) Then
```

```
        Do sth
Else
        Do sth else
        %This.CheckPassCreated();
End-If;
end-method;
```

341. How to insert a new row into a table using PeopleCode?

When inserting rows using PeopleCode, you can either use the Insert method of a record object or create a SQL insert statement using a SQL object. If you need to do a single-row insert, use the record insert method. If you need to insert multiple rows at once, use the SQL to insert.

The SQL object uses dedicated cursors and if the database you are working with supports it, it will do bulk insert.

A dedicated cursor means that the SQL gets compiled only once on the database, so PeopleTools looks for the meta-SQL only once. This can increase performance.

For bulk insert, inserted rows are buffered and sent to the database server only when the buffer is full or a commit occurs. This reduces the number of round-trips to the database. The following is a code example of using the record insert method:

```
&REC = CreateRecord(Record.GREG);
&REC.DESCR.Value = "Y" | &I;
&REC.EMPLID.Value = &I;
&REC.Insert();
```

The following is a code example using a SQL object to insert rows:

```
&SQL = CreateSQL("%INSERT(:1)");
&REC = CreateRecord(Record.GREG);
&SQL.BulkMode = True;
For &I = 1 to 10
```

271

```
&REC.DESCR.Value = "Y" | &I;

&REC.EMPLID.Value = &I;

&SQL.Execute(&REC);

End-For;
```

342. How to pass a URL to a PeopleCode built-in function?

If a variable is passed to a built-in function, it is treated as a plain string and not as a URL identifier object. To make sure you call a URL Identifier and not a string, you should use @(&URL).

A code example is shown below:

```
If Exact(Left(&URL_ID, 4), "URL.") Then

        &RETCODE = AddAttachment(@(&URL_ID),
        &ATTACHSYSFILENAME, &FILEEXTENSION, &ATTACHUSERFILE,
        &FILESIZE);

Else

        &RETCODE = AddAttachment(&URL_ID, &ATTACHSYSFILENAME,
        &FILEEXTENSION, &ATTACHUSERFILE, &FILESIZE);

End-If;
```

343. How to set a dynamic prompt table in PeopleCode?

The SetEditTable method works with the ExecuteEdits method. It is used to set the value of a field on a record that has its prompt table defined as %EDITTABLE value. %EDITTABLE values are used to dynamically change the prompt record for a field.

Use SetEditTable to dynamically set the prompt table.

```
If %PanelGroup = PanelGroup.RUN_HPRETDISTSRCH Then

        DERIVED.EDITTABLE = "SETID_TBL";

        GetRecord(Record.RUN_HPDISTSRCH).SetEditTable("%EDITTA
        BLE", Record.SETID_TBL);
```

272

```
Else

       DERIVED.EDITTABLE = "HP_RDIST_TRIGVW";

       GetRecord(Record.RUN_HPDISTSRCH).SetEditTable("%EDITTA
       BLE", Record.HP_RDIST_TRIGVW);

End-If;
```

344. How to call a java class in PeopleCode?

You can refer to the following code example.

```
local JavaObject &glmCalVal_obj;

try

       &glmCalVal_obj =
       CreateJavaObject("XXX.CalendarValidation");
       &glmCalValStatus =
       &glmCalVal_obj.validateJournalDate(&mill, &BU,
       &JRNL_DT_STR, &ps_home);
       &glmCalVal_obj = Null;

end-try;
```

XXX is the name of the application package. CalendarValidation is the name of the java class.

The following sample code shows how to access a Java class so you can manipulate it in PeopleCode. The code will force the program to sleep for 100 seconds before moving on to the next step.

```
GetJavaClass("java.lang.Thread").sleep(160000); /* 100 second
nap */
```

345. How to debug code by writing variable values to a file?

The WinMessage() function and the MessageBox() function are very useful for debugging. You can use any of them to display a debug message in a message box. But in some scenarios these two functions may not work. On the other hand, tracing may not be available sometime.

You can write variable values to an output file when you cannot use the MessageBox() function or the WinMessage() function to display debug variable values.

You can refer to the following code example.

```
&MYFILE = GetFile("debug-file.txt", "W");
If &MYFILE.IsOpen Then


      &MYFILE.WriteLine("Here is my First Variable");
      &MYFILE.WriteLine(&MyVariable);
      &MYFILE.WriteLine("Here is another Variable");
      &MYFILE.WriteLine(&MySecondVariable);
      &MYFILE.Close();


End-If;
```

This example code shows how to write variables to a debug file. The output file can be found in the app server directory for debugging online pages, and the process monitor for debugging a batch program. Remember that WriteLine() will overwrite any existing files with the same file name.

This technique is especially useful when MessageBox() or WinMessage() is not working and tracing is also not available.

346. How to set trace in PeopleCode?

Other than setting trace flags on the login page, traces can be set within the PeopleCode by wrapping around the code to be traced.

Here is an example of setting trace on submitting a form for approval.   When it works, the trace can be ignored and deleted, but when an issue occurs again, the problem will have been captured. The trace will go into the application server log file, i.e., APPSRV_MMDD.log.

```
method DoSubmit
Local string &default;
Local string &msg;
Local Exception &base;
SetTraceSQL(31);
SetTracePC(4044);
If (Not %This.submitEnabled) Then
     %This.RequireAppDef();
     %This.RequireNewOrNoAppInst();
     %This.RequireNoEndedAppInst();
     &default = "Unexpected situation: submit is disabled.
     (Process id = '" | %This.txn.awprcs_id | "').";
     &msg          =          MsgGetText(&utils.MSG_CATALOG,
     &utils.MSG_SUBMIT_DISABLED,              &default,
     %This.txn.awprcs_id);
     &base       =          CreateException(&utils.MSG_CATALOG,
     &utils.MSG_SUBMIT_DISABLED,              &default,
     %This.txn.awprcs_id);
     throw    create    EOAW_CORE:EXCEPTIONS:AppError(&base,
     &msg);
End-If;
&txn.possible_preview = False;
%This.PrepareToSubmit();
&appInst.Launch();
SetTraceSQL(0);
SetTracePC(0);
end-method;
```

347. How to find records and fields used in a PeopleSoft Page using a SQL query?

You may often come across a situation when you need to find records behind a page or records associated with a field and so on. Here are a few helpful SQL queries, which will come handy in such situations.

1) SQL query to find all the Records and Fields used in a PeopleSoft page

```
SELECT  recname, fieldname
FROM    pspnlfield
WHERE   pnlname = {PageName}
ORDER BY recname;
```

2) SQL query to find all the Records where a particular PeopleSoft field is used

```
SELECT DISTINCT recname, fieldname
FROM    psrecfield
WHERE   fieldname = {FieldName};
ORDER BY recname;
```

3) SQL query to find all the page names where a field is used from a particular record

```
SELECT pnlname
FROM    pspnlfield
WHERE   recname = {RecordName}
AND fieldname = {FieldName};
```

348. What are the PeopleCode functions available for file attachments?

AddAttachment(): Uploads a user selected file to destination. Think-time function

PutAttachment(): Uploads a a file available on application server file system to destination.

ViewAttachment(): Downloads a user requested file available in destination system and opens it in browser. Think-time function

GetAttachment(): Downloads a user requested file available in destination system to application server file system.

DetachAttachment(): Downloads a user requested file available in destination system and prompts the user with Save Open dialog. Think-time function

DeleteAttachment(): Deletes the user requested file from destination system.

CopyAttachments(): Copies the files from a source system to a destination system.

The supported protocols of above attachment function functions are FTP, FTPS, SFTP, HTTP and HTTPS.

349. How to use the %EffdtCheck meta-sql element to select the effective date rows?

You can use the %EffdtCheck meta-sql element to select the effective date rows in the record view SQL. An example is as follows,

```
SELECT A.SETID
, A.CONTACT_ID
, B.CUSTOMER_SETID
, B.CUST_ID
, B.CNTCT_SEQ_NUM
FROM PSOPRALIAS A
, PS_CONTACT_CUST B
 WHERE A.SETID = B.SETID
AND A.CONTACT_ID = B.CONTACT_ID
AND A.OPRALIASTYPE = 'CNT'
AND A.OPRALIASVALUE = B.CONTACT_ID
AND %EffdtCheck(CONTACT_CUST X, B, %CurrentDateIn)
AND B.EFF_STATUS = 'A';
```

%EffdtCheck is a very handy meta-sql element. It writes effective date logic for you. For example, you can write a view that returns the maximum effective dated and active subject from the subject table.

Note the %EffDtCheck construct expands into an effective date subquery suitable for a Where clause. However, it cannot be used with records that contain EFFSEQ as part of the key. This also applies to other records that contain EFFDT field + additional fields after EFFDT that indicate a parent-child relationship.

350. How to increment the number automatically with strings?

In the following code example, values are incremented as SY00000001, SY00000002, SY00000003.....etc.

```
Local string &MaxRequestID;
If %Component = Component.XXX_AWE_LR Then
  If %Mode = "A" Then
      SQLExec("select max(REQUEST_ID) from PS_XXX_AWE_LR",
      &MaxRequestID);
      If &MaxRequestID = "" Then
          XXX_AWE_LR.REQUEST_ID = "SY00000001";
      Else
          &RequestId1 = Substring(&MaxRequestID, 1, 2);
          &RequestId2 = Substring(&MaxRequestID, 3, 10);
          &RequestId2 = Value(&RequestId2) + 1;
          &newnbr = Rept("0", 8 - Len(&RequestId2)) |
          &RequestId2;
          &newnbr1 = &RequestId1 | &newnbr;
          XXX_AWE_LR.REQUEST_ID.Value = &newnbr1;
      End-If;
  End-If;
End-If;
```

351. How to clear the default values of a drop-down list and create a new drop-down list?

You can refer to the following code example.

```
&FLD.GetRecord(Record.PERSONAL_PHONE).GetField(Field.PHONE_TYP
E);
```

```
&FLD.ClearDropDownList();

&FLD.AddDropDownItem("BUSN", "Business");

&FLD.AddDropDownItem("HOME", "Home");

&FLD.AddDropDownItem("MAIN", "Main");

&FLD.AddDropDownItem("OTR", "Other");
```

352. How to create a drop-down list of the months in the order from January to December?

Here is a code example,

```
Local Rowset &rsXlat;

&rsXlat = CreateRowset(Record.PSXLATITEM);

&rsXlat.Flush();

&rsXlat.Fill("WHERE    fieldname    =    'XXX_MONTH'    ORDER    BY
fieldvalue");

XXX_RC_SGS_WKH.XXX_MONTH.ClearDropDownList();

&j = &rsXlat.ActiveRowCount + 1;

For &i = 1 To &rsXlat.ActiveRowCount

    &Value = &rsXlat.GetRow(&i).PSXLATITEM.FIELDVALUE.Value;

    &Descr = &rsXlat.GetRow(&i).PSXLATITEM.XLATLONGNAME.Value;

    XXX_RC_SGS_WKH.XXX_MONTH.AddDropDownItem(&Value,
    Rept(Char(9), &j - &i) | &Descr);

End-For;
```

353. How to display items in a drop-down list in a particular order?

Here is a code example. It creates a drop-down list of the months from September to August next year.

```
XXX_RC_SGS_WKH.XXX_MONTH.ClearDropDownList();
```

```
XXX_RC_SGS_WKH.XXX_MONTH.AddDropDownItem("09", Rept(Char(9),
12) | "September");

XXX_RC_SGS_WKH.XXX_MONTH.AddDropDownItem("10", Rept(Char(9),
11) | "October");

XXX_RC_SGS_WKH.XXX_MONTH.AddDropDownItem("11", Rept(Char(9),
10) | "November");

XXX_RC_SGS_WKH.XXX_MONTH.AddDropDownItem("12", Rept(Char(9),
9) | "December");

XXX_RC_SGS_WKH.XXX_MONTH.AddDropDownItem("01", Rept(Char(9),
8) | "January");

XXX_RC_SGS_WKH.XXX_MONTH.AddDropDownItem("02", Rept(Char(9),
7) | "February");

XXX_RC_SGS_WKH.XXX_MONTH.AddDropDownItem("03", Rept(Char(9),
6) | "March");

XXX_RC_SGS_WKH.XXX_MONTH.AddDropDownItem("04", Rept(Char(9),
5) | "April");

XXX_RC_SGS_WKH.XXX_MONTH.AddDropDownItem("05", Rept(Char(9),
4) | "May");

XXX_RC_SGS_WKH.XXX_MONTH.AddDropDownItem("06", Rept(Char(9),
3) | "June");

XXX_RC_SGS_WKH.XXX_MONTH.AddDropDownItem("07", Rept(Char(9),
2) | "July");

XXX_RC_SGS_WKH.XXX_MONTH.AddDropDownItem("08", Rept(Char(9),
1) | "August");
```

This drop-down list is displayed as follows,

Here is another example.

```
XXX_SC_REC.PriorityButton.ClearDropDownList();

XXX_SC_REC.PriorityButton.AddDropDownItem("L", Rept(Char(9),
5) | "Low");

XXX_SC_REC.PriorityButton.AddDropDownItem("M", Rept(Char(9),
4) | "Medium");

XXX_SC_REC.PriorityButton.AddDropDownItem("H", Rept(Char(9),
3) | "High");

XXX_SC_REC.PriorityButton.AddDropDownItem("O", Rept(Char(9),
2) | "Other");
```

This drop-down list is displayed as follows,

354. How to load a flat file with a control file using a file layout, save the data into a table with edit, save any errors into a log file, and send out a notification email if the file cannot be found in a folder?

```
Import PT_MCF_MAIL:MCFOutboundEmail;
```

```
Function EditRecord(&REC As Record) Returns boolean;
   Local integer &E;
   REM    &REC.ExecuteEdits(%Edit_Required + %Edit_DateRange +
%Edit_YesNo + %Edit_TranslateTable + %Edit_PromptTable +
%Edit_OneZero);
&REC.ExecuteEdits(%Edit_Required + %Edit_DateRange +
%Edit_YesNo + %Edit_OneZero);
   If &REC.IsEditError Then
     For &E = 1 To &REC.FieldCount
       &MYFIELD = &REC.GetField(&E);
        If &MYFIELD.EditError Then
           &MSGNUM = &MYFIELD.MessageNumber;
           &MSGSET = &MYFIELD.MessageSetNumber;
           &LOGFILE.WriteLine("****Record:" | &REC.Name | ",
      Field:" | &MYFIELD.Name );
            &LOGFILE.WriteLine("****" | MsgGet(&MSGSET,
      &MSGNUM, ""));
         End-If;
     End-For;
     Return False;
   Else
     Return True;
   End-If;
End-Function;

Function ImportSegment(&RS2 As Rowset, &RSParent As Rowset)
   Local Rowset &RS1, &RSP;
   Local string &RecordName;
   Local Record &REC2, &RECP;
   Local SQL &SQL1;
   Local integer &I, &L;
```

282

```
&SQL1 = CreateSQL("%Insert(:1)");
&RecordName = "RECORD." | &RS2.DBRecordName;
&REC2 = CreateRecord(@(&RecordName));
&RECP = &RSParent(1).GetRecord(@(&RecordName));
For &I = 1 To &RS2.ActiveRowCount
    &RS2(&I).GetRecord(1).CopyFieldsTo(&REC2);
    If (EditRecord(&REC2)) Then
        &SQL1.Execute(&REC2);
        &RS2(&I).GetRecord(1).CopyFieldsTo(&RECP);
        For &L = 1 To &RS2.GetRow(&I).ChildCount
&RS1 = &RS2.GetRow(&I).GetRowset(&L);
            If (&RS1 <> Null) Then
                &RSP = &RSParent.GetRow(1).GetRowset(&L);
ImportSegment(&RS1, &RSP);
            End-If;
        End-For;
        If &RSParent.ActiveRowCount> 0 Then
            &RSParent.DeleteRow(1);
        End-If;
Else
   &LOGFILE.WriteRowset(&RS);
   &LOGFILE.WriteLine("****Correct error in this record and
delete all error messages");
   &LOGFILE.WriteRecord(&REC2);
        For &L = 1 To &RS2.GetRow(&I).ChildCount
&RS1 = &RS2.GetRow(&I).GetRowset(&L);
            If (&RS1 <> Null) Then
&LOGFILE.WriteRowset(&RS1);
            End-If;
        End-For;
    End-If;
End-For;
```

```
End-Function;

Function MissingFileEmailTrigger()
    Local PT_MCF_MAIL:MCFOutboundEmail&eMail;
    &eMail = create PT_MCF_MAIL:MCFOutboundEmail();
    SQLExec("SELECT DBNAME FROM PSDBOWNER", &DBName);

    &EmailIDSQL = CreateSQL("SELECT STRING_TEXT FROM
%Table(STRINGS_TBL) WHERE PROGRAM_ID='CSUEMAIL' AND STRING_ID
BETWEEN '1' and '99'");
    While &EmailIDSQL.fetch(&eMailID)
        &SendTo = &SendTo | "," | &eMailID;
    End-While;

    &MAIL_TO = &SendTo;
    &eMail.Subject = &DBName | ": " | "Invoice Processing - No
Files Found";
    &eMail.Text = MsgGetExplainText(30000, 5, "No File Found ",
&FileDate);
    &eMail.From = "DoNotReply@abc.com";
    &eMail.Recipients = &MAIL_TO;
    &eMail.CC = "";

    /* Send the email */
    &result = &eMail.Send();

    Evaluate &result
    When %ObEmail_Delivered
        &done = True;
        MessageBox(0, "", 0, 0, "No file found email sent");
        Break;
```

```
    When %ObEmail_NotDelivered

    When %ObEmail_PartiallyDelivered

    When %ObEmail_FailedBeforeSending

        &done = False;

        MessageBox(0, "", 0, 0, "Error sending email for no file
found");

        Break;

    End-Evaluate;


End-Function;


rem
*************************************************************
***;
rem * PeopleCode to Import Data
*;
rem
*************************************************************
***;
Local File &FILE1;
Local Record &REC1;
Local SQL &SQL1;
Local Rowset &RS1, &RS2;
Local integer &M;
Component string &FileDate;


SQLExec("SELECT STRING_TEXT FROM PS_STRINGS_TBL WHERE
PROGRAM_ID = 'CSUDIST' AND STRING_ID = 'FILEPATH'",
&FilePath);
SQLExec("SELECT STRING_TEXT FROM PS_STRINGS_TBL WHERE
PROGRAM_ID = 'CSUDIST' AND STRING_ID = 'FILENAME_IN'",
&FileName);
```

```
If &FileName = Upper("NONE") Then
   &File_Pattern = &FilePath | "*VISA_OOP_" |
DateTimeToLocalizedString(%Date, "MMddyy") | ".TXT";
   &FileDate = DateTimeToLocalizedString(%Date, "MMddyy");
Else
   &File_Pattern = &FilePath | &FileName;
   &FileDate = Substring(&FileName, 17, 6);
   MessageBox(0, "", 0, 0, "Loading file date: " | &FileDate);
End-If;
XXX_CS_VCHR_AET.DATE_FIELD.Value = &FileDate;
MessageBox(0, "", 0, 0, "Loading file pattern: " |
&File_Pattern);


&FNAMES = FindFiles(&File_Pattern, %FilePath_Absolute);


If &FNAMES.Len = 0 Then
   MissingFileEmailTrigger();
   Exit (1);
End-If;


While &FNAMES.Len> 0
   &MYFILE = GetFile(&FNAMES.Shift(), "R",
%FilePath_Absolute);
   &asDir = Split(&MYFILE.Name, "/");
   /* Get the last string... */
   &sFileName = &asDir [&asDir.Len];
End-While;


&ControlFileName = &FilePath | "CTRL_" |
XXX_CS_VCHR_AET.DATE_FIELD.Value | ".TXT";
```

```
MessageBox(0, "", 0, 0, "Control File Name: " |
&ControlFileName);

If FileExists(&ControlFileName, %FilePath_Absolute) Then
    &ControlFile = GetFile(&ControlFileName, "r", "a",
%FilePath_Absolute);
    &ControlFile.ReadLine(&Control_String);

    &AS = Split(&Control_String, "     ");
    XXX_CS_VCHR_AET.DATE_CHAR.Value = &AS [1];
    XXX_CS_VCHR_AET.INVOICE_COUNT.Value = &AS [2];
    XXX_CS_VCHR_AET.CONTROL_AMT.Value = &AS [3];
    XXX_CS_VCHR_AET.CONTROL_PAY_AMT.Value = &AS [4];

    MessageBox(0, "", 0, 0, "" |
XXX_CS_VCHR_AET.DATE_CHAR.Value | "_" |
XXX_CS_VCHR_AET.INVOICE_COUNT.Value | "_" |
XXX_CS_VCHR_AET.CONTROL_AMT.Value | "_" |
XXX_CS_VCHR_AET.CONTROL_PAY_AMT.Value);
Else
    MissingFileEmailTrigger();
    Exit (1);
End-If;

If FileExists(&FilePath | &sFileName, %FilePath_Absolute) Then

    &FILE1 = GetFile(&FilePath | &sFileName, "r", "a",
%FilePath_Absolute);
    &FILE1.SetFileLayout(FileLayout.XXX_CSPYMT_STG_FL);
    &RS1 = &FILE1.CreateRowset();
    &RS = CreateRowset(Record.XXX_CSPYMT_STG);
```

287

```
&SQL1 = CreateSQL("%Insert(:1)");
&RS1 = &FILE1.ReadRowset();
While &RS1 <>Null;
    ImportSegment(&RS1, &RS);
    &RS1 = &FILE1.ReadRowset();
End-While;


&FILE1.Close();
End-If;
```

To import a file with a file layout that has multiple levels, such as file header, invoice header and invoice line, use the following command to create rowsets.

```
&RS = CreateRowset(Record.XXX_FL_HDR,
CreateRowset(Record.XXX_VCHR_HDR,
CreateRowset(Record.XXX_VCHR_LN)));
```

355. How to export data from a table to a flat file using a file layout?

Here is a code example,

```
/* Generate Report */
&filename = %FilePath | "XXX_ITA_MAX_PENSION_SALARY_WORK" |
".CSV";
/* set run date for report header */
&RundateStr = "Run Date: " | %Date;
/* attempt to read from file - just to see if it is open or
not, or if it exists */
&FILE = GetFile(&filename, "W", %FilePath_Absolute);
If &FILE.IsOpen Then
/* write header rows */
```

```
&FILE.WriteLine("ITA Max Pension Salary Load - Applicable
Employees Report");

&FILE.WriteLine(&RundateStr);

&FILE.WriteLine(" ");

&FILE.WriteLine("Employee
ID,EmplRcd,BenefitRcd,FirstName,LastName,Status,Full/Par
Time,Reg/Temp, EE
Class,Union,SalaryPlan,Grade,FTHours,FTE,ActualHours,Hourly
Rate,PlanType,BenefitPlan,CoverageDate,PensionBase,Pension
Base-No Cap,Comments");

/* write data rows using a file layout */

&XXX_PENS_ITA = CreateRecord(Record.XXX_PENS_ITA);

&FILE.SetFileLayout(FileLayout.XXX_PENS_ITA);

/* populate rowset from the table. select only the records
created in this run - by using processinstance */

&SQL1 = CreateSQL("%selectall(:1) order by emplid",
&XXX_PENS_LD_TMP);

/* write each record out to report file */

While &SQL1.Fetch(&XXX_PENS_ITA)

   &FILE.WriteRecord(&XXX_PENS_ITA);

End-While;

Else

   MessageBox(0, "", 0, 0, "Error cannot open file %1",
&filename);

End-If;

&FILE.Close();
```

356. How to export data from a table or a view to a flat file and save the data into a history table
     with the same table structure?

Here is a code example,

```
If &OutFile.SetFileLayout(FileLayout.XXX_PC_FIN_PLAN_FL) Then

        &RecFinPlan = CreateRecord(Record.XXX_PC_FP_VW);
        &SQLSelect = CreateSQL("%Selectall(:1)", &RecFinPlan);


        &RecFinPlanHist = CreateRecord(Record.XXX_PC_FP_HIS);
        &SQLInsert = CreateSQL("%Insert(:1)");


        &Count = 0;


        While &SQLSelect.Fetch(&RecFinPlan)


            /* save into the h
istory table */
            &RecFinPlan.CopyFieldsTo(&RecFinPlanHist);
            &SQLInsert.Execute(&RecFinPlanHist);


            /* write to the extract file */
            &OutFile.WriteRecord(&RecFinPlan);


            &Count = &Count + 1;


        End-While;


Else
        /* do error processing - file layout not correct */
```

```
      MessageBox(0, "", 0, 0, "File layout cannot be openned");


End-If;
```

357. How to perform record field edit from PeopleCode?

Here is a code example,

```
Function EditRecord(&REC As Record) Returns boolean;
Local integer &E;
REM    &REC.ExecuteEdits(%Edit_Required + %Edit_DateRange +
%Edit_YesNo + %Edit_TranslateTable + %Edit_PromptTable +
%Edit_OneZero);
rem &REC.ExecuteEdits(%Edit_Required + %Edit_DateRange +
%Edit_YesNo + %Edit_OneZero);
&REC.ExecuteEdits();
If &REC.IsEditError Then
   For &E = 1 To &REC.FieldCount
   &MYFIELD = &REC.GetField(&E);
     If &MYFIELD.EditError Then
         &MSGNUM = &MYFIELD.MessageNumber;
         &MSGSET = &MYFIELD.MessageSetNumber;
         REM &LOGFILE.WriteLine("**** Record:" | &REC.Name |
         ", Field:" | &MYFIELD.Name);
         &LOGFILE.WriteLine("**** Record:" | &REC.Name | ",
         Field:" | &MYFIELD.Name | ", Value:" |
         &REC.GetField(&E).Value);
         &LOGFILE.WriteLine("**** " | MsgGet(&MSGSET,
         &MSGNUM, ""));
      End-If;
```

```
    End-For;

    Return False;

  Else

  Return True;

  End-If;

  End-Function;
```

358. How to delete the data from another table when deleting a row from a grid on a page?

You can refer to the following code example. It is used in the SavePostChange event of the main record of the grid.

```
Local Rowset &WRK_ROWSET1, &WRK_ROWSET2, &DELETE_RS;

Local Record &WRK_REC, &DELETE_REC;

Local Row &ROW;

Local integer &J, &K;

&WRK_ROWSET1 = GetLevel0();

&WRK_ROWSET2 =

&WRK_ROWSET1.GetRow(1).GetRowset(Scroll.PATS_APPL_SEQ);

For &J = 1 To &WRK_ROWSET2.RowCount

    &ROW = &WRK_ROWSET2.GetRow(&J);

    If &ROW.IsDeleted Then

    &WRK_REC = &ROW.GetRecord(Record.PATS_APPL_SEQ);

    &DELETE_RS = CreateRowset(Record.PATS_APPL_BRAN);

    &DELETE_RS.Fill("WHERE PATS_APPL_ID = :1 And

    PATS_APPL_TYPE_ID = :2 And PATS_SEQ_NO >= :3",

    &WRK_REC.PATS_APPL_ID.Value,

    &WRK_REC.PATS_APPL_TYPE_ID.Value,

    &WRK_REC.PATS_SEQ_NO.Value);

        For &K = 1 To &DELETE_RS.ActiveRowCount
```

```
              &DELETE_REC =
              &DELETE_RS(&K).GetRecord(Record.PATS_APPL_BRAN);
              &DELETE_REC.Delete();
        End-For;
     End-If;
  End-For;
```

359. How to get the website name from a signout URL?

Here is a code example.

```
Local integer&POS, &POS2, &POS3, &I;
&strLogoutURL = %Request.LogoutURL;
&POS = (Find("/psp/", &strLogoutURL) + 5);
&POS2 = Find("/", &strLogoutURL, &POS);
Local string &SiteName, &Char, &ParseSiteName;
&SiteName = Substring(&strLogoutURL, &POS, &POS2 - &POS);
&POS3 = 0; /* code to remove any _number from the signout URL
*/
For &I = 1 To Len(&SiteName)
   &Char = Substring(&SiteName, &I, 1);
   If &Char = "_" Then
      &POS3 = &I;
   End-If;
End-For;
If &POS3 <> 0 Then
&ParseSiteName = Substring(&SiteName, &POS3 + 1,
Len(&SiteName) - &POS3);
   If IsNumber(&ParseSiteName) Then
        &SiteName = Substring(&SiteName, 1, &POS3 - 1);
```

```
  End-If;
 End-If;
```

360. How to build a file validation routine?

Here is a code example to retrieve multiple file names from a directory so that you can do the validation and delete the file if it is not a valid name.

```
&FileRepository = GetURL(@("URL." | "XXX_" | %DbName |
"_FILE_REPOSITORY"));
&ArrFileNames = FindFiles(&FilePathName, %FilePath_Absolute);
For &FileIdx = 1 To &ArrFileNames.Len
   &FileName = &ArrFileNames [&FileIdx];
   &InFileName = Substitute(&FileName, &FileDir, "");
   &LogFile.WriteLine(" ");
   &LogFile.WriteLine(" File Name: " | &InFileName);
   &InFile = GetFile(&FileName, "R", %FilePath_Absolute);
   &InFile.Close();
   If &DelSrc = "Y" Then
   &LogFile.WriteLine(" *** Deleting Source ***");
   &InFile = GetFile(&FileName, "R", %FilePath_Absolute);
   &InFile.Delete();
   &InFile.Close();
   End-If;
End-For;
```

361. How to schedule and run a PS query report from within an Application Engine?

PS query can be called from Application Engine.

Here is a code example,

```
Local ApiObject &aRunQry;
```

```
&PSQry = %Session.GetQuery();
&qryName = "PS Query Name";


/* State Record is Prompt field in PS Query*/
&process_instance = PT_TEST_AET.PROCESS_INSTANCE;


If (&PSQry.Open(&qryName, True, True) <> 0) Then


    &fileLogLM.WriteLine("Cannot Open the Query");


Else

    &aQryPromptRec = &PSQry.PromptRecord;


    /*This instance of the PromptRecord can be passed to
    the PeopleCode Prompt function to prompt the user for
    the runtime values, as follows*/

    &nResult = Prompt(&strQryName | " Prompts", "",
    &aQryPromptRec);

    /* Populate the runtime parameters */
    If &aQryPromptRec <> Null Then
    &nResult = Prompt(&strQryName | " Prompts", "",
    &aQryPromptRec);
    End-If;


    &Date_Format = DateTimeToLocalizedString(%Date, "dd-MMM-
yyyy");


    /* Output File */
    &strFile = "FILE_" | &process_instance;
```

```
                /* Use the RunToFile method to execute the Query and
        return the result to the file specified with Destination.*/
                    &outStrFile = %FilePath | &strFile;
                    MessageBox(0, "", 0, 0, "Query Out File : " |
        &outStrFile);


                    If (&PSQry.RunToFile(&aQryPromptRec, &outStrFile,
        %Query_XLS, 0) = 0) Then


                        MessageBox(0, "", 0, 0, "Result Set saved into file
        successfully.");
                    Else
                        MessageBox(0, "", 0, 0, "Failed to save Result set
        into file.");
                    End-If;
        End-If;
```

362. How to schedule and run a PS query-based BI Publisher report from within an Application Engine?

You can refer to the following code example.

```
/* Reference the report application package at the beginning
of the event */
import PSXP_RPTDEFNMANAGER:*;
/* Local variables declaration* /
Local Record &rcdQryPrompts;
Local string &LanguageCd, &MyTemplate, &MyReportName,
&OutFormat, &State;
Local date &AsOfDate;
```

```
Local PSXP_RPTDEFNMANAGER:ReportDefn&oReportDefn;
/* Need to DoSaveNowincase they have updated any data before
printing */
DoSaveNow();
/* Set XML Publisher report required parameters */
&MyReportName = "XXX_AR_RCPT";
&MyTemplate = "XXX_AR_RCPT_1";
&LanguageCd = "ENG";
&AsOfDate = %Date;
&OutFormat = "PDF";
/* Instantiate (construct) your Report Definition Object */
&oReportDefn = create
PSXP_RPTDEFNMANAGER:ReportDefn(&MyReportName);
/* Get a handle on your Report Definition */
&oReportDefn.Get();
/* Since there are prompts to the query used in this report,
you need to
provide the values for the prompts */
&rcdQryPrompts = &oReportDefn.GetPSQueryPromptRecord();
If Not&rcdQryPrompts = Null Then
 &oReportDefn.SetPSQueryPromptRecord(&rcdQryPrompts);
 &rcdQryPrompts.DEPOSIT_BU.Value =
 DEPOSIT_CONTROL.DEPOSIT_BU;
 &rcdQryPrompts.DEPOSIT_ID.Value =
 DEPOSIT_CONTROL.DEPOSIT_ID;
 &rcdQryPrompts.PAYMENT_SEQ_NUM.Value =
 PAYMENT.PAYMENT_SEQ_NUM;
End-If;
/* Kick of the report process */
```

297

```
&oReportDefn.ProcessReport(&MyTemplate, &LanguageCd,
&AsOfDate, &OutFormat);
CommitWork();
/* Display Report to the user */
&oReportDefn.DisplayOutput();
```

363. How to schedule and run a process from PeopleCode?

There are two ways to do it.

You can schedule to run a process from PeopleCode using the ScheduleProcess() function.

```
&&PROCESS_NAME = "SQRNAME";
&&PROCESS_TYPE = "SQR Report";
&&RUN_CNTL_ID = "YOUR_RUN_ID";
&&RUN_CONTROL = ScheduleProcess(&PROCESS_TYPE,
&&PROCESS_NAME, "2", &RUN_CNTL_ID, &PRCS_INST);
If &&RC != 0   /*"1" = client "2" = server */
   Winmessage("Error: Error Scheduling SQR Process,
   RC="/&RUN_CONTROL);
End-If;
```

You can also schedule/run a process from PeopleCode using the CreateProcessRequest() function.

```
&RQST = CreateProcessRequest();
&RQST.JobName = "CreateLPOReport";
&RQST.RunControlID = XXX_LPSDATA_AET.XXX_LPS_ID;
&RQST.RunLocation = "PSUNX";
&RQST.RunDateTime = %Datetime;
&RQST.TimeZone = %ServerTimeZone;
```

298

```
&RQST.ProcessType = "SQR Report";

&RQST.ProcessName = {ProcessName};
```

364. How to use the SendMail function to send an Email?

You can refer to the following code example.

```
Local string &MAIL_CC, &MAIL_TO, &MAIL_BCC, &MAIL_SUBJECT,
&MAIL_TITLES, &MAIL_TEXT, &MAIL_FILES, &MAIL_FROM, &REPLYTO,
&SENDER;
Local number &MAIL_FLAGS, &RET;
&MAIL_FLAGS = 0;
&MAIL_TO = "";
&MAIL_CC = "";
&MAIL_BCC = "";
&MAIL_SUBJECT = "Test Email";
&MAIL_TEXT = "Sending an Email from PeopleCode.";
&MAIL_FILES = "";
&MAIL_TITLES = "";
&MAIL_FROM = "";
&MAIL_SEP = ";";
&CONTTYPE = "";
&REPLYTO = "";
&SENDER = "";
&RET = SendMail(&MAIL_FLAGS, &MAIL_TO, &MAIL_CC, &MAIL_BCC,
&MAIL_SUBJECT, &MAIL_TEXT, &MAIL_FILES, &MAIL_TITLES,
&MAIL_FROM, &MAIL_SEP, &CONTTYPE, &REPLYTO, &SENDER);
If &RET <> 0 Then
MessageBox(0, "", 0, 0, "Return code from SendMail= " |
&RET);
```

```
    /*Do error processing here*/
End-If;
```

Note: Make sure your SMTP server is configured properly, or the SendMail function will fail.

In order to send a HTML based email, you need to specify the variable for the content type as follows,

```
&CONTTYPE = "Content-type: text/html";
```

Note the SendMail function has been deprecated. Use the MCFOutboundEmailapplication class of the PT_MCF_MAIL application package instead.

365. How to use the PT_MCF_MAIL application package to send an Email?

```
Import PT_MCF_MAIL:*;
Local string &JRNL_ID, &JRNL_BU, &TEXT1, &TEXT2, &MAIL_TEXT;
Local date &JRNL_DT;
Local integer &I, &RET;
Local Rowset &RS;
Local PT_MCF_MAIL:MCFMailUtil&emailUtil = create
 PT_MCF_MAIL:MCFMailUtil();
Local PT_MCF_MAIL:MCFOutboundEmail&email = create
 PT_MCF_MAIL:MCFOutboundEmail();
&email.Subject = MsgGetText(25003, 42, "In Flight Journals -
 Forced Error");;
&email.ContentType = "text/html";
/* Get the email Address of the user */
If All(XXX_JNLLAP_AET.OPRID) Then
```

```
SQLExec("Select EMAILID From PSUSEREMAIL Where OPRID = :1",
XXX_JNLLAP_AET.OPRID, &MAIL_TO);
End-If;
/* Initiatite the email sent status to not successful */
&RET = 1;
If All(&MAIL_TO) Then
&MAIL_TEXT = "";
&TEXT1 = MsgGetExplainText(25003, 42, "Message not found");
&TEXT2 = "<table border=0 cellspacing=0 cellpadding=0
width=700 >" | "<tr><td width=140 valign=top
><p><b><u>Business Unit</u></b></p></td>" | "<td width=140
valign=top ><p><b><u>Journal ID</u></b></p></td>" | "<td
width=140 valign=top ><p><b><u>Journal
Date</u></b></p></td></tr>";
/* For each journal the user submitted and has been errored
 out by this program, provide the journal id, date and BU of
 the journal */
&RS = CreateRowset(Record.XXX_JNIF_TMP);
&RS.Fill("Where PROCESS_INSTANCE = :1 And SUBMIT_OPRID = :2",
XXX_JNLLAP_AET.PROCESS_INSTANCE, XXX_JNLLAP_AET.OPRID);
&RS.Sort(XXX_JNIF_TMP.JOURNAL_DATE, "A");
/* Get Journal ID and date of the journals errored out and
 add the info into the email body */
For &I = 1 To &RS.ActiveRowCount
&JRNL_BU = &RS.GetRow(&I).XXX_JNIF_TMP.BUSINESS_UNIT.Value;
&JRNL_ID = &RS.GetRow(&I).XXX_JNIF_TMP.JOURNAL_ID.Value;
&JRNL_DT = &RS.GetRow(&I).XXX_JNIF_TMP.JOURNAL_DATE.Value;
&TEXT2 = &TEXT2 | "<tr><td width=140 valign=top ><p>" |
 &JRNL_BU | "</p></td>" | "<td width=140 valign=top ><p>" |
```

```
 &JRNL_ID | "</p></td>" | "<td width=140 valign=top ><p>" |
 &JRNL_DT | "</p></td></tr>";
End-For;
&MAIL_TEXT = "<html><body><p>" | &TEXT1 | "</p><p>" | &TEXT2
 "</table></p></body></html>";
If &emailUtil.ValidateAddress(&MAIL_TO) Then
&email.From = "peoplesoft@xxx.com";
&email.Recipients = &MAIL_TO;
&email.Text = &MAIL_TEXT;
&response = &email.Send();
&validSentAddr = &email.ValidSentAddresses;
&invalidAddr = &email.InvalidAddresses;
&validUnsentAddr = &email.ValidUnsentAddresses;
&errDescr = &email.ErrorDescription;
rem &errDetails = &email.ErrorDetails;
Evaluate &response
When %ObEmail_Delivered
&RET = 0;
MessageBox(0, "", 0, 0, "Email delivered to " | &emailAddr |
 ".");
Break;
When %ObEmail_NotDelivered
MessageBox(0, "", 0, 0, "Email NOT delivered to " |
 &emailAddr | ".");
If All(&invalidAddr) Then
MessageBox(0, "", 0, 0, &invalidAddr | " is not a valid email
 address.");
End-If;
If All(&validUnsentAddr) Then
```

```
MessageBox(0, "", 0, 0, "Email has not been sent to " |
 &validUnsentAddr | " due to system problems.");
End-If;
Break;
When %ObEmail_PartiallyDelivered
MessageBox(0, "", 0, 0, "Email partially delivered.");
If All(&validSentAddr) Then
MessageBox(0, "", 0, 0, "Email delivered to " |
 &validSentAddr | ".");
End-If;
If All(&invalidAddr) Then
MessageBox(0, "", 0, 0, &invalidAddr | " is not a valid email
 address.");
End-If;
 If All(&validUnsentAddr) Then
 MessageBox(0, "", 0, 0, "Email has not been sent to " |
  &validUnsentAddr | " due to system problems.");
 End-If;
 Break;
 When %ObEmail_FailedBeforeSending
 MessageBox(0, "", 0, 0, "Email failed before sending. Error
  Descr: " | &errDescr);
 Break;
 End-Evaluate;
 Else
 MessageBox(0, "", 0, 0, &emailAddr | " is not valid email
  address.");
 End-If;
 End-If;
```

```
 /* Update the table with email sent status */

If &RET = 0 Then

/* Email sent successfully */

Else

/* Email sending failed */

End-If;
```

366. How to display a message by executing PeopleCode immediately upon user sign on?

For our first example, a simple welcome message is displayed to the user.

Firstly, create a new work record and insert a single field into the record:

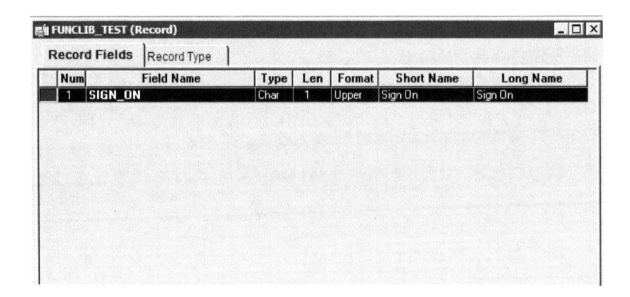

In the FieldFormula event, add your Sign-on PeopleCode as a function:

```
Function ShowMessage

Local Record &Operator_Rec = CreateRecord(Record.PSOPRDEFN);

&Operator_Rec.OPRID.Value = %SignonUserId;

&Operator_Rec.SelectByKey();

SetAuthenticationResult(True, %SignonUserId, "Welcome " |

&Operator_Rec.OPRDEFNDESC.Value, False, 0);

End-Function;
```

This displays a welcome message to the user based on the system variable %SignonUserId. The usual message functions, such as 'MessageBox' do not work in Sign-on PeopleCode. To get around this (in a quick-and-dirty kind of way), I am using the 'SetAuthenticationResult' function, passing in a piece of text as a third parameter.

Now open up the delivered record FUNCLIB_PWDCNTL. Open the FieldChange event on

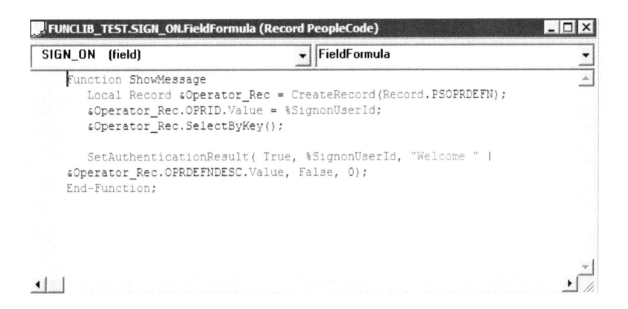

the PWDCNTL field. At the top of the code, add a reference to your new function:

And then, in the function itself, make a call to the 'ShowMessage' function. When developing Sign-on PeopleCode, it's important to wrap the code with your own user ID, at least as a starting point. That way, your change should not impact other users:

```
PWDCNTL  (field)                                    ▼   FieldChange

    Declare Function ShowMessage PeopleCode FUNCLIB_TEST.SIGN_ON FieldFormula;

    Function PASSWORD_CONTROLS();
        rem get values from psoprden and pssecoptions;
        Local string &USERID = %SignonUserId;
        Local number &FailedNum, &AccountLock;
        Local date &LASTCHANGE;
        Local boolean &PSAuthResult, &Ext_Auth_Value;
        /* 8.50 Replacing SQL object by SQLExec below */ /*
            &REC = CreateRecord(Record.PSOPRDEFN);
            &SQL = CreateSQL("%SELECTALL(:1) WHERE OPRID =:2", &REC, &USERID);
            While &SQL.Fetch(&REC)
                &FailedNum = &REC.FAILEDLOGINS.VALUE;
                &LASTCHANGE = &REC.LASTPSWDCHANGE.VALUE;

        If %SignonUserId = "XYZ" Then
            ShowMessage();
        End-If;

        SQLExec("SELECT ACCTLOCK, FAILEDLOGINS, %DateOut(LASTPSWDCHANGE) from PSOPRDEFN WHERE
    OPRID =:1", &USERID, &AccountLock, &FailedNum, &LASTCHANGE); /* PP replaces above SQL
    object */
        rem SetAuthenticationResult( True, %SignonUserId, "Test Message Delivered", False,
```

Now try logging into the system via the browser. You should receive a simple welcome message:

Welcome [PS] Peoplesoft Superuser

Sign in to PeopleSoft

This is not a very helpful example, as you can't do anything further after receiving the message except return to the sign-on page. But it does help to quickly demonstrate how Sign-on PeopleCode works without getting into too many complexities.

D. Example 2 – Transfer to Component

Next, let us look at a slightly more useful example. This function transfers the user directly to a component via the use of 'GeneralComponentContentURL' and 'SetAuthenticationResult'. Note that any form of 'transfer' function will produce an error if the user does not have security over the destination page.

You can create your 'Transfer' code as a function, and use the same record, field, and event as before

```
01
02    Function TransferUser
03    Local string &url
04    = GenerateComponentContentURL(Portal.EMPLOYEE,
05    Node.HRMS, MenuName.MAINTAIN_SECURITY, %Market,
06    Component.CHANGE_PASSWORD, Page.CHANGE_PASSWORD,
07    %Action_UpdateDisplay);
08    &message_text = "Your password needs to change. <a href="" |
09    &url | "">Click here to continue</a><p>";
10    SetAuthenticationResult(True, %SignonUserId, &message_text, False);
11    End-Function;
12
```

```
SIGN_ON  (field)                                              ▼  FieldFormula
  Function ShowMessage
      Local Record &Operator_Rec = CreateRecord(Record.PSOPRDEFN);
      &Operator_Rec.OPRID.Value = %SignonUserId;
      &Operator_Rec.SelectByKey();

      SetAuthenticationResult( True, %SignonUserId, "Welcome " | &Operator_Rec.OPRDEFNDESC.Value, False, 0);
  End-Function;

  Function TransferUser
      Local string &url = GenerateComponentContentURL(Portal.EMPLOYEE, Node.HRMS, MenuName.MAINTAIN_SECURITY, %Market, Component.CHANGE_PASSWORD,
  Page.CHANGE_PASSWORD, %Action_UpdateDisplay);

      &message_text = "Your password needs to change. <a href='" | &url | "'>Click here to continue</a><p>";

      SetAuthenticationResult( True, %SignonUserId, &message_text, False);

  End-Function;
```

Then, in the FUNCLIB_PWDCNTL record, you need to modify the code you previously added to call the new TransferUser function:

Upon logging, the user should receive the message about changing their password:

Your password needs to change. Click here to continue

Sign in to PeopleSoft

367. How to control component save processing?

There are a couple of methods and properties which controls or depends on the component save flag.

This is how the Save Warning is triggered for a component. When a component is loaded, the Component Processor maintains a flag value that indicates whether the component has been modified. This flag is set when the user modifies a field value on the online page or when a field value is changed via PeopleCode logic. With this flag value, whenever the user tries to navigate away from the component, the Component Processor checks the flag. If the

309

flag is set, a Save Warning is issued; otherwise, the user is logged out of the component. The value of this specific flag is reset after each database insertion (after SavePreChange), which prevents the warning from appearing when the user has already saved the component. However, a code in your Save Post Change could set the flag again.

Here are some of the functions and properties which could be potentially helpful in tackling the Save Warning issues.

ComponentChanged() – This function will return a Boolean value based on if the component was changed after last save. You could use this function to determine the component level flag value and based on that you could write your logic.

```
If ComponentChanged() Then

    WinMessage("Your Message Text",0);

Else

    Transfer(….);

End-If;
```

SetComponentChanged() – This function enables you to programmatically set the flag at the component level. In some cases, it might be necessary for the system to perform the save processing even if the user hasn't modified any values on the page. This function accomplishes that by triggering the Save Warning or Save Processing, regardless of whether any changes have been made to the component.

```
SetComponentChanged();

DoSaveNow();
```

Note you can use the SetComponentChanged() function in the PageActivate PeopleCode of a page, such as a run control page, so that the theSaveEdit PeopleCode can be triggered even there hasn't been any change to the page when user clicksa button, such as a Run button, to go to the next page.

SetSaveWarningFilter() – Use this function to supress the Save Warning irrespective of whether the component level flag is set or not. If you use this function the component processor will ignore the component level flag value and let the user to navigate away from the component without issuing any Save Warning. This function takes a Boolean value as argument. Passing True will direct the component processor to ignore the flag whereas passing an argument of False will make the component behave in its normal way.

310

```
&myRec.DESCR.Value = "My Description";

SetSaveWarningFilter(True);
```

Set Component Changed (Page Field Property) – Sometimes, for certain fields, even if the user changes some value on the online page we may not require to initiate the Save Processing or issue the Save Warning. This page field level property comes handy in those scenarios.

This property can be found in the Use tab of the page field property. This will determine if the component flag needs to be set when the user changes the value of the field. This property determines the behavior only for user intervention and does not govern the PeopleCode changes.

Disable Saving Page (Component property) – If the entire purpose of the component you have designed is to just display information or to act as an intermediate component, then you can use this property to avoid the Save warning. This property can be found on the Use tab of the component.

Checking this field will hide the save button from the component and will suppress the save warning. If you want to permanently suppress the Save Warning for the entire component this is the best option to choose as it provides the mechanism to achieve the objective with minimal impact.

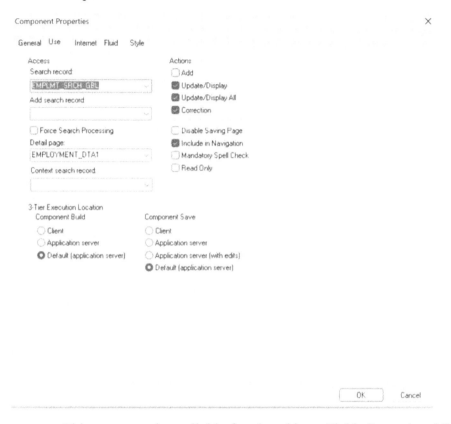

IsChanged Property – This property is available for the objects Field, Record and Row. This property will return a Boolean value indicating whether the object has changed or not. This property will be helpful in doing some special processing for which you need to dynamically know which object has changed.

```
Local Number &I;

&I = 1;

For &I = 1 To &myRecord.FieldCount

    If &myRecord.GetField(&i).IsChanged Then

    End-If;

End-For;
```

SetComponentChanged (Property) – This property is read-write and can be accessed at both the Field and Rowset Level. When this value is set to True, it informs the component processor that any modifications made to the Field/Rowset using PeopleCode will trigger the component save flag and prompt a Save Warning. Conversely, if the value is set to False, the component changed flag will not be set when the Field/Rowset value is altered programmatically using PeopleCode. The example below demonstrates the usage of this property, where a field's value is programmatically modified without requiring or initiating a Save Warning.

```
&myRec.DESCR.SetComponentChanged = False;

&myRec.DESCR.Value = "New Description";

&myRec.DESCR.SetComponentChanged = True;
```

368. How to work with collections in CI?

In simple words collection is same as a rowset in your component buffer. You can navigate through the collection and update/delete any row in the collection as you do with rowset in the component. Let's see how this can be achieved by PeopleCode.

To assign the collection (rowset) to a variable you can use the below code.

```
&CI = %Session.GetCompIntfc(CompIntfc.MY_CI);
&CI.KEY ="Key";
&CI.Get();
/* Get the collection(rowset) */
&Collection = &CI.MY_COLLECTION;
```

Your collection name may not always be same as the rowset. So you should verify with the CI to get the correct collection name.

To get the number of rows in the rowset, similar to the ActiveRowCount property in the rowsets you can use the Count property.

```
/* To get the number of rows */
&nRows = &Collection.Count;
```

Now to insert a new row to the collection you can use InserItem method. You need to specify the index (row number in rowset) while using the method.
&myItem = &Collection.InsertItem(1);

The above code will insert a new row at the first row. It is, the new row's row count will be 2. This is similar to clicking the + button in the PIA page. If we click the + button on the first row, the new row will be inserted as the second row.

Now to update the value in this row, you can directly call the property (corresponding to Field in component) and assign.

```
&myItem.NAME = "My Name";
```

Now if your component interface is in interactive mode and your grid in the component has some code to sort the grid at field change you should be very careful. Eg: when you change a date, the grid will sort based on the ascending value of date. In such case it can happen that when you enter the value, the rowset will get sorted and when you update the second field, you may be actually updating the second field in some other row as the index has changed due to sorting. In that case you need to loop back and get the original Item(row) and then proceed with updating.

Now to get the Nth row of the collection (rowset) you can use the below code.

```
&myItem = &Collection.Item(&RowNumber);
```

Now to delete the row from the component, you can deleteItem method. When using the method, you should specify the index of the row to be deleted.

```
&Collection.DeleteItem(2);
```

If your component is effective dated, to get the effective dated row you can use CurrentItem method.

```
&effDatedItem = &Collection.CurrentItem;
```

To fetch the row number of the effective dated row, you can directly use the CurrentItemNum property.

```
&CurrentRowNumber = &Collection.CurrentItemNum;
```

All these above logics can be clubbed to loop up to level 3. For example you can use the below code.

```
&CI  = %Session.GetCompIntfc(CompIntfc.MY_CI);

/* Pass the Key */
&CI.KEY = "Key";
&CI.Get();

/* Get Level 1 Collection */
&Collection1 = &CI.COLLECTION_ONE;
&MyItem1 = &Collection1.Item(1);

/*Get Level 2 Collection */
&Collection2 = &MyItem1.COLLECTION_TWO;
```

314

```
&MyItem2 = &Collection2.Item(1);

/*Get Level3 Row */
&Collection3 = &MyItem2.COLLECTION_THREE;
&MyItem3 = &Collection3.Item(1);

/* Updating Level 3 row */
&MyItem3.FIELD_PROPERTY = "My Value";
```

369. How to create a new style and change the style of a page element?

Are you tired of using the same set of styles and colors every day? PeopleSoft offers a wide range of options to completely transform the appearance of the application. You have the ability to modify the style of the entire application, create new styles, and dynamically change the styles of page elements using PeopleCode.

Style sheets are essentially a collection of different style classes. Each style class has its own properties such as font, color, size, and background color. Once you create a style sheet, you can apply the styles to multiple objects, ensuring consistency throughout your application.

PeopleSoft comes with a few pre-defined styles, but you can customize the theme and styles of the application by navigating to the following link: PeopleTools -> Utilities -> Administration -> PeopleTools Options.

Here, you can modify the styles by changing the value in the "Style Sheet Name" field. After logging out and logging back in, you will see the changes take effect. In some cases, you may need to clear the web server and browser cache to ensure the changes are properly reflected.

To create your own styles, open the application designer and go to File -> New, then select Style Sheet. For simplicity, you can choose the standard style sheet. If you're familiar with CSS, you can explore other options as well.

To define your style, double-click on the object within the free form object, and then double-click again to see the list of objects such as edit boxes and hyperlinks. Similar to working in MS Word, you can make changes to the object to achieve your desired style. Don't forget to save your changes, and you're all set with your new style!

The PeopleSoft Field objects have an associated style property. You can use this property to set the style of the object.

```
&fField = GetRecord(Record.MY_REC).GetField(Field.MY_FLD);
/* Seeting the style to editbox error */
&fField.Style = "PSERROR";
```

The style you mention must be defined inside the style sheet you selected for the page. The default styles for any object can be found in the object properties box (Alt+Enter).

Here is an example to set the style dynamically.

```
&fField = GetRecord(Record.MY_REC).GetField(Field.MY_FLD);

/* Check if value is there */
If None(&fField.Value) Then

/* If no value then highlight the field in red and throw
error. */

&fField.Style = "PSERROR";
Error "Value is required for the field …";

Else
/* Change back the field to normal editbox style */
&fField.Style = "PSEDITBOX";
End-If;
```

370. **Error**: "Java Exception: java.lang.OutOfMemoryError: Java heap space"

Cause: The java heap size on the web server is not big enough.

Solution: Ask PS Admin to increase the heap size on the web server.

371. **Error**: "Invalid row number 1 for class Rowset method GetRow"

Cause: When looping through rows of a scroll or a grid to get the value of a record field on a row, it finds an extra row or it is missing one row.

Solution: Check all the rows in the table involved when looping through and make sure row counts match.

PEOPLESOFT INSTALLATION

372. How to run PeopleTools locally?

Depending on where you work, you may either run PeopleTools (Application Designer, data mover, etc.) locally or across the network. Typically shortcuts are created to run PeopleTools over the network.

The main reason for running PeopleTools locally is Performance. You don't have to worry about issues related to network glitches or the file server being down

You can roll your own configuration file with the configuration you want.

To run PeopleTools locally, there are two things you'll need to do:

Copy the relevant files from the network to a local directory (e.g. C:\Oracle\PeopleSoft)

Create or copy an existing configuration file and load it through Configuration Manager

Copying the relevant files to a local directory

You can install PeopleSoft files under C:\PTools. You can use any directory

you want but use a path without spaces so C:\Program Files is not ideal.

Copy everything under the PeopleTools folder

from the PeopleSoft file server. This can be around 10GB, so make sure you have enough space! Note that the directories in the setup folder are required for generating browser compare reports.

Creating and updating the configuration file

To start the configuration manager, run pscfg.exe under PS_HOME\bin\client\winx86 on your local machine:

E.g. C:\Oracle\PeopleSoft\bin\client\winx86\pscfg.exe.

The best way to go here is to just copy an existing configuration (.cfg) file from the file server where you run PeopleTools and then modify it. To load an existing configuration file, go to the Import/Export tab in the configuration manager and press the Import From a File button and select the appropriate configuration (.cfg) file.

To roll your own configuration file, start the configuration manager and specify at least the following:

Startup tab:

Database type

Server name

Database name

Connect ID

Connect Password & Confirmation Password

Profile tab -> Edit Default

Database connection type & Database name

If you want three-tier (application server) access, you also need to specify the application server name, machine name/IP address, and port number.

Navigate to Import/Export tab and export your configuration file to store a copy on file. Otherwise, the settings will only be maintained in the Windows registry.

Test login to Application Designer

To start Application Designer, run pside.exe under PS_HOME\bin\client\winx86.

E.g. C:\Oracle\PeopleSoft\bin\client\winx86\pside.exe.

First try a two-tier login. Then if you have an application server configured, try a three tier login using Application Server as the database type. Hopefully it all works for you.

If you receive error messages starting configuration manager or Application Designer make sure that you have copied the relevant files locally. If files are missing you may get a tuxedo error.

Useful tweaks

In the startup tab, specify the user ID you commonly use to login to Application Designer

In the startup tab, you can specify the location of the local cache in the cache files section

Use the Client Setup tab to create shortcut icons on your start menu. You need to tick the links you want (e.g.Application Designer, Configuration Manager, Data Mover) as well as ticking Install Workstation. Then press apply.

373. How to run SQR locally?

To run SQRs locally, copy the SQRs/SQCs from the file server to a local directory (e.g. C:\Oracle\PeopleSoft\sqr), go to the following settings in Profile -> Edit Default Profile -> Process scheduler; change SQR executables (e.g. C:\Oracle\PeopleSoft\bin\sqr\...\binw), and change the SQR report search path to where you copied the SQRs (e.g. C:\Oracle\PeopleSoft\sqr),. Clear out SQR report search path or set these to point to your file server as fall backs if the SQR/SQC is not found on your local machine.

Make sure you have a copy of the pssqr.ini file in your local SQR folder

PIA

381. How to navigate to a page in PeopleSoft with a URL directly?

The format of a URL to directly navigate to a page with portal navigation is,

http://server/servlet_name/SiteName/PortalName/NodeName/content_type/content_id?content_parm

For components, content parameters are:

Page=pagename&action=action_value&key_id=key_value

If you do not specify the Page then it goes to the first page in component.

Action = A - Add, U - Update/Display, L - Update/Display All, C – Correction

KeyIDs are actual Field Name of the Search record that has search key attribute set.

To display a page and navigate to that page for e.g the URL Maintenance Page in PeopleTools, the URL will be

https://servername/psp/ps/EMPLOYEE/EMPL/c/UTILITIES.URL_TABLE.GBL?Page=URL_TABLE&Action=U&URL_ID=CMDOCDB

Here is an example:

https://servername:port/psc/instance
name/EMPLOYEE/Node/c/XXX_MENU.XXX_COMP_CMP.GBL?page=XXX_PAGE_NM

382. How to use SQL to obtain the navigation path of a component?

Instead of using Find Object Navigation via PIA, you can use the following SQL to get the navigation path of a component.

```
SELECT level3.PORTAL_URI_SEG2, LEVEL0.PORTAL_LABEL || ' > '
|| LEVEL1.PORTAL_LABEL || ' >'  || LEVEL2.PORTAL_LABEL || ' >
'  || level3.PORTAL_LABEL PATH_TO_COMPONENT
FROM PSPRSMDEFN level3
, PSPRSMDEFN level2
, PSPRSMDEFN level1
```

```
, PSPRSMDEFN LEVEL0
WHERE level3.PORTAL_URI_SEG2 = 'NAME_OF_THE_PS_COMPONENT'
AND level3.PORTAL_PRNTOBJNAME = level2.PORTAL_OBJNAME
AND level2.PORTAL_PRNTOBJNAME = level1.PORTAL_OBJNAME
AND level1.PORTAL_PRNTOBJNAME = LEVEL0.PORTAL_OBJNAME
AND level3.PORTAL_NAME = level2.PORTAL_NAME
AND level2.PORTAL_NAME = level1.PORTAL_NAME
AND level1.PORTAL_NAME = LEVEL0.PORTAL_NAME;
```

For example, you can use the following SQL to get the navigation path of all components with their names starting as VCHR.

```
SELECT level3.PORTAL_URI_SEG2, LEVEL0.PORTAL_LABEL || ' > '
   || LEVEL1.PORTAL_LABEL || ' >'  || LEVEL2.PORTAL_LABEL ||
   ' > '  ||  level3.PORTAL_LABEL PATH_TO_COMPONENT
FROM PSPRSMDEFN level3
, PSPRSMDEFN level2
, PSPRSMDEFN level1
, PSPRSMDEFN LEVEL0
WHERE level3.PORTAL_URI_SEG2 LIKE '%VCHR'
AND level3.PORTAL_PRNTOBJNAME = level2.PORTAL_OBJNAME
AND level2.PORTAL_PRNTOBJNAME = level1.PORTAL_OBJNAME
AND level1.PORTAL_PRNTOBJNAME = LEVEL0.PORTAL_OBJNAME
AND level3.PORTAL_NAME = level2.PORTAL_NAME
AND level2.PORTAL_NAME = level1.PORTAL_NAME
AND level1.PORTAL_NAME = LEVEL0.PORTAL_NAME;
```

The query result of the above SQL is as follows,

321

PORTAL_URI_SEG2	PATH_TO_COMPONENT
1 VCHR_ACCTG_ENTRIES	Accounts Payable > Review Accounts Payable Info >Vouchers > Accounting Entries
2 VCHR_ACCTG_ENTRIES	Navigation Collections > Payables >My Reporting & Analysis >
3 VCHR_WTHUPD_WRK	Accounts Payable > Vouchers >Maintain > Selective Withholding Update
4 VCHR_ACCTG_UNBAL	Accounts Payable > Review Accounts Payable Info >Vouchers > Unbalanced Accounting Entries
5 VCHR_APPROVE	Accounts Payable > Vouchers >Approve > Approve Voucher
6 VCHR_APPROVE	Navigation Collections > Buyer >Approvals >
7 VCHR_APPROVE	Navigation Collections > Manage Departments >Review and Approve Purchases >
8 VCHR_APPROVE	Navigation Collections > Manage Practice >Review & Approve Purchases >

PROCESSES

383. A run control record must have OPRID and RUN_CNTL_ID, and both fields should be key fields.

384. If a process doesn't show up on the process request page, check if the process has been defined in the process definition page, and if the process has appropriate process groups in the definition (try process group for the module, e.x., PCALL, GLALL), and user's permission to access to the process group.

385. Process run notification distribution list is set in Process Definition -> Notification.

386. Process Output Destination is only available when Output Type selected is File or Printer.

387. To send report output directly to a printer, in the Destination tab of the process definition, set Type to 'Printer', Destination Source to 'Process Definition', and Output Destination to the printer queue name.

388. The notification and distributions can also be stored at the job, and jobset level, where jobs give you the option to override the process definition; and jobsets will always override job and process definitions.

389. To stop a recurring process permanently, cancel the queued process request and then delete the request. Note you might have to login in as the user id which was used to create the process request in order to delete the request.

390. You can check the PSPRCSRQST table for all historical process requests and their run statuses.

```
SELECT * FROM PSPRCSRQST;
```

391. How to check which processes a user has recently run?

You can check the PS_PMN_PRCSLIST table to see if a process has been run through a process scheduler and which user has run that process at what time.

```
SELECT * FROM PS_PMN_PRCSLIST;
```

392. **Error**: Process stuck at the queued status and are never initiated

Cause:

1. A server agent (NT/Unix) has not been selected to run the process, and there is no default server agent set for the process in the process definition.

2. Process scheduler server agent on which the process runs is down or crashed.

393. **Error**: "You are not authorized to run the process"

Cause: The process profile and primary permission list may not have been set up properly in the user profile.

Solution: The process profile contains the permissions a user requires for running batch processes through process scheduler. The primary permission list determines which data permissions to grant to a user.

394. **Error**: A process doesn't show up on the process list after it is kicked off from the System Process Requests page

Cause:

1. Process definition for the process may not have been defined.

2. Process Group configuration may not be right in the process definition.

3. User profile file may need to add System Administrator role.

PS QUERY

395. You can have trees and tree nodes in a PS query.

396. You can use 'like' or 'not like' as an operator in the query expression.

Comparison value used in a 'like' expression may be a string that contains wildcard characters. The wildcard characters that PeopleSoft Query recognizes are % and _.

% matches any string of zero or more characters. For example, C% matches any string starting with C, including C alone.

_ matches any single character. For example, _ones matches any five-character string ending with ones, such as Jones or Cones.

PeopleSoft Query also recognizes any wild-card characters.

To use one of the wild-card characters as a literal character (for example, to include a % in your string), precede the character with a \ (for example, percent\%).

397. If the performance of a query is very slow, try to flatten out the SQL behind the query. If the performance of the SQL is slow, try to avoid using any views in it, and use physical tables instead. This is because it takes more time to retrieve data from a view comparing with from a physical table.

398. If a query has a performance issue and it is very slow, you can turn off Query Statistics. Go to Run Query Statistics in Utilities -> Query Administration -> Settings and see if it is checked, and uncheck it if so.

399. How to show all PS queries that reference a particular record or a particular field?

The following SQL can show you all PS Queries that reference a particular record:

```
SELECT A.OPRID, A.QRYNAME
FROM PSQRYRECORD
WHERE RECNAME = 'PERSONAL_PHONE';
```

This can be expanded to all queries that reference any record included in a project:

```
SELECT A.OPRID, A.QRYNAME
FROM PSQRYRECORD A, PSPROJECTITEM B
WHERE A.RECNAME = B.OBJECTVALUE1
AND B.OBJECTTYPE = 0
AND B.PROJECTNAME = 'PROJECT NAME';
```

Finally, here are the two equivalent statements for fields:

```
SELECT A.OPRID, A.QRYNAME
FROM PSQRYFIELD A
WHERE A.FIELDNAME = 'BIRTHDATE';
```

```
SELECT A.OPRID, A.QRYNAME
FROM PSQRYFIELD A, PSPROJECTITEM B
WHERE A.FIELDNAME = B.OBJECTVALUE1
AND B.OBJECTTYPE = 2
AND B.PROJECTNAME = 'PROJECT_NAME';
```

400. You can turn on Query Logging for each query. This will give you information on each query that is executed, including userid, row counts, and timings.

This is on the same navigation/component as the Query Statistics but on the first tab (Admin). Search for the query you want to add Logging to, then select Logging On.

PeopleSoft Query uses query access group trees to control the security of the tables You can grant and restrict access to entire query trees or portions of them through the Permission List Access Groups page (PeopleTools -> Security -> Permission & Roles -> Permission Lists -> Query -> Access Group Permissions).

401. The Query Access Group Manager is located at PeopleTools -> Maintain Security -> Query Security.

You may need to run Enable Access List Cache, when adding/removing records from a query access list tree, adding/removing a query access list tree from a permission list or a role. (Maintain Security -> Query Security -> Enable Access List Cache)

402. Exporting a file as a CSV can lead to formatting issues due to line feeds, carriage returns, and commas. These formatting issues can cause problems when using data visualization tools that connect to the data file, such as Excel or PowerBI. To address this, you can utilize expressions to eliminate these characters from the fields. For instance, the provided sample expression removes commas, carriage returns (char(13)), and line feeds (char(10)) from a DESCRLONG_NOTES field.

```
REPLACE (REPLACE (REPLACE (DESCRLONG_NOTES, ',' , ''),
CHAR(13) , ''), CHAR(10), '')
```

403. You can concatenate related parent/child fields to create unique values in a column for data analysis. The following sample expression combines two fields with a dash separator,

```
CONCAT(B.PROJECT_ID,'-',B.SUB_PROJECT_NUM)
```

404. You can set the following security in Permission List -> Query -> Query Profile.

    Only allowed to run Queries

    Allow creation of Public Queries,

    Allow creation of Role, Process and Archive Queries

    Allow use of Distinct

    Allow use of 'Any Join'

    Allow use of Subquery/Exists

    Allow use of Union

    Allow use of Expressions

    Maximum Rows Fetched

Maximum Run Time in Minutes

Maximum Joins Allowed

Maximum 'In Tree' Criteria

Query Output

Query Output to Excel

405. **Error**: user gets "You are not authorized to access this component" when clicking a report link in the system generated email sent by a recurring query

   Cause: User doesn't have access to the Report Index component

   Solution: Grant access to the component CDM_RPT (Report Index) to the permission list of an appropriate role of the user.

406. **Error**: "QDM could not load query definition"

   Cause: The primary cause of this error message is the Record is NOT contained in a Query Access Group attached to a permission list in the User Profile.

   Solution: If you know for certain that the record(s) involved is in your profile, then it is likely your Definition of Security is not correct. You would need to add the PeopleTools definition security (in order to run the delivered Security Queries) to your Primary Permission.

RUN CONTROL

407. The run control id field must be set as a search key in the run control record, otherwise, the search page may not show up, or the Add button on the run control page may not work.

408. Use the PRCSRUNCNTL_SBP subpage as the subpage of a standard run control page.

409. Use the PRCSRUNCNTL record as the run control record, if Oprid and Process Instance are the only two required parameters and no other parameters are required.

410. How to delete a run control id from a list of run control ids from behind the scenes?

To delete a run control id from the list of the run control ids from PIA, you can delete it from the PS_PRCSRUNCNTL table from behind the scenes.

```
DELETE FROM PS_PRCSRUNCNTL
WHERE OPRID = 'USER_ID';
```

To delete a run control for an Application Engine process, you can go to the PS_AERUNCONTROL table to delete a run control id that will not be needed anymore.

```
DELETE FROM PS_AERUNCONTROL
WHERE OPRID = 'USER_ID';
```

SECURITY

411. How to implement row-level data security?

You can use the PERALL_SEC_QRY, PERS_SRCH_QRY, POI_SEC_QRY or EMPLMT_SRCH_QRY table to join other tables to implement the row-level data security in HCM.

412. What is the use of the primary permission list in PeopleSoft user security?

Primary permission lists typically control row level security. For example, in HCM, primary permission lists are used to control access to departments. Row level security gives specific users access to specific data.

413. If you have done everything for granting access to a component, including adding a permission list to the right menu in the Structure and Content, log off and clear the browser cache, run portal sync, you still can't access the component, or you are getting authorization issue with the page, you should try ask PS Admin to bounce the application server and web server, and clear cache.

414. To find out which permission lists have access to a specific page or a specific component, you can check in the PSAUTHITEM table. The description of the CLASSID field (permission list) in the table can be found in the PSCLASSDEFN table.

You can use SQL to insert/update PSAUTHITEM table to add or change a permission list's access to a component or a page, and its result is the same as what you do in PeopleTools -> Security via PIA.

415. How to lock and unlock a user profile using SQL commands?

To lock a user profile, use

```
UPDATE PSOPRDEFN SET ACCTLOCK = 1 WHERE OPRID = ' ';
```

The user will get the Invalid Userid/Password error and will not be able to log in with the change.

To unlock a user profile, set the value of ACCTLOCK to 0 as follows,

```
UPDATE PSOPRDEFN SET ACCTLOCK = 0 WHERE OPRID = ' ';
```

Note you need to have the update privilege in the database in order to execute above SQL commands.

416. Here are SQL statements that access the primary security tables and SQL statements that join the relevant tables to determine who can access what and what can be accessed by whom.

```
/* all User IDs */
SELECT OPRID
FROM PSOPRDEFN
ORDER BY OPRID;
```

332

```
/* all role names */
SELECT ROLENAME
FROM PSROLEDEFN
ORDER BY ROLENAME;
/* all permission lists (class names) */
SELECT CLASSID
FROM PSCLASSDEFN
ORDER BY CLASSID;
/* users --> roles */
SELECT ROLEUSER, ROLENAME
FROM PSROLEUSER
ORDER BY ROLEUSER, ROLENAME;
/* users --> permission lists (class names) */
SELECT DISTINCT UR.ROLEUSER, RP.CLASSID
FROM PSROLEUSER UR, PSROLECLASS RP
WHERE UR.ROLENAME = RP.ROLENAME
ORDER BY UR.ROLEUSER, RP.CLASSID;
/* users --> components */
SELECT DISTINCT UR.ROLEUSER, PC.MENUNAME, PC.BARNAME,
PC.BARITEMNAME, PC.PNLITEMNAME
FROM PSROLEUSER UR, PSROLECLASS RP, PSAUTHITEM PC
WHERE UR.ROLENAME = RP.ROLENAME
AND RP.CLASSID = PC.CLASSID
ORDERY BY UR.ROLEUSER, PC.MENUNAME, PC.BARNAME,
PC.BARITEMNAME, PC.PNLITEMNAME;
/* roles --> permission lists (class names) */
SELECT ROLENAME, CLASSID
FROM PSROLECLASS
ORDER BY ROLENAME, CLASSID;
/* roles --> components */
SELECT DISTINCT RP.ROLENAME, PC.MENUNAME
, PC.BARNAME, PC.BARITEMNAME, PC.PNLITEMNAME
```

333

```
FROM PSROLECLASS RP, PSAUTHITEM PC
WHERE RP.CLASSID = PC.CLASSID;
```

417. How to migrate data in PeopleTools security tables?

To import & export PeopleTools security tables, find the tools delivered security import/exports DMS scrips at the $PS_HOME/scripts on the app server.

PeopleTools provides a set of DataMover scripts to EXPORT and IMPORT your security. The provided scripts transfer User Profiles.

The EXPORT/IMPORT scripts export and import ALL security tables (all UserProfiles, Roles, and Permission Lists). The USEREXPORT/USERIMPORT scripts export and import ALL User Profiles. From Application Designer, you can only copy Roles and Permission Lists (not User Profiles). The scripts are for use in situations where you need to move all the security from one database to another. Use Application Designer if you just need to copy a few select Roles and/or Permission Lists between databases.

This USEREXPORT.DMS script looks like below and these tables are Security Tables:

```
SET OUTPUT SECURITYEXPORT.DAT;
SET LOG SECURITYEXPORT.LOG;
-- ACCESS PROFILES
EXPORT PSACCESSPRFL;
-- USERS
EXPORT PSOPRDEFN;
EXPORT PSOPRALIAS;
EXPORT PSROLEUSER;
EXPORT PSUSERATTR;
EXPORT PSUSEREMAIL;
EXPORT PSUSERPRSNLOPTN;
EXPORT PS_ROLEXLATOPR;
EXPORT PS_RTE_CNTL_RUSER;
-- ROLES
EXPORT PSROLEDEFN;
```

```
EXPORT PSROLEDEFNLANG;
EXPORT PSROLECANGRANT;
EXPORT PSROLECLASS;
-- PERMISSION LISTS
EXPORT PSCLASSDEFN;
EXPORT PSAUTHBUSCOMP;
EXPORT PSAUTHCHNLMON;
EXPORT PSAUTHCUBE;
EXPORT PSAUTHITEM;
EXPORT PSAUTHOPTN;
EXPORT PSAUTHPRCS;
EXPORT PSAUTHSIGNON;
EXPORT PSPRCSPRFL;
EXPORT PS_MC_OPR_SECURITY;
EXPORT PS_MC_OPRID;
EXPORT PS_SCRTY_ACC_GRP;
EXPORT PS_SCRTY_QUERY;
-- DEFINITION SECURITY
EXPORT PSOBJGROUP;
EXPORT PSOPROBJ;
-- PERSONALIZATIONS
EXPORT PSUSEROPTNDEFN;
EXPORT PSUSEROPTNLANG;
EXPORT PSOPTNCATGRPLNG;
EXPORT PSOPTNCATGRPTBL;
EXPORT PSOPTNCATTBL;
EXPORT PSOPTNCATLANG;
-- SECURITY OPTIONS
EXPORT PSSECOPTIONS;
-- SECURITY LINKS
EXPORT PSUSEROTHER;
EXPORT PSUSERSELFOTHER;
```

```
EXPORT PSROLEOTHER;

EXPORT PSPERMLISTOTHER;

-- USER ID TYPES

EXPORT PSOPRALIASTYPE;

EXPORT PSOPRALIASFIELD;

-- DELETE USER BYPASS TABLE

EXPORT PS_BYPASS_TABLE;

-- EMAIL TEXT

EXPORT PSPSWDEMAIL;

-- PASSWORD HINTS

EXPORT PSPSWDHINT;

-- SIGNON PEOPLECODE

EXPORT PSSIGNONPPC;
```

418. **Error**: "You do not have permission to edit or view <OBJECT NAME>" when opening a PeopleTools object, such as a page, In Application Designer

Cause: Issue was caused due to missing Definition Security under Primary Permission List associated with User Profile.

Solution: User accessing Application Designer objects (without having Peoplesoft Admin Role) should have Definition Security associated to his Primary Permission List and provided respective access under definition types (read, no access, full access) Then the permission list should be added as Primary Permission list under User Profile to allow access to Tools pages.

419. **Error**: "No rows exist for the specified keys."

Solution: You should first check that the data is present in the system or not. If data is available, the next point to check is the Search Record of the Component underlying the CI.

You should check if it has keys like OPRCLASS or ROWSECCLASS. These are used for setting up Row-level security.

If any of these are present, check the user's User Profile to see what Primary Permission list / Row Security permission list they are having.

The most common cause would be that the user's Row-level security doesn't allow access to the data pertaining to the employee.

SELF SERVICE

420. The value of the Emplid field on an HCM Self Service page is populated by the Emplid field SearchInit event PeopleCode of the search record HR_SS_PERS_SRCH for all HCM components.

421. To change the Emplid tied to a user id, go to Maintain Security -> User profile -> ID page. The Emplid and the UserID mapping is stored in the PSOPRDEFN table.

SQL

422. A string comparison of the two values using '=' or 'like' as the operator is case sensitive.

423. The underscore character '_' used in a LIKE condition finds matches with same length of string but different letter in the string. f.i.,

```
SELECT * FROM SYSIBM.SYSKEYS
WHERE IXNAME LIKE 'PS_XXX_SUMM_REPORT';
```

will find PS_XXX_SUMM_REPORT as well as PSAXXX_SUMM_REPORT.

Wildcard	Description
%	A substitute for zero or more characters
_	A substitute for a single character

424. You can specify the range of numbers, dates, and text using BETWEEN operator in a SQL.

425. How to grant access to a table to the public in SQL Developer?
Execute the following command,

```
GRANT ALL ON SYSADM.PS_XXX_ACAD_PROG TO PUBLIC;
```

426. How to change a date column from not allowing a null value to allowing a null value?

```
ALTER TABLE PS_JRNL_HEADER
```

339

```
ALTER COLUMN OPRID_APPROVED_BY CHAR(30) NULL;
```

427. How to use Case When with an aggregation (SUM, COUNT, etc.) function and where clause in a SQL select statement?

Case When can be used with an aggregation (SUM, COUNT, etc.) function in a SQL Select statement.

```
SELECT DISTINCT RE.BUSINESS_UNIT, RE.PROJECT_ID,
RE.ACTIVITY_ID, RE.DEPTID, 'A', '2005', 12, '03/31/2005
00:00:00', (CASE WHEN RE.ANALYSIS_TYPE = 'PMA' THEN 'PMA'
ELSE ' ' END) AS USER_KEY2, ' ', (CASE WHEN RE.ANALYSIS_TYPE
= 'PMA' THEN 'PMA Approval' ELSE ' ' END) AS USER_FIELD_2, '
', ' ', ' ', ' ', ' ', ' ', ' ', ' ', ' ', SUM
(RESOURCE_AMOUNT)
```

It can also be used in the where clause.

```
SELECT %DateOut(BEGIN_DT)
FROM PS_CAL_DETP_TBL
WHERE SETID = 'HYDRO'
AND CALENDAR_ID = 'FY'
AND FISCAL_YEAR = (CASE WHEN %Bind(FISCAL_YEAR) = 2006
AND %Bind(FISCAL_MONTH) = 1 THEN 2006 WHEN %Bind(FISCAL_YEAR)
> 2006
AND %Bind(FISCAL_MONTH) = 1 THEN %Bind(FISCAL_YEAR) - 1 ELSE
%Bind(FISCAL_YEAR) END)
AND ACCOUNTING_PERIOD = (CASE WHEN %Bind(FISCAL_YEAR) = 2006
AND %Bind(FISCAL_MONTH) = 1 THEN 1 WHEN %Bind(FISCAL_YEAR) >
2006
```

```
AND %Bind(FISCAL_MONTH) = 1 THEN 12 ELSE %Bind(FISCAL_MONTH)
- 1 END);
```

It can be used in the ORDER BY clause as well. Here is an example,

```
SELECT XXX_REQUEST_TYPE
, XXX_RETURN_DATE
FROM PS.PS_XXX_ADR_INT_
WHERE XXX_PLATE like 'AAAA%' AND XXX_REQUEST_TYPE IN
('PD','IS','PI','RM','RR')
ORDER BY CASE XXX_REQUEST_TYPE WHEN 'PD' THEN '01' WHEN 'RM'
THEN '02' WHEN 'NP' THEN '03' WHEN 'IS' THEN '04' WHEN 'PI'
THEN '05' WHEN 'RR' THEN '06' ELSE '10' END
FETCH FIRST 1 ROWS ONLY;
```

428. You can do Insert Select without specifying allthe column names.

```
INSERT INTO PS_XXX_TM_HIS (
SELECT * FROM PS_XXX_TM);
```

You can also add other fieldvalues if the target table has more fields than the source table.

```
INSERT INTO PS_XXX_TM_HIS (
SELECT A.*, SYSDATE FROM PS_XXX_TM A);
```

429. What is the difference between truncating a table and deleting data in a table?
The difference between truncating a table and deletingdata in a table is as follows,

Truncate

- DDL statement

341

- No rollback segment needed

- Much faster than delete

- Data cannot be retrieved in normal conditions

- Does not need an explicit commit

Delete

- DML statement

- A bit slower

- Selective data can be deleted using where condition

- Commit needs to be done to complete the transaction

430. How to do a left outer join or a right outer join to one table that is inner joined with a few other tables?

A code example is as follows,

```
SELECT ...
FROM PS_CUSTOMER A, PS_CUST_ADDRESS B, PS_XXX_CUST_INF C LEFT
OUTER JOIN PS_CUST_AGING D ON C.CUST_ID = D.CUST_ID
WHERE A.SETID = B.SETID
AND A.CUST_ID = B.CUST_ID
AND B.SETID = C.SETID
AND B.CUST_ID = C.CUST_ID;
```

431. How to do left outer join or right outer join on multiple tables?

You can do left outer join or right outer join on multiple tables.

An example is as follows,

```
SELECT A.COURSE, A.SESSION_NBR, A.SESSION_NBR, P.EMPLID,
P.LETTER_CD, F.LETTER_CD
FROM SYSADM.PS_CRSE_SESSN_TBL A, SYSADM.PS_COURSE_TBL
B,(SYSADM.PS_TRAINING P LEFT OUTER JOIN  SYSADM.PS_DEPT_TBL C
ON  C.DEPTID = P.DEPTID LEFT OUTER JOIN
SYSADM.PS_STANDRD_LTR_TBL F ON F.LETTER_CD = P.LETTER_CD)
WHERE A.COURSE = 'CH0036'
AND A.SESSION_NBR = '0001'
AND A.COURSE = B.COURSE
AND A.SESSION_NBR = P.SESSION_NBR
AND P.COURSE_START_DT = A.COURSE_START_DT;
```

Outer join can be perfomred to any table, not just the last table that was added.

432. You can use the query result of a SQL select statement as a table.

```
SELECT TITLE, SECTION FROM (
SELECT ISBN, TITLE, DECODE(SECTION_ID, 10, 'Fiction', 5,
'Romance', 6,
'Science Fiction', 7, 'Science', 9, 'Reference', 11, 'Law',
'Unknown')
SECTION FROM BOOK
) WHERE ISBN > 100;
```

433. A subquery can be replaced by a more efficient join if the result of the subquery is from one table only. If you can avoid a subquery and replace it with a JOIN clause, you should do so without hesitation.

434. To get the correct result of aggregation values when using GROUP BY in table joins, you can use a subquery or join all tables with proper join conditions, to eliminate duplicated rows being returned.

435. What are the differences between UNION, UNION All, INTERSECT and MINUS?

The UNION query allows you to combine the result sets of 2 or more "select" queries.

The UNION ALL query allows you to combine the result sets of 2 or more "select" queries. It returns all rows (even if the row exists in more than one of the "select" statements). Each SQL statement within the UNION ALL query must have the same number of fields in the result sets with similar data types.

The INTERSECT query allows you to return the results of 2 or more "select" queries. However, it only returns the rows selected by all queries. If a record exists in one query and not in the other, it will be omitted from the INTERSECT results. Each SQL statement within the INTERSECT query must have the same number of fields in the result sets with similar data types.

The MINUS query returns all rows in the first query that are not returned in the second query. Each SQL statement within the MINUS query must have the same number of fields in the result sets with similar data types.

436. Dynamic SQL incurs overhead because the cost of the dynamic bind, or PREPARE, must be added to the processing time of all dynamic SQL programs. But this overhead is not quite as costly as many people seem to think it is.

437. The driving table of a SQL join is the last table in the FROM clause moving from right to left or first nested select. To improve performance, you can make the table with the least number of rows the driving table.

438. To tune the performance of a SQL with lots of table joins, start from one table first, and then add more tables one by one and test the performance in the SQL client. The sequence of adding tables into joining should start with the key table first, then big tables, and lastly, small tables.

439. You can add secondary indexes to a big table to improve the performance of a SQL when its join columns are not used as its primary index. Note creating and maintaining an index on a huge table can be costly.

440. How to use a database index as a hint to enhance the performance of a SQL statement?

A database hint provides a directive to the optimizer in choosing an execution plan for the SQL statement being executed. The database INDEX hint instructs the optimizer to use an index scan for the specified table.

The syntax of using a database index as a hint is as follows,

```
SELECT /*+ORDERED INDEX(A PSGLEDGER) */  A.BUSINESS_UNIT ,
A.ACCOUNT.... FROM PS_LEDGER;
```

Because the database query optimizer typically selects the best execution plan for a query, it is recommended that database hints be used only as a last resort by experienced developers and database administrators.

441. How to get the refresh date of a non-production environment?

You can query the maximum value of the last updated date time from a table with generated every day, f.i. PS_JRNL_HEADER table. Use the following SQL:

```
SELECT MAX(JRNL_CREATE_DTTM) FROM PS_JRNL_HEADER;
```

442. How to identify all duplicated rows in a select insert SQL that error out?

You need to create a query with all the key fields with group by and pull only those combinations with count great than 1.

Here is an example,

```
SELECT  SUPER_EMPLID,  SUPER_EMPL_RCD,  EMPLID,  EMPL_RCD,
COUNT(*)
FROM
(SELECT DISTINCT SUPER.EMPLID as SUPER_EMPLID,
SUPER.EMPL_RCD as SUPER_EMPL_RCD,
POS.EMPLID as EMPLID,
POS.EMPL_RCD as EMPL_RCD,
POS.EMPL_STATUS ,
POS.EFFDT ,
POS.POSITION_NBR ,
POS.EFFDT ,
POS.REPORTS_TO ,
POS.POSITION_OVERRIDE ,
POS.HR_DR_LEVEL ,
'N' ,
DRILL_DOWN_FLAG
FROM PS_JOB SUPER ,
PS_DR_RPT_TO_TMP POS
WHERE POS.REPORTS_TO = SUPER.POSITION_NBR
AND SUPER.EFFDT
= (SELECT MAX(JOB2.EFFDT)
FROM PS_JOB JOB2
WHERE SUPER.EMPLID= JOB2.EMPLID
AND SUPER.EMPL_RCD= JOB2.EMPL_RCD
```

```
AND   JOB2.EFFDT         <=   TO_DATE(TO_CHAR(SYSDATE,'YYYY-MM-
DD'),'YYYY-MM-DD')
)
AND POS.REPORTS_TO > ' '
AND SUPER.EFFSEQ   =
(SELECT MAX(JOB3.EFFSEQ)
FROM PS_JOB JOB3
WHERE SUPER.EMPLID=JOB3.EMPLID
AND SUPER.EMPL_RCD=JOB3.EMPL_RCD
AND SUPER.EFFDT   =JOB3.EFFDT
)
AND POS.EMPL_STATUS IN ('A','L','P','W', 'S'))
GROUP BY SUPER_EMPLID, SUPER_EMPL_RCD, EMPLID, EMPL_RCD
HAVING COUNT(*) > 1;
```

443. The following SQL can be used to check roles, permission lists, and navigations.

```
SELECT DISTINCT
d.roleuser,
a.rolename,
b.classid              AS PERMISSION_LIST,
b.menuname,
b.baritemname          AS "COMPONENT NAME",
b.pnlitemname,
c.descr                AS "PAGE DESCRIPTION",
Decode(b.displayonly, 1, 'Y',   'N')   AS "DISPLAY ONLY?",
e.navigation
FROM   sysadm.psroleclass a,
```

```
sysadm.psauthitem b,

sysadm.pspnldefn c,

sysadm.psroleuser d,

SELECT LEVEL0.portal_label

|| ' > '

|| LEVEL1.portal_label

|| ' > '

|| LEVEL2.portal_label

|| ' > '

|| level3.portal_label AS navigation,

level3.portal_uri_seg2 AS component

FROM   psprsmdefn level3,

psprsmdefn level2,

psprsmdefn level1,

psprsmdefn LEVEL0

WHERE level3.portal_prntobjname = level2.portal_objname

AND level2.portal_prntobjname = level1.portal_objname

AND level1.portal_prntobjname = LEVEL0.portal_objname

AND level3.portal_name = level2.portal_name

AND level2.portal_name = level1.portal_name

AND level1.portal_name = LEVEL0.portal_name) e

WHERE   a.classid = b.classid

AND b.pnlitemname = c.pnlname

AND a.rolename = d.rolename

AND d.roleuser = 'CR_CHENS'

--AND b.baritemname = 'COMPONENT NAME'

--AND d.rolename = 'ROLENAME'

AND b.classid = 'XXX_CUSTOM'
```

```
AND e.component = b.baritemname
ORDER BY 1, 2, 3, 4, 5, 6;
```

444. How to use SQL to get the formats of all fields in a record?

The following SQL can be used to get the formats of all fields in a record.

```
SELECT
A.RECNAME,
A.FIELDNAME,
CASE
WHEN B.FIELDTYPE = 0 THEN
'CHAR'
WHEN B.FIELDTYPE = 1 THEN
'LONG CHAR'
WHEN B.FIELDTYPE = 2 THEN
'NUMBER'
WHEN B.FIELDTYPE = 3 THEN
'SIGNED NBR'
WHEN B.FIELDTYPE = 4 THEN
'DATE'
WHEN B.FIELDTYPE = 5 THEN
'TIME'
WHEN B.FIELDTYPE = 6 THEN
'DATETIME'
WHEN B.FIELDTYPE = 7
OR B.FIELDTYPE = 8 THEN
'IMAGE'
ELSE NULL
```

```
END AS FIELDTYPE,
CASE
WHEN B.FIELDTYPE = 2
OR B.FIELDTYPE = 3 THEN
TRIM(TO_CHAR(B.LENGTH)) || '.' || TO_CHAR(B.DECIMALPOS)
ELSE TO_CHAR(B.LENGTH)
END AS FLDLEN,
CASE
WHEN bitand(A.USEEDIT, 256) > 0 THEN
'YES'
ELSE 'NO'
END AS REQ,
CASE
WHEN bitand(A.USEEDIT, 1) > 0 THEN
'KEY'
WHEN bitand(A.USEEDIT, 2) > 0 THEN
'DUP'
WHEN bitand(A.USEEDIT, 16) > 0 THEN
'ALT'
ELSE NULL
END AS KEY_TYPE,
CASE
WHEN bitand(A.USEEDIT, 64) > 0 THEN
'DESC'
WHEN ( bitand(A.USEEDIT, 1) > 0
OR bitand(A.USEEDIT, 2) > 0
OR bitand(A.USEEDIT, 16) > 0 )
AND bitand(A.USEEDIT, 64) = 0 THEN
```

```
'ASC'

ELSE NULL

END AS DIR,

CASE

WHEN bitand(A.USEEDIT, 2048) > 0 THEN

'YES'

ELSE 'NO'

END AS SRCH,

CASE

WHEN bitand(A.USEEDIT, 32) > 0 THEN

'YES'

ELSE 'NO'

END AS LIST,

CASE

WHEN bitand(A.USEEDIT, 4) > 0 THEN

'YES'

ELSE 'NO'

END AS SYS,

CASE

WHEN TRIM(A.DEFRECNAME) = '' THEN

A.DEFFIELDNAME

ELSE

TRIM(A.DEFRECNAME) || '.' || A.DEFFIELDNAME

END AS DEFAULT_VALUE,

CASE

WHEN bitand(A.USEEDIT, 8) > 0

AND bitand(A.USEEDIT, 128) = 0

AND bitand(A.USEEDIT, 1024) = 0 THEN
```

351

```
'A'
WHEN bitand(A.USEEDIT, 8) > 0
AND bitand(A.USEEDIT, 128) > 0
AND bitand(A.USEEDIT, 1024) = 0 THEN
'AC'
WHEN bitand(A.USEEDIT, 8) > 0
AND bitand(A.USEEDIT, 128) > 0
AND bitand(A.USEEDIT, 1024) > 0 THEN
'ACD'
WHEN bitand(A.USEEDIT, 8) = 0
AND bitand(A.USEEDIT, 128) > 0
AND bitand(A.USEEDIT, 1024) = 0 THEN
'C'
WHEN bitand(A.USEEDIT, 8) = 0
AND bitand(A.USEEDIT, 128) > 0
AND bitand(A.USEEDIT, 1024) > 0 THEN
'CD'
WHEN bitand(A.USEEDIT, 8) = 0
AND bitand(A.USEEDIT, 128) = 0
AND bitand(A.USEEDIT, 1024) > 0 THEN
'D'
ELSE NULL
END AS AUDT,
CASE
WHEN bitand(A.USEEDIT, 16384) > 0 THEN
'PROMPT'
WHEN bitand(A.USEEDIT, 512) > 0 THEN
'XLAT'
```

```
WHEN bitand(A.USEEDIT, 8192) > 0 THEN
'Y/N'
ELSE NULL
END AS EDIT,
A.EDITTABLE AS PROMPT_TABLE,
A.SETCNTRLFLD AS SET_CONTROL_FLD,
CASE
WHEN bitand(A.USEEDIT, 4096) > 0 THEN
'YES'
ELSE 'NO'
END AS REASONABLE_DT,
CASE
WHEN bitand(A.USEEDIT, 32768) > 0 THEN
'YES'
ELSE 'NO'
END AS AUTO_UPDT,
CASE
WHEN bitand(A.USEEDIT, 262144) > 0 THEN
'FROM'
WHEN bitand(A.USEEDIT, 524288) > 0 THEN
'THROUGH'
ELSE NULL
END AS SEARCH_FIELD,
CASE
WHEN A.SUBRECORD = 'Y' THEN
'YES'
ELSE 'NO'
END AS SUBRECORD,
```

```
A.LASTUPDDTTM,

A.LASTUPDOPRID

FROM sysadm.PSRECFIELD A,

sysadm.PSDBFIELD B

WHERE (A.RECNAME = UPPER('&RecordName') OR A.RECNAME =

UPPER('&RecordName'||'_SBR'))

AND A.FIELDNAME = B.FIELDNAME

ORDER BY A.RECNAME,FIELDNUM;
```

445. How to use SQL to get the properties of all the fields on a page?

The following SQL can be used to get the page field properties.

```
SELECT

  PNLNAME AS "Page Name"

, PNLFLDID AS "Page Field ID"

, PNLFIELDNAME AS "Page Field Name"

, DECODE(FIELDTYPE,

0,'Text',

        1,'Frame',

        2,'Group Box',

        3,'Static Image',

        4,'Edit Box',

        5,'Dropdown List',

        6,'Long Edit Box',

        7,'Check Box',

        8,'Radio Button',

        9,'Image',

        10,'Scroll Bar',
```

```
        11,'Subpage',

        12,'Push Button/Link (PeopleCode)',

        13,'Push Button/Link (Scroll Action)',

        14,'Push Button/Link (Toolbar Action)',

        15,'Push Button/Link (External Link)',

        16,'Push Button/Link (Internal Link)',

        17,'Push Button/Link (Process)',

        18,'Secondary Page',

        19,'Grid',

        20,'Tree',

        21,'Push Button/Link (Secondary Page)',

        22,'UNKNOWN',

        23,'Horizontal Rule',

        24,'Tab Separator',

        25,'HTML Area',

        26,'Push Button/Link (Prompt Action)',

        27,'Scroll Area',

        28,'UNKNOWN',

        29,'Push Button/Link (Page Anchor)',

        30,'Chart',

        31,'Push Button/Link (Instant Messaging)') AS
  "Field Type"
, 'DSPLFORMAT Flags-->|' AS DUMMY
, CASE WHEN bitand(DSPLFORMAT,1) > 0 THEN 'Y' END AS
  "Alignment: Left"
, CASE WHEN bitand(DSPLFORMAT,2) > 0 THEN 'Y' END AS
  "Alignment: Center"
, CASE WHEN bitand(DSPLFORMAT,4) > 0 THEN 'Y' END AS
  "Alignment: Right"
```

```
, CASE WHEN bitand(DSPLFORMAT,8) > 0 THEN 'Y' END AS
  "Alignment: Auto"

, CASE WHEN bitand(DSPLFORMAT,16) > 0 THEN 'Y' END AS "Show
  Currency Symbol"

, CASE WHEN bitand(DSPLFORMAT,32) > 0 THEN 'Y' END AS "1000
  Separator"

, CASE WHEN bitand(DSPLFORMAT,64) > 0 THEN 'Y' END AS
  "UNKNOWN"

, CASE WHEN bitand(DSPLFORMAT,128) > 0 THEN 'Y' END AS
  "Display Zero"

, CASE WHEN bitand(DSPLFORMAT,256) > 0 THEN 'Y' END AS
  "UNKNOWN"

, CASE WHEN bitand(DSPLFORMAT,512) > 0 THEN 'Y' END AS "Auto
  Fill"

, CASE WHEN bitand(DSPLFORMAT,1024) > 0 THEN 'Y' END AS "Auto
  Decimal"

, CASE WHEN bitand(DSPLFORMAT,2048) > 0 THEN 'Y' END AS
  "Image Size: Scale"

, CASE WHEN bitand(DSPLFORMAT,4096) > 0 THEN 'Y' END AS
  "UNKNOWN"

, CASE WHEN bitand(DSPLFORMAT,8192) > 0 THEN 'Y' END AS
  "UNKNOWN"

, CASE WHEN bitand(DSPLFORMAT,16384) > 0 THEN 'Y' END AS
  "Image Size: Size"

, CASE WHEN bitand(DSPLFORMAT,32768) > 0 THEN 'Y' END AS
  "Password"

, CASE WHEN bitand(DSPLFORMAT,65536) > 0 THEN 'Y' END AS
  "Display Century"

, CASE WHEN bitand(DSPLFORMAT,131072) > 0 THEN 'Y' END AS
  "Displayed: Xlat Short"
```

```
, CASE WHEN bitand(DSPLFORMAT,262144) > 0 THEN 'Y' END AS
  "Displayed: Xlat Long"
, CASE WHEN bitand(DSPLFORMAT,524288) > 0 THEN 'Y' END AS
  "Label Alignment: Left"
, CASE WHEN bitand(DSPLFORMAT,1048576) > 0 THEN 'Y' END AS
  "Label Alignment: Centered"
, CASE WHEN bitand(DSPLFORMAT,2097152) > 0 THEN 'Y' END AS
  "Label Alignment: Right"
, CASE WHEN bitand(DSPLFORMAT,4194304) > 0 THEN 'Y' END AS
  "First occurs only"
, CASE WHEN bitand(DSPLFORMAT,8388608) > 0 THEN 'Y' END AS
  "Show Prompt Button (OFF)"
, CASE WHEN bitand(DSPLFORMAT,16777216) > 0 THEN 'Y' END AS
  "UNKNOWN"
, CASE WHEN bitand(DSPLFORMAT,33554432) > 0 THEN 'Y' END AS
  "UNKNOWN"
, CASE WHEN bitand(DSPLFORMAT,67108864) > 0 THEN 'Y' END AS
  "UNKNOWN"
, CASE WHEN bitand(DSPLFORMAT,134217728) > 0 THEN 'Y' END AS
  "UNKNOWN"
, CASE WHEN bitand(DSPLFORMAT,268435456) > 0 THEN 'Y' END AS
  "UNKNOWN"
, CASE WHEN bitand(DSPLFORMAT,536870912) > 0 THEN 'Y' END AS
  "Display Time Zone"
, '|<--DSPLFORMAT Flags' AS DUMMY
, DECODE(LBLTYPE,
         0,'None',
         1,'Text',
         2,'RFT Short',
         3,'RFT Long',
```

```
                4,'XLAT Short',
                5,'XLAT Long',
                6,'Default',
7,'Message Catalog') AS "Label Type"
, LABEL_ID AS "Label ID"
, LBLTEXT AS "Label Text"
, 'FIELDUSE Flags-->|' AS DUMMY
, CASE WHEN bitand(FIELDUSE,1) > 0 THEN 'Y' END AS "Display
  Only"
, CASE WHEN bitand(FIELDUSE,2) > 0 THEN 'Y' END AS "UNKNOWN"
, CASE WHEN bitand(FIELDUSE,4) > 0 THEN 'Y' END AS
  "Invisible"
, CASE WHEN bitand(FIELDUSE,8) > 0 THEN 'Y' END AS "Display
  Control Field"
, CASE WHEN bitand(FIELDUSE,16) > 0 THEN 'Y' END AS "Related
  Field"
, CASE WHEN bitand(FIELDUSE,32) > 0 THEN 'Y' END AS "Multi-
  Currency Field"
, CASE WHEN bitand(FIELDUSE,64) > 0 THEN 'Y' END AS "No Auto
  Select"
, CASE WHEN bitand(FIELDUSE,128) > 0 THEN 'Y' END AS "No Auto
  Update"
, CASE WHEN bitand(FIELDUSE,256) > 0 THEN 'Y' END AS "No Row
  Insert"
, CASE WHEN bitand(FIELDUSE,512) > 0 THEN 'Y' END AS "No Row
  Delete"
, CASE WHEN bitand(FIELDUSE,1024) > 0 THEN 'Y' END AS
  "UNKNOWN"
```

```
, CASE WHEN bitand(FIELDUSE,2048) > 0 THEN 'Y' END AS "Freeze
  Grid Column"
, CASE WHEN bitand(FIELDUSE,4096) > 0 THEN 'Y' END AS
  "UNKNOWN"
, CASE WHEN bitand(FIELDUSE,8192) > 0 THEN 'Y' END AS
  "UNKNOWN"
, CASE WHEN bitand(FIELDUSE,16384) > 0 THEN 'Y' END AS
  "UNKNOWN"
, CASE WHEN bitand(FIELDUSE,32768) > 0 THEN 'Y' END AS
  "UNKNOWN"
, CASE WHEN bitand(FIELDUSE,65536) > 0 THEN 'Y' END AS
  "UNKNOWN"
, CASE WHEN bitand(FIELDUSE,131072) > 0 THEN 'Y' END AS
  "UNKNOWN"
, CASE WHEN bitand(FIELDUSE,262144) > 0 THEN 'Y' END AS
  "Enable When Page Display Only"
, CASE WHEN bitand(FIELDUSE,524288) > 0 THEN 'Y' END AS
  "UNKNOWN"
, CASE WHEN bitand(FIELDUSE,1048576) > 0 THEN 'Y' END AS
  "UNKNOWN"
, CASE WHEN bitand(FIELDUSE,2097152) > 0 THEN 'Y' END AS
  "UNKNOWN"
, CASE WHEN bitand(FIELDUSE,4194304) > 0 THEN 'Y' END AS
  "UNKNOWN"
, CASE WHEN bitand(FIELDUSE,8388608) > 0 THEN 'Y' END AS
  "UNKNOWN"
, CASE WHEN bitand(FIELDUSE,16777216) > 0 THEN 'Y' END AS
  "UNKNOWN"
, CASE WHEN bitand(FIELDUSE,33554432) > 0 THEN 'Y' END AS
  "UNKNOWN"
```

```
, CASE WHEN bitand(FIELDUSE,67108864) > 0 THEN 'Y' END AS
  "Hide Border"
, '|<--FIELDUSE Flags' AS DUMMY
, 'FIELDUSETMP Flags-->|' AS DUMMY
, CASE WHEN bitand(FIELDUSETMP,1) > 0 THEN 'Y' END AS
  "Activate by Enter key"
, CASE WHEN bitand(FIELDUSETMP,2) > 0 THEN 'Y' END AS "Enable
  Spell Check"
, CASE WHEN bitand(FIELDUSETMP,4) > 0 THEN 'Y' END AS
  "Disabled Edit Control"
, CASE WHEN bitand(FIELDUSETMP,8) > 0 THEN 'Y' END AS "Set
  Component Changed (OFF)"
, CASE WHEN bitand(FIELDUSETMP,16) > 0 THEN 'Y' END AS
  "UNKNOWN"
, CASE WHEN bitand(FIELDUSETMP,32) > 0 THEN 'Y' END AS "Set
  Component Changed "
, CASE WHEN bitand(FIELDUSETMP,64) > 0 THEN 'Y' END AS "Wrap
  Long Words"
, '|<--FIELDUSETMP Flags' AS DUMMY
, DECODE(DEFERPROC,
         0,'Interactive',
         1,'Allow deferred processing') AS "Deferred
Processing Mode"
, OCCURSLEVEL AS "Occurs level"
, RECNAME AS "Record Name"
, FIELDNAME AS "Field Name"
, FIELDSTYLE AS "Page Field Style Class"
, DECODE(FIELDSIZETYPE,
         0,'Average',
```

```
                1,'Maximum',

                2,'Custom ') AS "Field Size Type"

, DECODE(LABELSIZETYPE,

                0,'Left',

                1,'Custom',

                2,'Top') AS "Label Position"

, DECODE(PTADJHIDDENFIELDS,

                0,'Disable Adjust Layout for Hidden Fields',

                1,'Enable Adjust Layout for Hidden Fields') AS "Adj
Layout for Hidden Fields"

, DECODE(PTCOLLAPSEDATAAREA,

                0,'Disable Collapsible Data Area',

                1,'Enable Collapsible Data Area') AS "Collapsible
Data Area"

, DECODE(PTDFLTVIEWEXPANDED,

                0,'Disable Default Initial View to Expanded State',

                1,'Enable Default Initial View to Expanded State')
AS "Default View to Expanded"

, DECODE(PTHIDEFIELDS,

                0,'Disable Hide all Fields when Group Box Hidden',

                1,'Enable Hide all Fields when Group Box Hidden')
AS "Hide Flds when Grp Box Hidden"

, DECODE(PTLEBEXPANDFIELD,

                0,'Disable Expand Field When Display Only',

                1,'Enable Expand Field When Display Only') AS
"Expand Field When Display Only"

, DECODE(ENABLEASANCHOR,

                0,'Disable as Page Anchor',

                1,'Enable as Page Anchor') AS "Enable As Anchor"
```

```
FROM SYSADM.PSPNLFIELD

WHERE PNLNAME = '&PAGENAME'

ORDER BY PNLNAME, PNLFLDID;
```

446. How to use SQL to get a list of all objects in a project, and the object type, last updated date, and last updated OPRID of each object?

The following SQL can be used to get a list of all objects in a project, and the object type, last updated date, and last updated oprid of each object.

```
SELECT A.PROJECTNAME

,(CASE OBJECTTYPE WHEN 0 THEN 'Record'

WHEN 1 THEN 'Index'

WHEN 2 THEN 'Field'

WHEN 3 THEN 'Field Format'

WHEN 4 THEN 'Translate Value'

WHEN 5 THEN 'Pages'

WHEN 6 THEN 'Menus'

WHEN 7 THEN 'Components'

WHEN 8 THEN 'Record PeopleCode'

WHEN 9 THEN 'Menu PeopleCode'

WHEN 10 THEN 'Query'

WHEN 11 THEN 'Tree Structures'

WHEN 12 THEN 'Trees'

WHEN 13 THEN 'Access group'

WHEN 14 THEN 'Color'

WHEN 15 THEN 'Style'

WHEN 16 THEN 'N/A'

WHEN 17 THEN 'Business process'

WHEN 18 THEN 'Activity'
```

```
WHEN 19 THEN 'Role'

WHEN 20 THEN 'Process Definition'

WHEN 21 THEN 'Server Definition'

WHEN 22 THEN 'Process Type Definition'

WHEN 23 THEN 'Job Definitions'

WHEN 24 THEN 'Recurrence Definition'

WHEN 25 THEN 'Message Catalog'

WHEN 26 THEN 'Dimension'

WHEN 27 THEN 'Cube Definitions'

WHEN 28 THEN 'Cube Instance Definitions'

WHEN 29 THEN 'Business Interlink'

WHEN 30 THEN 'SQL'

WHEN 31 THEN 'File Layout Definition'

WHEN 32 THEN 'Component Interfaces'

WHEN 33 THEN 'AE program'

WHEN 34 THEN 'AE section'

WHEN 35 THEN 'Message Node'

WHEN 36 THEN 'Message Channel'

WHEN 37 THEN 'Message'

WHEN 38 THEN 'Approval rule set'

WHEN 39 THEN 'Message PeopleCode'

WHEN 40 THEN 'Subscription PeopleCode'

WHEN 41 THEN 'N/A'

WHEN 42 THEN 'Component Interface PeopleCode'

WHEN 43 THEN 'AE PeopleCode'

WHEN 44 THEN 'Page PeopleCode'

WHEN 45 THEN 'Page Field PeopleCode'

WHEN 46 THEN 'Component PeopleCode'
```

```
WHEN 47 THEN 'Component Record PeopleCode'
WHEN 48 THEN 'Component Rec Fld PeopleCode'
WHEN 49 THEN 'Image'
WHEN 50 THEN 'Style sheet'
WHEN 51 THEN 'HTML'
WHEN 52 THEN 'Not used'
WHEN 53 THEN 'Permission List'
WHEN 54 THEN 'Portal Registry Definitions'
WHEN 55 THEN 'Portal Registry Structures'
WHEN 56 THEN 'URL Definitions'
WHEN 57 THEN 'Application Packages'
WHEN 58 THEN 'Application Package Peoplecode'
WHEN 59 THEN 'Portal Registry User Homepage'
WHEN 60 THEN 'Problem Type'
WHEN 61 THEN 'Archive Templates'
WHEN 62 THEN 'XSLT'
WHEN 63 THEN 'Portal Registry User Favorite'
WHEN 64 THEN 'Mobile Page'
WHEN 65 THEN 'Relationships'
WHEN 66 THEN 'Component Interface Property Peoplecode'
WHEN 67 THEN 'Optimization Models'
WHEN 68 THEN 'File References'
WHEN 69 THEN 'File Type Codes'
WHEN 70 THEN 'Archive Object Definitions'
WHEN 71 THEN 'Archive Templates (Type 2)'
WHEN 72 THEN 'Diagnostic Plug In'
WHEN 73 THEN 'Analytic Model'
ELSE 'UNKNOWN OBJECT TYPE' END) AS OBJECTTYPE
```

```
, RTRIM(RTRIM(OBJECTVALUE1) || '.' || RTRIM(OBJECTVALUE2) ||
'.' || RTRIM(OBJECTVALUE3) || '.' || RTRIM(OBJECTVALUE4),'.')
OBJECTNAAM

, B.LASTUPDDTTM

, B.LASTUPDOPRID

FROM SYSADM.PSPROJECTITEM A,

SYSADM.PSPROJECTDEFN B

WHERE A.PROJECTNAME = 'AY_BPI_LN_CR61' --- Replace with your
project name...

AND A.PROJECTNAME = B.PROJECTNAME

ORDER BY OBJECTTYPE, OBJECTVALUE1, OBJECTVALUE2,
OBJECTVALUE3;
```

SQL (DB2)

447. The command to set the current SQL operator ID is

```
SET CURRENT SQLID = 'PS';
```

448. To select top n rows of a table, use FETCH FIRST.

```
SELECT name,
description
FROM TABLE
ORDER
BY NAME
FETCH FIRST 10 ROWS ONLY
OPTIMIZE FOR 10 ROWS;
```

OPTIMIZE FOR 10 ROWS tells DB2 to select an access path that returns the first qualifying row quickly. This means that whenever possible.

449. To find a starting position of the first occurrence of one string within another string, use the built-in function 'Locate'.

450. To add a day to the current date, use

```
SELECT CURRENT DATE + 1 DAY FROM {TABLE};
```

To get the difference between the two dates,

```
SELECT DAYS('2022-07-27') - DAYS('2019-04-18')
```

```
FROM {TBNAME};
```

451. You can define a temporary table by using With AS.

    Here is an example,

    ```
    WITH B AS
    (SELECT DISTINCT CUST_ID, CONTACT_ID
    FROM PS.PS_CONTACT_CUST)
    SELECT B.CUST_ID, COUNT(B.CONTACT_ID)
    FROM B
    GROUP BY CUST_ID
    HAVING COUNT(B.CONTACT_ID) >1;
    ```

452. The SYSTABLES table contains one row for each table or view.

    The SYSCOLUMNS table contains one row for every column of each table and view.

    The SYSINDEXES table contains one row for every index.

    The SYSKEYS table contains one row for each column of an index key.

    The schema to use for the above tables is SYSIBM.

SQL (ORACLE)

453. How to change the current session's schema?

   The following statement sets the schema of the current session to the schema name specified in the statement.

   ```
   ALTER SESSION SET CURRENT_SCHEMA = <SCHEMA>;
   f.i.
   ALTER SESSION SET CURRENT_SCHEMA = SYSADM;
   ```

454. How to spell out words from numbers?

   You can use the below SQL to convert numbers to words,

   ```
   SELECT TO_CHAR(TO_DATE(108, 'J'),'JSP') FROM DUAL;
   ```

   The result is one hundred eight.

455. Use the CREATE SYNONYM statement to create a synonym, which is an alternative name for a table.   You can create a synonym for the remote table using the dblink.

   ```
   CREATE DATABASE LINK MY_DB_LINK CONNECT TO USER IDENTIFIED BY
   PASSWD USING 'ALIAS';
   CREATE SYNONYM MY_TABLE FOR REMOTE_TABLE@MY_DB_LINK;
   ```

   Now, you could query the remote table using the synonym:

   ```
   SELECT * FROM MY_TABLE;
   ```

456. How to create a public synonym for a table in Oracle?

   The syntax is as follows,

   create public synonym <table name> for sysadm.<table name>;

Here is a SQL example to drop a public synonym, recreate it and grant access privilege.

```
DROP PUBLIC SYNONYM PS_XXX_RUN_CTAP;
CREATE PUBLIC SYNONYM PS_XXX_RUN_CTAP FOR PS_XXX_RUN_CTAP;
GRANT SELECT ON PS_XXX_RUN_CTAP TO PS_ROLE_RO;
GRANT SELECT INSERT, UPDATE, DELETE ON PS_XXX_RUN_CTAP TO
PS_ESB_ROLE;
```

457. How to load data from a different database, such as MS-Access database, to Oracle?

There are two ways that you can use to load data from the other database to Oracle.

1) Export the data in other database to a flat file and then load the flat file data import through the SQL Developer;

2) Export table in the other database to a flat file and then load the flat file through an Application Engine/File program;

458. You can use materialized views to enhance the performance of complex SQLs which take long time to run. Materialized views can pre-summarize aggregations and pre-join tables, making SQL run super-fast in systems with low volume update activity.

459. How to generate a random number in Oracle?

Use the function dbms_random.random() to generate a random number.

The following SQL selects a random row from a table.

```
SELECT COLUMN FROM
(SELECT COLUMN FROM MYTABLE
ORDER BY DBMS_RANDOM.VALUE)
WHERE rownum = n;
```

460. The NVL function lets you substitute a value when a null value is encountered.

The syntax for the NVL function is,

```
NVL (STRING1, REPLACE_WITH)
```

An example is as follows,

```
SELECT NVL (SUPPLIER_CITY, 'N/A') FROM SUPPLIERS;
```

String1 can be a select statement, use bracket to include.

461. The DECODE function allows you to add procedural if-then-else logic to the query. DECODE compares the expression to each search value one by one.If expression is equal to a search, then Oracle Database returns the corresponding result . If no match is found, then Oracle returns default. If default is omitted, then Oracle returns null.

The syntax for the DECODE function is:

```
DECODE (EXPRESSION, SEARCH, RESULT [, SEARCH, RESULT]... [,
DEFAULT]);
```

An example is as follows,

```
DECODE (PFI_LVL8_ID, ' ', PROJECT_ID, PFI_LVL8_ID);
```

462. To get the first day of the month, quarter, or year in Oracle, use the TRUNC(date) function.

```
TRUNC(TO_DATE('22-AUG-03'), 'YEAR')    would return '01-JAN-
03'
```

```
TRUNC(TO_DATE('22-AUG-03'), 'Q')       would return '01-JUL-
03'
```

```
TRUNC(TO_DATE('22-AUG-03'), 'MONTH')   would return '01-AUG-
03'
```

463. You can add and subtract constants to and from a Date value, and these numbers will be interpreted as numbers of days. For example, SYSDATE + 1 will be tomorrow.

464. How to obtain the total count of all distinct field value combinations?

To get the total count of all distinct field value combinations from a table, you can use the COUNT function along with the DISTINCT keyword. Here's a general approach:

1) **Concatenate the fields**: Combine the fields you want to consider as distinct.

2) **Count the distinct combinations**: Use the COUNT function with DISTINCT on the concatenated fields.

One way to do this is

```
SELECT COUNT ( DISTINCT CONCAT (field1, field2, field3))
AS distinct_count
FROM your_table;
```

Here is an example,

```
SELECT COUNT( DISTINCT CONCAT(EMPLID, EMPL_RCD)) AS
distinc_count FROM PS_JOB;
```

Another way to do this is using the concatenation operator ||

```
SELECT COUNT ( DISTINCT (field1 || field2 || field3)) AS
distinct_count
FROM your_table;
```

Here is an example,

```
SELECT COUNT(DISTINCT(EMPLID || EMPL_RCD)) AS distinct_count
FROM PS_JOB;
```

Note the above SQLs are for Oracle. For other databases, you can use the same approach with similar functions.

465. How to obtain the number of rows affected by the last executed SQL in Oracle?

You can use the SQL%ROWCOUNT. The value of the SQL%ROWCOUNT attribute refers to the most recently executed SQL statement.

466. How to change a column from not allowing null value to allowing null value?

```
ALTER TABLE "SYSADM"."PS_XXX_PCCAPWP_AET" MODIFY("END_DT"
NULL);
```

467. DUAL is the dummy table in Oracle.

```
SELECT 123 *456 AS RESULT FROM DUAL;
```

468. The ALL_TABLES table contains one row for each table or view.

The ALL_TAB_COLUMNS table contains one row for every column of each table and view.

The ALL_INDEXES table contains one row for every index. The schema is SYSADM.

The ALL_IND_COLUMNS table contains one row for each column of an index key.

The schema to use for the above tables is SYSADM.

469. **Error:** "A table may be outer joined to at most one other table"

Cause: A table cannot be outer joined to more than one table in Oracle

For example, when you run the following query, you will get the error

```
SELECT T1.ID, T1.NAME, T2.T3_ID FROM T1, T2, T3 WHERE T1.ID
= T2.ID(+)
AND T3.ID = T2.ID(+);
```

Solution: To resolve this error, you should remove the second outer join as follows.

```
SELECT T1.ID, T1.NAME, T2.T3_ID FROM T1, T2, T3 WHERE T1.ID
= T2.ID(+)
AND T3.ID = T2.ID;
```

470. In Oracle SQL Developer, you can use Ctrl + Enter shortcut to execute the current statement without highlighting it.

You can use Ctrl + Shift + N to open a new tab with a dedicated connection.

471. How to create multiple SQL insert statements at once based on the result of a SQL select in Oracle SQL Developer?

In Oracle SQL Developer, you can create many SQL insert statements at once based on the result of a SQL select by clicking Export and choose Insert, and replace the EXPORT TABLE with the target table name.

472. **Error**: "Invalid Character"

Cause: Special characters are valid only in certain places. If special characters other than $, _, and # are used in a name, and the name is not enclosed in double quotation marks ("), this message will be issued. One exception to this rule is for database names; in this case, double quotes are stripped out and ignored.

Solution: Remove the invalid character from the SQL statement or enclose the object name in double quotation marks.

473. **Error**: "Unable to extend tablespace"

Cause: The tablespace is nearly full.

Solution: Ask DBA to extend the tablespace.

474. **Error**: "Looping chain of synonyms" error message shows up when granting access privilege by using the following SQL

```
GRANT SELECT ON <Table_Name> TO <Role_Name>
```

Cause: The table or the view to grant privilege may not exist.

Solution: Create the table or the view.

475. **Error**: "Error Position: 304 Return: 1722 - ORA-01722: invalid number"

Failed SQL stmt: INSERT INTO PS_DEPT_BUDGET_ERN…"

Solution: Error Position number is the actual position where the field is failed to insert, use this info to find out which field the insertion is failed on. Check those fields before and after the Error Position number. The position is counted from the first word (INSERT).

476. **Error:** "inconsistent datatypes: expected – got CLOB"
Cause: You can not put long field in where clause or in a SQL union statement
Solution: Use to_char(longfield2) in the SQL.

```
SELECT field1, to_char(longfield2) from Table1 UNION SELECT
field1,to_char(longfield2) from Table2
```

477. **Error**: "TNS: could not resolve the connect identifier specified"

Cause: You are trying to connect to a database name that is unknown to the system.

Solution: The most common cause are typos in your connection string or network configuration file. Make sure the network configuration file is in the folder specified in Oracle Client->Net Manager -> File -> Open Network Configuration.

478. How to update a field of a table with values from another table on each row in SQL Server? Here is an example,

```
UPDATE A SET A.INTEREST_RATE_ID = (SELECT MAX(B.ID) FROM
INTEREST_RATE B WHERE B.INTEREST_START_DATE <=
A.INTEREST_DATE)
FROM dbo.SECURITYMIG_INTEREST A;
```

479. To get the count of the distinct rows, use

```
SELECT COUNT(DISTINCT {COLUMN}) FROM {TABLE};
```

480. The NULLIF expression accepts two arguments and returns NULL if two arguments are equal. Otherwise, it returns the first expression.
The syntax for using NULLIF() function in SQL is as follows :

```
NULLIF(first_expression,second_expression);
```

Here is an illustration of NULLIF as a CASE statement.

```
CASE WHEN first_expression = second_expression
THEN NULL
ELSE first_expression
END;
```

481. To get the table description in SQL Server, use the sp_help command. or, use Object Browser in the SQL Management Studio.

482. To check indexes of a particular table, use the following command in the SQL Management Studio.

```
EXEC SYS.SP_HELPINDEX @OBJNAME ='PS_ITEM';
```

483. The COALESCE function in SQL Server receives a list of parameters that are separated by comma. The function returns the value of the first of its input parameters that is not NULL. Its syntax is,

```
COALESCE (expression [ ,...n ]) ;
```

484. The TABLES table contains one row for each table or view.

The COLUMNS table contains one row for every column of each table and view.

The INDEXES table contains one row for every index.

The INDEX_COLUMNS table contains one row for each column of an index key.

The schema to use for the above tables is SYS.

485. How to check the primary key fields in a table?

Here is an example,

```
SELECT A.TABLE_NAME, A.CONSTRAINT_NAME
FROM SYS.TABLE_CONSTRAINTS A
WHERE A.TABLE_NAME = '{TableName}';
SELECT A.TABLE_NAME, A.CONSTRAINT_NAME, B.COLUMN_NAME
FROM SYS.TABLE_CONSTRAINTS A, SYS.CONSTRAINT_COLUMN_USAGE B
WHERE CONSTRAINT_TYPE = 'PRIMARY KEY' AND A.CONSTRAINT_NAME =
B.CONSTRAINT_NAME
AND A.TABLE_NAME = '{TableName}';
```

486. **Error**: "Unable to get a stable set of rows in the source tables" shows up when running a Merge Into statement in SQL Server

Cause: This is usually caused by duplicates in the query specified in USING clause in the Merge Into statement.

Solution: Modify the update SQL to make sure there are no duplicates returned from the query in USING clause.

487. **Error**: "Cannot resolve the collation conflict between 'Latin1_General_BIN' and 'SQL_Latin1_General_CP1_CI_AS' in the equal to operation"

Cause: This issue occurs in cross database join in SQL Server

Solution: To resolve it requires use of the COLLATE keyword. The COLLATE keyword, in the context of a SELECT statement, allows you to cast the collation of a column just as you would use CAST function to alter the implied data type of a column. The following query casts the output for the [name] column into the Latin1_General_BIN collation so it can then be compared to the values in sys.database.

An example is as follows,

```
SELECT SD.name

FROM sys.database SD

WHERE database_nm NOT IN

(

SELECT database_nm COLLATE Latin1_General_BIN

FROM backup.database

);
```

Another example of it is

```
SELECT *

FROM PSARSRC.PSPROD07.PS_XXX_SC_EST_PYOT A.PS_XXX_CUST_MAP B
```

```
WHERE A.BUSINESS_UNIT = B.BUSINESS_UNIT COLLATE
Latin1_General_BIN
AND A.CUST_ID = B.CUST_ID COLLATE Latin1_General_BIN
```

SQR

488. SQR commands and variables are CASE INSENSITIVE.

489. SQR has four scalar data types. Database column variables begin with "&". Numeric variables begin with "#". Character variables and date variables begin with "$".

490. You must specify each individual column of a table in a SQL SELECT statement. SELECT * FROM {Table} is not allowed in SQR.

491. 'Setup01.sqc' (or Setup02.sqc) has to be included in a SQR program at the beginning in order to assign the database owner id 'PS' for running the SQR.
    The differences between setup01.sqc and setup02.sqc are,
    Setup01.sqc: Orientation on page is portrait. 8 lines per inch;
    Setup02.sqc: Orientation on page is landscape. 6 lines per inch.

492. You can use the count and exit-select within the main select to test a SQR program.

```
let #testcount = #testcount + 1
if #testcount > 10000
exit-select
end-if
```

493. You can use the 'Stop' command within an SQR program to exit from the SQR program anytime.

494. How to create dynamic SQL in SQR?
    You can use [] to create dynamic SQL. F.I.

```
let $and_customer_type = ' AND A.CUSTOMER_TYPE = ' || '''' ||
$customer_type || ''''
WHERE A.XXX_DELINQUENT = 'Y'
  [$and_customer_type]
```

495. Mostly used SQR Predefined Variables are as follows,

#current-column   The current column on the page.

$current-date The current date-time on the local machine when SQR starts running the program.

#current-line Refers to the physical line number on the page.

#page-count   The current page number.

#return-status Value to be returned to the operating system when SQR exits.

#sql-count   The count of rows affected by a DML statement (insert, update and delete).

$sql-error   The text message from the database explaining the most recent error.

#sql-status   The status value from the database after each query is compiled or executed.

$sqr-hostname The name of the machine that this SQR is running on.

#sqr-pid   The process ID of the current SQR process.

$sqr-program The name of the SQR program file.

$sqr-report   The name of the report output file.

$username   The database username specified on the command line.

496. How to put a SQR program in debug mode?

To put a SQR program in debug mode and show debug messages when running the program, append the parameter -debug to the process definition for the SQR program, and use the following statement in the SQR.

```
#debug show '$Emplid: '    $Emplid
#debug show '$PayEndDt: ' $PayEndDt
```

380

497. **Error**: "(SQR 3301) Program stopped by user request"

Cause: This can be caused by an internal logic issue. One possible cause for the error is that a piece of customized code hasn't been retrofitted to the new release during an upgrade process. Once the customization code has been retrofitted, the issue may be resolved.

TRACE

498. Trace can be turned on or off globally by switching on and off a trace flag in the app server configuration file.

499. How to enable online tracing?

You can set all of the trace parameters from the PeopleSoft sign-in page. Just beneath the Sign In button, click the link that opens the trace flags page. This enables you to set the trace options and then sign into the system. It only affects the user who signs in and doesn't affect any other users.

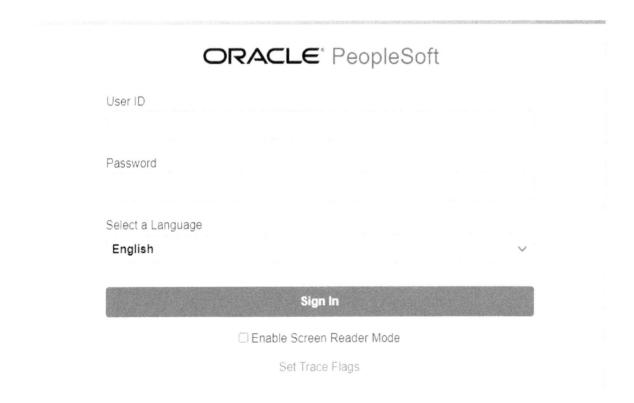

When you click the Set Trace Flags link, you will see all of the trace options.

SQL trace settings	PeopleCode trace settings	Component Processor trace settings	Page Generation trace settings
☐ SQL statements	☐ Evaluator instructions	☐ Page Structures at Init	☐ Log page generation errors
☐ SQL statement variables	☐ List program	☐ Component Buffers at Init	☐ Show table layout
☐ SQL connect, disconnect, commit, rollback	☐ Variable assignments	☐ Component Buffers before/after service	☐ Source annotation for overlap
☐ SQL fetch	☐ Fetched values	☐ Component Buffers after scrollselect	☐ Detailed table gen trace
☐ All other SQL API calls except SSBs	☐ Evaluator stack	☐ Component Buffers after modal page	☐ Inline stylesheet
☐ Set select buffer calls (SSBs)	☐ Program starts	☐ Component Buffers before Save	☐ Unminified javascript
☐ Database-specific API calls	☐ External function calls	☐ Component Buffers after row insert	☐ Extra markup needed for QA
	☐ Internal function calls	☐ Default Processing	☐ Format source
	☐ Function parameter values	☐ PRM Contents	☐ Save source in files
	☐ Function return values	☐ Internal counters (debug build only)	☐ Include Javascript debugging
	☐ Each statement	☐ Memory stats at Init	☐ Log form data
	☐ Suppress logs in loop	☐ Keylist Generation	☐ Log unknown parameters
		☐ Work Record Flagging	
		☐ Related Displays	

Note the signon tracing link can be disabled through web profile settings. However, there's a way around this. If you notice your URL when you click the hyperlink it changes and includes a trace directive.

Regular signon URL is something like this:

```
https://server:port/psp/ps/?cmd=login
```

With tracing, the signon URL includes the trace directive:

```
https://server:port/psp/ps/?cmd=login&trace=y
```

So, regardless of whether you can see the hyperlink, you can still turn on signon tracing using the trace directive.

500. How to enable application engine trace?

You can set the trace from the Process Definition.

PeopleTools –> Process Scheduler –> Processes

Go to the Override Options tab and set the Parameter List to append.

Here are a few commonly used Application Engine process trace parameters.

-TRACE 7 -TOOLSTRACESQL 31 -TOOLSTRACEPC 3596

Using both the -TOOLSTRACEPC & -TOOLSTRACESQL together should only be done when required, as the output from both go into the same file, making it very large and difficult to read. For normal program tracing using just

-TRACE 7 -TOOLSTRACEPC 3596

give the application engine trace, which traces the SQL and PeopleCode in an App Engine program.

To get the timing of SQLs for an application engine program when tracing, use the following trace flag.

-TRACE 135-TOOLSTRACESQL 31-TOOLSTRACEPC 3596

This can help find why an Application Engine takes very long time to run.

Note, if an Application Engine program trace log file doesn't show up in the process monitor as expected, check first if you have a process scheduler admin role, then check with the PS admin whether AE tracing has been turned on by looking at the AE trace flag value in the App Server config file, the value should be set to 2 or 4.

Commonly Used Tables

Commonly Used Tables in PeopleSoft Financials and Supply Chain Management

MODULE/SUB AREA	TABLE NAME	DESCRIPTION
REQUISITIONS	REQ_HDR	Requisition Header
	REQ_LINE	Requisition Line
	REQ_LINE_DISTRIB	Requisition Accounting Distribution
	REQ_LINE_SHIP	Requisition Shipment Details
	REQ_APPROVAL	Requisition Approval
PURCHASE ORDERS	PO_HDR	PO Header
	PO_LINE	PO Line
	PO_LINE_DISTRIB	PO Line Distribution
	PO_LINE_SHIP	PO Line Shipment Details
	PO_APPROVAL	PO Approval
SUPPLIERS	VENDOR	Vendor Header
	VENDOR_LOC	Vendor Location
	VENDOR_ADDR	Vendor Address Information
ACCOUNTS PAYABLES	VOUCHER	Voucher Header
	VOUCHER_LINE	Voucher Line
	DISTRIB_LINE	Voucher Distribution
	VCHR_ACCTG_LN	AP Accounting Entries
BILLING	BI_HDR	Bill Header
	BI_LINE	Bill Line
	BI_ACCT_ENTRY	Billing Accounting Entries
CUSTOMERS	CUSTOMER	Customer Header
	CUST_ADDRESS	Customer Address Information
	CUST_CONTACT	Customer Contact Details

	CUST_DATA	Customer Info / Balances
	CUST_AGING	Customer Aging Detail
RECEIVALBES	ITEM	Items
	ITEM_ACTIVITY	Item Activities
	ITEM_DST	Item Distributions
	DEPOSIT_CONTROL	Customer Deposit Information
	PENDING_ITEM	Pending Items
PAYMENTS	PAYMENT_ID_CUST	Payment Customer Identification
	PAYMENT_ID_ITEM	Payment Item Identification
	PAYMENT	Customer Payment Information
	PAY_MISC_DST	Non-Customer Payment Distribution
EXPENSE REPORTS	EX_SHEET_HDR	Expense Sheet Header
	EX_SHEET_LINE	Expense Sheet Line
	EX_SHEET_DIST	Expense Sheet Distribution
	EX_ACCTG_LINE	Expense Accounting Line
CASH ADVANCES	EX_ADV_HDR	Cash Advance Header
	EX_ADV_LINE	Cash Advance Line
	EX_ADV_DIST	Cash Advance Distribution
	EX_ADV_APPRVR	Cash Advance Approval
ASSETS	BOOK	Asset Book transactions
	COST	Asset Cost Transactions
	INTFC_PRE_AM	Pre-Interface Table to AM
	INTFC_FIN	Interface Accounting Details
	ASSET	Asset General Information
	ASSET_ACQ_DET	Asset Acquisition Details
	ASSET_NBV_TBL	Asset Net Book Value Detail
	DIST_LN	AM Accounting Entries

GENERAL LEDGER	JRNL_HEADER	Journal Header Data
	JRNL_LN	Journal Line Data
	LEDGER	Ledger Data
COMMITMENT CONTROL	LEDGER_KK	Commit Control Ledger Data
	KK_BUDGET_HDR	Commit Control Budget Header
	KK_BUDGET_LINE	Commit Control Budget Line
	KK_ACTIVITY_LOG	Commit Control Budget Activities
CHARTFIELDS	DEPT_TBL	Departments
	PROJECT	Projects
	GL_ACCOUNT_TBL	Accounts
	PROGRAM_TBL	Programs
	FUND_TBL	Funds
	CLASS_CF_TBL	Class of Trades
	BUD_REF_TBL	Budget References
	ALTACCT_TBL	Alternate Accounts
	SPEEDTYP_TBL	SpeedTypes
	COMBO_DATA_TBL	Chartfield Combo Data

Commonly Used Tables in PeopleSoft Human Capital Management

MODULE/SUB AREA	TABLE NAME	DESCRIPTION
HR DATA	PERSONAL_DATA	Personal Data
	PERSON	Person Data
	PERS_NID	Person National IDs
	NAMES	Person Names
	PERS_DATA_EFFDT	Effective Dated Personal Data

	ADDRESSES	Person Addresses
	PERSON_ADDRESS	Person's Current Addresses
	PERSON_PHONE	Person Phone Numbers
	EMAIL_ADDRESSES	Email Addresses
	PER_ORG_ASGN	Person Org Assignments
	PER_ORG_INST	Person Org Instance
	PER_POI_TYPE	Person Poi Type
	REG_REGION_TBL	Regulatory Region
	DIVERS_ETHNIC	Ethnic Diversity
	UNION_TBL	Union Codes
	ACTION_TBL	Job Actions
	ACTN_REASON_TBL	Job Action Reasons
	COMPANY_TBL	Company Data
	PAYGROUP_TBL	Pay Groups
JOB	JOB	Job Data
	JOBCODE_TBL	Job Codes
	CURRENT_JOB	Current Job Data
	COMPENSATION	Employee Compensation Data
	EMPLOYMENT	Employment Data
	EMPLOYEES	Non-Terminated Employees
	POSITION_DATA	Position Data
PAYROLL	PAY_CALENDAR	Pay Calendar Data
	PAY_PAGE	Pay Page Data
	PAY_LINE	Pay Check Line Data
	PAY_EARNINGS	Pay Earning Data
	PAY_OTH_EARNS	Pay Other Earning Data
	PAY_GARN_OVRD	Payroll Garnishment Override

	PAY_ONE_TIME	Payroll Deduction Override
	PAY_DEDUCTION	Pay Deductions
	PAY_CHECK	Pay Check Data
	PAY_TAX	Pay Tax Data
	PAY_ERN_DIST	Pay Earning Distributions
	PAY_DED_DIST	Pay Deduction Distributions
	PAY_TAX_DIST	Pay Tax Distributions
	PAY_TAX_OVRD	Payroll Deduction Override
	PAY_DISTRIBUTN	Payroll Deposit Distribution
	PAY_GARNISH	Payroll Garnishment
	DEDUCTION_TBL	Deduction Plan and Deduction Code Combinations
	GENL_DEDUCTION	General Deductions
	GENL_DED_CD	General Deduction Codes
	DEDUCTION_CLASS	Deduction Classifications
	ADDL_PAY_EFFDT	Additional Pay Effective Dates
	ADDL_PAY_DATA	Additional Pay Data
	ADDL_PAY_ERNCD	Additional Pay Earning Codes
	DIRECT_DEPOSIT	Direct Deposits
	DIR_DEP_DISTRIB	Direct Deposit Distributions
	GARN_SPEC	Garnishment Specifications
	GARN_RULE	Garnishment Rules
	GARN_EMPL_DED	Garnish Employee Deductions
	RETROPAY_EARNS	Retroactive Pay Earnings
	PAY_CHECK_REVRS	Pay Check Reverse Data
	EARNINGS_BAL	Earnings Balance s
	DEDUCTION_BAL	Deduction Balance
	DED_ARREARS	Deduction Arrears

	GARN_BALANCE	Garnishment Balances
	TAX_BALANCE	Tax Balance Data
	HR_ACCTG_LINE	Payroll Accounting Line Data
TIME & LABOR	EMPL_DATA	Workgroup, Taskgroup and Time Reporter Status
	TL_RPTD_TIME	Time Reported by Employees
	TL_PAYABLE_TIME	Final Processed Time Ready to Be Sent to Payroll
	TL_TR_STATUS	Employee Time Reporting Status
	TL_IPT1	Intermediary Payable Time Table
	TL_EXCEPTION	Exceptions Details
	TL_TA_TRLIST	Time Reporters to Be Processed
	TL_RPTD_TIME	Punch Time Entries,
	TL_ATTEND_HIST	Attendance History Data
	TL_ATTENDANCE	Current Attendance Data
BENEFITS	BENEF_PLAN_TBL	Benefit Plans
	LEAVE_PLAN	Leave Plan Enrollment
	HEALTH_BENEFIT	Health Insurance Plan Enrollment
	SAVINGS_PLAN	Saving Plan Enrollment
	LIFE_ADD_BEN	Life Insurance Plan Enrollment
	RTRMNT_PLAN	Retirement Plan Enrollment
	DISABILITY_BEN	Disability Plan Enrollment
	LIFE_ADD_BEN	Life Ad/D Benefit Enrollment
	HEALTH_DEPENDNT	Health Plan Dependent
	LEAVE_ACCRUAL	Leave Accruals
	LIFE_ADD_BENEFC	Life Ad/D Beneficiaries
	PENSION_PLAN	Pension Plan Enrollment
	PENSION_BENEFC	Pension Beneficiaries

	SAVINGS_BENEFIC	Savings Plan Beneficiaries
	VACATION_BEN	Vacation Benefits Enrollment
ABSENCE MANAGEMENT	GP_PIN	Pin Details of All Elements
	GP_ABS_EVENT	Reported Absence
	GP_RSLT_ABS	Calculated Result of Reported Absence Takes
	GP_RSLT_ACUM	Results Of Accumulators
	GP_CAL_RUN	Calendar Group Id Details
	GP_PI_GEN_DATA	Positive Input for Processed Absences
	GP_ABS_SS_STA	Absence Event Workflow Status
TALENT MANAGEMENT	HRS_APPLICANT	Applicant Details
	HRS_RCMNT	Recruitment Tracking
	HRS_APP_STS	Applicant Status
	HRS_APP_PROFILE	Applicant Profiles
TAX	FED_TAX_DATA	Federal Tax Data
	STATE_TAX_DATA	State/Provincial Tax Data
TENURE	EG_TENURE_DATA	Tenure Data

Commonly Used Tables in PeopleSoft Campus Solutions

MODULE/SUB AREA	TABLE NAME	DESCRIPTION
SET UP SACR	INSTITUTION_TBL	Institutions
	CAMPUS_TBL	Campuses
	CAMPUS_LOC_TBL	Campus Locations
	HOME_CAMPUS_TBL	Home Campus
	ACAD_GROUP_TBL	Academic Groups
	ACAD_ORG_TBL	Academic Organizations
ACADEMIC CAREER	ACAD_CAR_TBL	Academic Career
	ACAD_CAR_PTRS	Academic Career Pointers
	CATLG_CAR_TBL	Academic Career Levels
	ACAD_CAL_DATA	Academic Career Calendars
	HOLIDAY_TBL	Holidays
PROGRAMS, PLANS AND DEGREES	ACAD_PROG_TBL	Academic Programs
	ACAD_PROG_OWNER	Academic Program Owners
	SSR_PRG_CD_TBL	Academic Program Codes
	ACAD_PLAN_TBL	Academic Plans
	DEGREE_TBL	Degrees
TERM AND SESSION	TERM_TBL	Terms
	TERM_VAL_TBL	Term Values
	SESSION_TBL	Term Session
	SESS_TIME_PEROD	Session Time Periods
LOAD/LEVEL RULES	LVL_LD_RULE_TBL	Academic Levels/Load Rules
	ACAD_LEVEL_TBL	Academic Levels

	ACAD_LOAD_TBL	Academic Load
	ACAD_LOAD2_TBL	Academic Load For Statistics
GRADING	GRADE_TBL	Grades
	GRADE_BASIS_TBL	Grading Basis
	GRD_BASE_CHOICE	Grading Basis Choices
	GRADESCHEME_TBL	Grading Schemes
	SSR_GRADE_FLAG	Grading Flags
APPLICANTS	ADM_APP_CAR_SEQ	Application Career Sequence
	ADM_APPL_DATA	Application Data
	ADM_APPL_PLAN	Application Plan
	ADM_APPL_PROG	Application Program
	ADM_APPL_RCR_CA	Recruiting Category
PROSPECTS	ADM_PRSPCT_CAR	Prospect Career
	ADM_PRSPCT_PLAN	Prospect Plan
	ADM_PRSPCT_PROG	Prospect Program
STUDENT FINANCIALS ACCOUNTS	ACCOUNT_SF	Student Accounts
	ITEM_SF	Student Account Items
	ITEM_LINE_SF	Student Account Item Lines
	ITEM_XREF	Student Item Cross Reference
	PAYMENT_TBL	Student Payments
	QUICK_POST_TBL	Quick Post
	QUICK_POST_ERR	Quick Post Errors
	ADM_APPL_DEP	Calculated Deposit Fees
BILLING	BI_BILL_HEADER	Billing Invoice Header

	BI_BILLING_LINE	Billing Line
	BI_BILL_MESSAGE	Bill Messages
	BI_STD_REQ_TBL	Billing Standard Requests
	BI_BILL_ERROR	Billing Errors
CREDIT HISTORY AND COLLECTIONS	CREDIT_HISTORY	Student Credit History
	COLLECTION_SF	Student Collections
	COLL_LTR_ITEM	Dunning/Collection Letters
	COLLECT_EFFORT	Student Collections Recovery Effort Data
CASHIERING	CSH_BD_CSH_TBL	Business Date Cashier Data
	CSH_BD_CSH_OPEN	Business Date Cashier Open Data
	CSH_BD_REG_OPEN	Business Date Register Open Data
	CSH_BD_REG_TBL	Business Date Register Data
	CSH_OFF_RECEIPT	Cashier Office Receipts
	CSH_OFF_RCPT_L	Cashier Office Receipt Line
	CSH_OFF_RCPT_T	Cashier Office Receipt Tender
	CSH_OFF_TBL	Cashiering Office Data
GL INTERFACE	SF_ACCTG_LN	Sf Accounting Line
	SF_ACCTG_ERROR	Sf Quick Posting Error Data
GROUP POST	GROUP_CONT_INFO	Control Group Info
	GROUP_LINE	Group Line Information/Check
ITEM TYPES	ITEM_TYPE_TBL	Item Type Data
	ITEM_ACCT_TYPE	Valid Account Types
	GL_INTERFACE	General Ledger Interface

OPTIONAL FEES	OPT_FEE_STDNT	Optional Fees by Student
	OPT_FEE_TBL	Optional Fees Data
	OPT_FEE_TERM	Optional Fee Terms
	OPT_FEE_VAL	Optional Fee Values
REFUNDS	REFUND_HDR	Refund Header
	REFUND_DTL	Refund Details
	REFUND_CHECK	Refund Check Information
	REFUND_WL	Refund Work Lists
TERM FEE	TERM_FEE_TBL	Term Fee Data
	TERM_FE_CD_TBL	Term Fee Code Data
	TERM_SF_CD_TBL	Term Sub Fee Code Data
	TERM_SUBFEE_TBL	Term Sub Fee Data
TUITION CALCULATION	TUIT_CALC_TBL	Tuition Calc Data
	CALC_MESSAGES	Tuition Calc Error/Warn Messages
	OPT_FEE_STDNT	Optional Fees by Student
TUITION GROUP	SEL_GROUP_TBL	Selector Group Data
	SEL_GROUP_CRITR	Selector Group Criteria
	GROUP_FEE_TBL	Group Fee Data
TUITION GROUP CRITERIA	SEL_CRITER_TBL	Group Selector Criteria
	SEL_CRITR_TBL	Group Selector Criteria
	SEL_VALUE_TBL	Selector Values
WAIVER	WAIVER_CODE_TBL	Waiver Codes

	WAIVER_GRP_DTL	Waiver Group Details
	WAIVER_GRP_TBL	Waiver Groups
	WAIVER_TBL	Waver Data
PERSON	PERSON	Core Person Data Including Birth and Death Information
	PERS_DATA_EFFDT	Core Person Data History Includes Martial Status and Gender
	PERSONAL_DATA	Snapshot Bio/Demo Data
	PER_POI_TYPE	Person Of Interest (POI) Types
	PER_POI_TRANS	Person Of Interest (POI) History
IDENTIFICATION	CITIZENSHIP	Citizenship Data
	SCC_CITIZ_HIST	Citizenship History
	CITIZEN_PSSPRT	Citizenship Passport Data
	DIVERS_ETHNICITY	Ethnicity Data
	DIVERSITY	Ethnicity Diversity Data
	PERS_NID	Persons National ID Data
	EXTERNAL_SYSKEY	External System Data (Key)
	EXTERNAL_SYSTEM	External System Data
	PER_ORG_ASGN	Organizational Relationships
BIOGRAPHIC/DEMOGRAPHIC	ADDRESSES	Address History
	EMAIL_ADDRESSES	Email Addresses
	NAMES	Names History
	PERSONAL_PHONE	Phone & Fax Data
3CS (COMMUNICATIONS, CHECKLISTS AND COMMENTS)	COMMUNICATION	Communication Data
	PERSON_CHECKLST	Checklist Data

	PERSON_COMMENT	Comment Data
	VAR_DATA_[AF]	Variable Data. Replace [AF] With Administrative Function E.G. SPRG
	LAST_3CS_TBL	Last SEQ_3C Value for A Student
CAMPUS EVENT PLANNING AND MEETINGS	CAMPUS_EVENT	Campus Events
	EVENT_MTG	Campus Event Meetings
SERVICE INDICATORS	SRVC_IND_DATA	Service Indicator Data
	SRVC_IN_RSN_TBL	Service Indicator Reasons
CURRICULUM MANAGEMENT COURSE DATA	CRSE_CATALOG	Course Catalogs
	CRSE_COMPONENT	Course Components
	CRSE_OFFER	Course Offerings
	CRSE_EQUIV_TBL	Course Equivalencies
	CRSE_LST_HDR_SF	Course List Header
	CRSE_LST_DTL_SF	Course List Details
	CRSE_TOPICS	Course Topics
CLASS DATA	CLASS_TBL	Class Data
	CLASS_ASSOC	Class Associations
	CLASS_ATTENDNCE	Class Attendance
	CLASS_COMPONENT	Class Components
	CLASS_INSTR	Class Instructors
	CLASS_NOTES	Class Notes
TERM ACTIVATION AND HISTORY	STDNT_CAREER	Student Careers

	STDNT_CAR_TERM	Student Career Term Activation
	STDNT_SESSION	Student Sessions
	TRNS_CRSE_SCH	Transfer Credit School
	TRNS_CRSE_TERM	Transfer Credit Course Term
	TRNS_TEST_MODEL	Test Transfer Credits Models
	TRNS_TEST_TERM	Test Transfer Credits Terms
PROGRAM/PLAN	ACAD_PROG	Student Program Data
	ACAD_PLAN	Student Plan Data
ENROLMENT	STDNT_ENRL	Student Enrolments
	CLASS_TBL_SE_VW	View That Combines Student Enrolment & Class Data
	ENRL_REQ_HEADER	Enrolment Request Header
	ENRL_REQ_DETAI	Enrolment Request Detail
GRADUATION/DEGREES	PS_ACAD_DEGR	Student Degree Data
	PS_ACAD_DEGR_PLAN	Student Degree Plan Data
	PS_ACAD_DEGR_HONS	Student Degree Honors Data
STUDENT GROUPS	STDNT_GRPS	Student Group Data
	STDNT_GRHIST	Student Group History
GRADE BOOK	STDNT_GRADE_DTL	Student's Grades Detail
	LAM_CLASS_ACTV	Class Assignments Information
STUDENT RECORDS SECURITY	SCRTY_TBL_INST	Institution Security

	SCRTY_TBL_ACAD	Academic Organization Security
	SCRTY_TBL_CAR	Academic Career Security
	SCRTY_TBL_PLAN	Academic Plan Security
	SCRTY_TBL_PROG	Academic Program Security
	SCRTY_ADM_ACTN	Admissions Action Security
	SCRTY_PROG_ACTN	Program Action Security
	SCRTY_APPL_CTR	Application Centre Security
	SCRTY_RECR_CTR	Recruiting Centre Security
	OPR_GRP_3C_TBL	3Cs Operator Group Security
	ENRL_ACCESS_GRP	Enrolment Access Group Security
	ENRMT_OVRD_TBL	Enrolment Override Security by Enrolment Access ID
	SCRTY_TBL_SRVC	Service Indicator Security
	SCRTY_TSCRPT	Transcript Type Security
	SAD_TEST_SCTY	Test ID Security
STUDENT FINANCIALS SECURITY	SEC_ISET_OPR	Operator Institution Set Security
	SEC_UNITSF_OPR	Operator Business Unit Security
	SEC_SETID_OPR	Operator SetID Security

Commonly Used Tables in PeopleTools

SUB AREA	TABLE NAME	DESCRIPTION
OBJECT DEFINITIONS	PSRECDEFN	Record Definitions
	PSRECFIELD	Fields in the Records
	PSRECFIELDALL	Fields in the Records (Including SubRecords)

	PSPNLDEFN	Page Definitions
	PSPNLFIELD	Fields on the Pages
	PSPNLGRPDEFN	Component Definitions
	PSPNLGROUP	Pages in the Components
	PSPROJECTDEFN	Project Definitions
	PSPROJECTITEM	Definitions in the Projects
	PSPCMPROG	PeopleCode Programs
	PSBUSPROCDEFN	Business Process Definitions
	PSFILEREDEFN	File References
	PSINDEXDEFN	Index Information
	PSKEYDEFN	The Index Key Information
	PSMPDEFN	Mobile Page Information
	PSMSGDEFN	Application Message Definitions
	PSMSGAGTDEFN	Application Message Agent Definitions
	PSDBFIELD	Fields in the System
	PSGATEWAY	Gateway URL
	PSPACKAGEDEFN	Application Packages Definitions
	PSQRYDEFN	Query Definitions
	PSSQLDEFN	SQL Object Definitions
	PSSQLTEXTDEFN	SQL Object's Text
	PSACTIVITYDEFN	Activity Definitions
	PSSTEPDEFN	Activity Step Information
	PSSTYLEDEFN	Style Definitions
	PSSTYLSHEETDEFN	Stylesheet Definitions
	PSSUBDEFN	Message Subscription Definitions
	PSTREEDEFN	Tree Definitions
	PSURLDEFN	Attachment Storage URL Definitions

COMPONENT INTERFACE	PSBCDEFN	Component Interface Header
FILE LAYOUT	PSFLDDEFN	File Layout Header
	PSFLDSEGDEFN	File Layout Segments
	PSFLDFIELDDEFN	File Layout Fields
APPLICATION ENGINE	PSAEAPPLSTATE	Application Engine State Records
	PSAEAPPLTEMPTBL	Application Engine Temporary Tables
	PSAESECTDEFN	Application Engine Section Definitions
	PSAESTEPDEFN	Application Engine Step Definitions
	PSAESTEPMSGDEFN	Application Engine Messages
	PSAESTMTDEFN	Application Engine Statements / Actions
MENU	PSMENUDEFN	Menu Definitions
	PSMENUITEM	Items / Components on the Menu
MESSAGE CATELOG	PSMSGCATDEFN	Message Catalogs
	PS_MSG_CAT_VW	Message Catalog Entries
	PS_MSG_CATLG_VW	Error Messages and Warnings
PROCESS	PS_PRCSDEFN	Process Definitions
	PS_PRCSDEFNGRP	Process Groups
	PS_PRCSJOBDEFN	Process Job Definitions
	PSPRCSRQST	Process Request Instances
	PS_PRCSDEFNPNL	Process Component
	PS_PRCSJOBITEM	Job Processes
	PSPRCSLOCK	Process Submitted
	PSPRCSQUE	Process Request Details
	PS_CDM_LIST	Process Instance Details
	PS_CDM_AUTH	Process Instance User Access Details
WORKFLOW	PS_APPR_RULE_HDR	Approval Rule Set Definitions

	PS_APPR_RULE_DETL	Approval Rule Definitions
	PS_APPR_RULE_FIELD	Approval Rule Definition Route Control
	PS_APPR_RULE_AMT	Approval Rule Amounts
	PS_RTE_CNTL_LN	Route Control Profile Line
	PS_RTE_CNTL_RUSER	RoleUser Route Control Profiles
	PS_RTE_CNTL_HDR	Route Control Types
TRANSLATE VALUES	PSXLATDEFN	Translate Fieldname and Version Number for Caching
	PSXLATITEM	Translate Fieldname and Their Values
PORTAL	PSPRSMDEFN	Content References and Folders
	PSPRUHTAB	Homepage Personalization
	PSPRUHTABPGLT	Homepage Pagelets
	PSPRSMDEFN	Portal Structure Definitions
	PSPRUFDEFN	Portal Registry Favorite Definitions
	PSPRUHDEFN	Portal User Homepage Definitions
	PSOPRDEFN	Operator ID Definitions
SECURITY	PSCLASSDEFN	Permission List Definitions
	PSROLEDEFN	Role Definitions
	PSROLEUSER	Roles Assigned to Each User
	PSROLECLASS	Permission Lists Associated to Each Role
	PSAUTHITEM	Menu Item Security by Permission List
	PSACCESSLOG	Login And Logout Information of Users
	PSACCESSPRFL	Symbolic Id, Accessid/Password Details
AUDIT	PSAUDIT	All The Changes for Panel/Record Modifications

CHANGE CONTROL	PSCHGCTLHIST	History of Locked Definitions
	PSCHGCTLLOCK	Currently Locked Definitions
VERSION	PSRELEASE	Application Release Details
	PSSTATUS	PeopleTools Information
LAUGUAGE	PSLANGUAGES	Languages Information
MODULES	PS_INSTALLATION	Modules Information

The End

www.ingramcontent.com/pod-product-compliance
Lightning Source LLC
LaVergne TN
LVHW082035050326
832904LV00005B/193